PREFACE

New ventures are always exciting. This is particularly true of
a project which is so perfectly in tune with the National
Library of Canada's mandate of stewardship and promotion of the nation's published heritage.

This anthology of essays is more than an example of the
Library extending its comprehensive collection of Canadian literature. It is more than a commemoration of a very special exhibition celebrating Canadian science fiction and fantasy. It is more
than a means of extending the reach and permanence of the ideas
and themes in the exhibition, although it is all these things. The
anthology is part of the published heritage of which the National
Library is the steward. By commissioning these essays, the
National Library has contributed to both an increasingly popular genre and a nation's collection.

And it is particularly appropriate that we should move in this
direction through the publication of *Out of This World*. Science
fiction and fantasy are genres that invite new points of view and
are open to new ventures. We are, after all, stepping out of this
world and into new realms, bounded only by the limits of our
imaginations. Through one of the fastest-growing areas of literature, we are able to view human interaction and motivation
through the mirror of possible future worlds, alternate histories,
time travel, horror stories and magic realism. The broad spec-
trum of ideas expressed through the essays touches every point
on the road from scholarly to personal. I am proud to be associated with a project that is truly out of this world.

Marianne Scott
National Librarian
National Library of Canada

OUT OF THIS WORLD

CANADIAN

SCIENCE FICTION

& FANTASY

LITERATURE

Compiled by
Andrea Paradis

Quarry Press
&
National Library of Canada

Canadian Cataloguing in Publication Data

Main entry under title:
    Out of this world : Canadian science fiction and fantasy literature

Co-published by: National Library of Canada.
Issued also in French under the title: Visions d'autres mondes.
Includes bibliographical references.
CCG cat. no. SN3-299/1995E
ISBN 1-55082-150-4

    1. Science fiction, Canadian — History and criticism.   2. Fantastic
fiction, Canadian — History and criticism.   I. National Library of Canada.

PS8191.S34088 1995   C813'.087609   C95-900399-1
PR9192.6.S34088 1995

Published by Quarry Press Inc. in cooperation with the National Library of Canada and the Canada Communication Group — Publishing, Supply and Services Canada.

Cover photograph of Canada from Outer Space courtesy of N.A.S.A. Cover painting entitled *La Chasse Galére,* depicting the devil leading a flying canoe of bûcherons on New Year's Eve, by Henri Julien, courtesy of the National Library of Canada. Author sketches by Heather Spears.

CONTENTS

FOREWORD
Something Else . . .
by Judith Merril

This is a book about *something else* — about the invention, design, and communication of other worlds, other times, other lifeforms, other beliefs and perceptions — "virtual realities" we have never experienced, and cannot experience, in everyday life.

The book itself is *something else* — a collection of statements, some personal, some scholarly, by people whose daily work is the creation and processing of these unique perceptions. Writers, editors, artists, and producers of fantastic and speculative literature have discussed their work in print before, but usually only in publications for insider genre audiences. This is the *first* time (not just 'first in Canada') that an anthology of this scope and authenticity has been published under prestigious literary auspices for the general reader. These auspices are *something else* again — this anthology celebrates OUT OF THIS WORLD, a major exhibit mounted by the National Library of Canada, the first time any major cultural institution (once again, not just in Canada) has honored the significance of the wide variety of other-worldly literature in the precarious rapid-change realities of the world today.

Forty-five years ago, when I began editing anthologies of science fiction and fantasy, there were no listings under those headings in standard library reference books. (Some science fiction was sometimes listed under the heading *Pseudoscience*!) In 1971, when the first Canadian academic conference on the literatures of *something else* was convened (The Secondary Universe Conference, jointly sponsored by The Toronto Public Libraries and McGill University), the reference books had revised their indexes to reflect a new respectability. Universities, even in America, were establishing courses in Science-Fiction and Utopian Studies; 'movies' were becoming 'cinema'; avant-gardists were beginning to talk seriously about comics and pop culture; and scholars were starting to write sober volumes of criticism about the kind of *something else* most people still thought of as the junk adolescents read by flashlight under the covers.

Even in America? In the United States, where contemporary science fiction and fantasy was born and flourished in pulp genre magazines and comic books, the only *respectable* fantastic fiction until twenty-five years ago was the supernatural horror story (preferably written by Hawthorne, Poe, or James). But in Britain and in Canada (as in most non-Anglophone countries), 'literary' authors were never limited to here-and-now-realism. And of course the fantasies, future-fictions, scientific romances, and utopian speculations of Swift, Verne, Wells, Shelley, Doyle, Chesterton, Kipling, Capek, Huxley, Lewis, Orwell, *et al*, had honored places *even* in American libraries.

In Canada, mainstream authors have never hesitated to cross the frontier into the uncharted worlds of something else, but up until fifteen years ago, professionally publishable genre writers in all forms of fantastic literature in this country could be counted on the fingers of two hands. This is a precise figure: when the first anthology of Canadian SF&F was published in 1979 (John Robert Colombo's *Other Canada*) it included ten selections by contemporary working genre writers. There were then no Canadian publishers, book or magazine, specializing in, or even emphasizing, speculative and fantastic literatures. The history, the significance, and the popularity of the explosion that has occurred since that time, as well as the feelings and philosophies of some of the most gifted writers, are documented in this book.

You may expect to be astonished. These authors are, quite simply, something *else*!

Judith Merril was the editor of the first Tesseracts anthology in 1985. A leading authority on SF, she has edited twenty other anthologies and written novels, short stories, and criticism. She was a founder of The Spaced-Out Library, The Merril Collection of Science Fiction, Speculation and Fantasy in Toronto, where she works as a broadcaster and consultant. She is also active in the peace movement.

INTRODUCTION
Aliens Among Us
by Allan Weiss and Hugh Spencer

THE PROJECT

Our assignment to curate the National Library's OUT OF THIS WORLD exhibition on Canadian science fiction and fantasy literature presented us with a set of paradoxes. The essential paradox was the project itself. An exhibition in an institution such as the National Library is as about as public and as credible an occurrence as can be imagined. Yet much of the appeal and power of fantasy and science fiction stems from the very private and incredible nature of the reading or viewing. The individual reader is often an imaginative collaborator in the experience of speculative fiction — setting the tonality of an alien language, filling the historical details in the societies where the stories are set, even assigning sex lives to heroes who seem to spend too much time with technology.

Another paradox was the very notion of *Canadian* science fiction and fantasy literature. We do not perceive ourselves as a particularly imaginative or fanciful nation. A common assumption is that fantasy and science fiction are something we import for our less responsible amusement — in much the same way that the Canadian Broadcasting Corporation used to air episodes of American soap operas such as *Dallas*. Canadians are too serious to produce science fiction and fantasy. If any fantastic literature was to be generated north of the 49th parallel, it would be a deviation, insignificant, works commercially-motivated for crass American markets, and certainly not worthy of treatment by a major national institution.

In the manner of many science fiction heroes, your curators responded by treating these paradoxes, not as barriers, but as challenges. We challenged these assumptions by researching Canada's literary heritage — as it is documented in the collections of the National Library of Canada and the Merril Collection of Science Fiction, Speculation and Fantasy, one of the world's premier reference libraries of fantastic literature. The fact that the Merril Collection is operated as part of the Toronto Public Library system was an early indication that Canadians may value the imagination and the fantastic more than one might think.

As curators we were determined that the exhibition would

be more than a three-dimensional coffee table book about science fiction, with pieces of Canadian trivia arising out of some homogenized overview of world-wide science fiction and speculation. We resolved to focus on the search for identity as a central theme which underlies much of Canadian SF and connects it to our wider literary traditions. The contributors to the exhibition anthology have taken this resolve even further, demonstrating new viewpoints and shedding new insight into Canada's imaginative heritage.

THE CONTEXT

It has become a truism in studies of Canadian literature and, to some extent, other media that our artists have worked within the documentary tradition. In other words, most people have assumed that the dominant mode in Canadian writing, film-making, radio drama, and so on has been the realist one, to the virtual exclusion of all others. The truth, however, is that fantastic literature has *always* played a central role in our literary tradition — right from the beginning. Indeed, the work identified as the first Québécois novel, *L'influence d'un livre* by Phillipe-Aubert de Gaspé (published in 1837), is also the first example of the form known as "le fantastique." The first Canadian science-fiction work we know of was Napoléon Aubin's "Mon voyage à la lune," published in his journal *Le fantasque* in 1839, while the oldest English-Canadian work (published in book form, at least) is *The Dominion in 1983* by the pseudonymous Ralph Centennius, published in 1883.

Our research of collections at institutions such as the National Library of Canada, the Merril Collection, and CBC Radio Archives has indicated that Canadian fantastic literature has been strongly influenced by international trends — especially those in Britain and the United States; however, we have also learned that certain features of the form and content of our fantastic literature *are* distinctly Canadian. Above all, Canadian fantastic literature frequently portrays the search for identity. This search occurs at the level of the individual — "Who am I?" — of the nation — "Who are we?" — and of the species — "What are we?" It would be a mistake to cite the theme of alienation as the defining characteristic of Canadian SF&F, since it is the chief preoccupation of all modern literature. But the theme has particular significance for us, since as Canadians we have long debated our national identity and even questioned whether we possess or will continue to possess one. Consider Northrop Frye's famous formulation of our national question: "Where is here?" If there is one thing that distinguishes Canadian science fiction from British or American science fiction, it is its political as opposed to its technological focus. Canadian writers have been less concerned with the effects of scientific and technological developments than political ones. What would happen if Quebec separated? Or if the United States (or Japan or Germany) invaded? In addition, political themes have been especially important in Québécois writing, but so have religious ones; the first book-length work of what is called QSF, Jules-Paul Tardivel's *Pour la patrie* (1895), neatly combines the two.

Throughout its history, then, Canadian fantastic literature in English and in French has been the product of both international and national forces. It has reflected the concerns of world and domestic developments in literature, culture, and technology. Thanks to the ability of Canadian writers to break into the American book market, particularly through the rise of science fiction and fantasy series (like Star Trek products), and the growth of Canadian publishers interested in the field, such as Press Porcépic/Tesseract Books, science fiction and fantasy have become the fastest growing genres in our literature. Canadian fantastic literature has always been a part of our heritage, but only now are we recognizing its increasing presence and importance.

THE VIEWPOINTS

The following essays bring together the views of scholars and authors in the field of Canadian SF&F literature and expression. We begin with the overviews of the English-Canadian scene by John Clute and John Robert Colombo. Providing a more recent interpretation are Robert Runté and Christine Kulyk. Jean-Louis Trudel and Jean-Marc Gouanvic perform the same service for the history of francophone fantastic literature, describing its earliest roots and tracing its developments to the present day. Stéphane Nicot supplies an international perspective.

Subsequent essays deal with some of the major themes explored in the genre. Canadian writers have frequently examined the strong role of the family in our culture and our sense of personal identity; the same is true for science fiction writers, as evidenced in Terence M. Green's discussion of family in his own work. Canadian science fiction tends to be of the "soft" variety, meaning that it emphasizes characterization and social issues rather than science and technology, and Green both represents and argues for this tendency. Ethnic background is also a key theme in Canadian literature, and Ven Begamudré, whose fiction arises out of the mythology of his Asian cultural background, presents a very personal account of writing in a "multicultural" context. Place is as important in Canadian fantastic literature as in mainstream works, a fact demonstrated in Lesley Choyce's discussion of Atlantic-Canadian SF and the history of his own writing and publishing career. A similar emphasis on place appears in the essay by Tanya Huff.

One of the most remarkable developments in fantastic literature here and elsewhere is the growing number of women writing in the field — in both science fiction and fantasy . . . contrary to the popular image of SF writers. Christine Kulyk, Élisabeth Vonarburg, and Francine Pelletier discuss the special problems and themes of women writers in both linguistic groups. Guy Bouchard takes a more academic, but no less interesting, approach as he analyzes the utopias and dystopias created by Canadian women writers.

Apart from science fiction, Canadian fantasy has grown remarkably in the past few years. Most recently, a number of writers such as Tanya Huff have begun to write "dark fantasy" — in other words, horror and related forms. Huff's article presents a personal perspective, while Robert Hadji, Canada's foremost expert in dark fantasy, surveys the sparse history of the field.

As well as the genres of science fiction and fantasy, we look at some related genres: surrealism, magic realism, and so on. Charles de Lint, one of Canada's best-known fantasists, writes on magic realism and his own work in high fantasy.

Out of This World covers not merely the authors but also the publishers and readers of fantastic literature in this country. Phyllis Gotlieb, Canada's foremost Canadian science fiction writer since the 1960s, describes the neglect and disdain that science fiction has been afforded by Canada's mainstream publishers. The fan magazine or fanzine has become a staple of the genre, and plays a particularly important role in Québécois science fiction. Essays by Joël Champetier and Marc Lemaire, editors respectively of the two most important Québec SF publications *Solaris* and *imagine* . . . , provide histories of their magazines and, by extension, QSF.

In Canada generally, but particularly in Québec, children's fantastic literature has blossomed, resulting in an unprecedented quantity and quality of fiction. The essays by Claire Le Brun and Daniel Sernine discuss the history of children's literature in Québec.

It may surprise some readers to learn how much Canadians have done in non-print media science fiction and fantasy. Upon examination, the situation becomes less surprising. Radio plays have been the main medium — Canadians have produced an astonishing number of plays in this format. Our fantastic radio has uniquely Canadian properties. The dramas were often produced as part of the nation-building function of the Canadian Broadcasting Corporation programing policy. CBC fantastic radio combined adaptations of classic works by international authors such as Arthur C. Clarke, John Wyndham, and Ray Bradbury with original anthology series such as *Vanishing Point* and *Nightfall* that drew on the suggestive and imaginative properties of radio drama to create fantastic realms and concepts. Some of this rich history is discussed in William Lane's essay.

Other artists have created or contributed to the creation of films and television programs. We were pioneers in television space opera with series such as *Space Command* in 1953 and *The Starlost* in 1973. But our more recent works feature genre excursions where Canadian cities and actors are disguised as American — such as *War of the Worlds* and *The X Files*. Canadian fantastic cinema includes practitioners such as Ivan Reitman and James Cameron — with the career of David Cronenberg perhaps representing the most personal and exploratory vision.

The longest-running and possibly most successful Canadian

SF television program is also something of a paradox. TVOntario's six-year series *Prisoners of Gravity* was called an "infotainment documentary about science fiction." *PoG* (as it was referred to in the SF community) was both innovative in its production techniques and dedicated to enhancing public understanding of fantastic literature and artistic expression. Greg Thurlbeck's essay describes how POG came to be created and the special role it played in his career as a television producer.

And as Michael Skeet reveals in his essay, Canadians have also frequently drawn on science fiction and fantasy themes in popular and rock music.

THE IMAGINATIVE HERITAGE

Both the National Library exhibit and the book *Out of This World* are public expressions of Canada's imaginative heritage, marking a watershed in our understanding of ourselves and our popular culture, prompting new discussion and further achievements. There is no area of artistic endeavor in which Canadians have not explored the themes and used the techniques of fantastic storytelling. The realistic mode may well have been the dominant one in our literature, filmmaking, and performing arts, but Canadian writers, producers, playwrights, and musicians have also explored other worlds and other times, reflecting our concerns, problems, and aspirations, questioning our identities as individuals, Canadians, and human beings, portraying the alienation and uncertainty that are so central to our culture. While their eyes are on other planets and other ages, they are really speaking of and for Canadians . . . and seeking the aliens among us.

Allan Weiss *is co-curator of the National Library exhibit* OUT OF THIS WORLD. *He is a Toronto based freelance writer and research consultant, who teaches at Woodsworth College and York University. He has had short stories published in numerous journals and anthologies, including* The Fiddlehead, The Windsor Review, Tesseracts[4], *and* Year's Best Horror Stories; *other stories will be appearing in*

Short Story *and* NorthWords. *His scholarly publications include* A Comprehensive Bibliography of English-Canadian Short Stories 1950-1983 *(1988).*

Hugh Spencer *(M.A. Social Anthropology — McMaster University, Master of Museum Studies — University of Toronto) has been active in the field of science fiction and public education for over twenty years. He has compiled a study of science fiction fan groups,* The Transcendental Engineers: The Fictional Origins of a Modern Religion, *hosted the Royal Ontario Museum's first science fiction film series in 1986-87, and currently serves as the Chair of the Friends of the Merril Collection of Science Fiction, Fantasy and Speculation. He has also published several science fiction short stories in* On Spec *magazine. As the Principal-in-Charge for the Exhibition Planning Division of Lord Cultural Resources Planning and Management Inc., Hugh has served as co-curator of the National Library exhibition* OUT OF THIS WORLD.

FABLES OF TRANSCENDENCE
The Challenge of
Canadian Science Fiction
by John Clute

We can call it a number of things. But what we call it gives us different starting points, and each time we start we end up with a different breed of fish. We can call it Utopian Discourse, and start off with Plato or Sir Thomas More — whose *Utopia* in 1516 gave this version of the genre a name — and end up with Zamiatin and Huxley and Orwell and Philip K. Dick as our touchstone figures. Or we can say it's a genre fundamentally devoted to the Fantastic Voyage, and start with Lucian or (say) Cyrano de Bergerac — who wrote a tale in 1659 about traveling to the Moon — and end up with Jules Verne, E.E. Smith, and Poul Anderson, whose romances of space are really romances of geography. Or we can say it is basically a form of Rationalized Gothic, and start off with Mary Shelley — whose *Frankenstein* in 1818 is thought by many to be the first tale genuinely to confront the impact of Progress and technology upon history — and end up with Theodore Sturgeon and Gene Wolfe as the carriers of the flame. Or we can call it Scientific Romance, and think of H.G. Wells — whose *Time Machine* in 1895 was the first text to treat this globe as time-bound in its round — and end up with Olaf Stapledon and Arthur C. Clarke and Brian Aldiss as figures who convey a view of the world that takes evolutionary perspectives as central.

Or we can call it science fiction.

But this means we must travel south. It is not, of course, an unusual direction for Canadians to take. We must go the United States, because it is there that science fiction (henceforth SF) began in the late 1920s; it is there that publishers and editors who thought of themselves as SF publishers and editors began to publish stories by SF writers who thought of themselves as SF writers — rather than writers who wrote popular fiction to order — and who sold the magazines in which these SF stories were published to an audience that thought of itself — within half a decade of the founding of *Amazing Stories* in 1926 — as making up a unique and privileged family of SF fans. From its beginning, SF was not, in other words, definable simply as a series of texts which expressed a characteristic take on the world (though see below); SF was a highly interactive affinity subculture, many of whose members played — either simultaneously or in turn — all the various roles available within that subculture. People like

Isaac Asimov, Damon Knight, Judith Merril, and Frederik Pohl were fans, editors, publishers, writers, convention organizers; and they also had a habit of marrying one another, too. They may have shared a take on the world (see below), but they were also a family.

This did not happen in Canada until much later. Which is the first thing to understand about Canadian SF. As a *family*, it is very recent. Those Canadians who wrote SF for Americans in (say) 1940, like A.E. Van Vogt, did not do so as members of a family. They wrote alone.

The second thing to understand about Canadian SF — and it's here we begin to enter deep waters — is that when we say it's not in fact American SF, it's almost as though we were saying it was not SF at all. We can argue against the narrowness of this view by arguing that the term SF was never really anything more than shorthand for the nest of widespread genres we've already listed above — a term used by American pirates to gather into a single hoard the Utopian Discourse, the Fantastic Voyage, the Rationalized Gothic, the Scientific Romance, and so forth — and that we're being unduly submissive when we allow the American SF tag to wag the Speculative Fiction dog in this fashion. And we can go on to argue that Canadian speculative fiction — *Consider Her Ways* (1947) by Frederick Grove, say — is just as much SF as the Lensman series by Doc Smith or *Sixth Column* (1949) by Robert A. Heinlein.

No.

In our hearts we must *know* this isn't good enough. In our hearts we must recognize that there was something about American SF in the days of its glory — from about 1925 to about 1965 or 1970 — that profoundly marked it precisely as American. The characteristic flavor of twentieth-century SF — I think we must recognize — was the flavor of America; and the characteristic plots of twentieth century SF were versions of the fable of America. This heartwood American SF story was the myth of a frontier-busting, gadget-loving, tall-tale-telling, melting-pot community, linked by blood or affinity into a genuine folk; exempt from mundane history; and guided by cantankerous Competent Men who created new scientific tools to mark the path, to challenge the frontier, to penetrate the barrier of the unknown, to conquer the aliens, to occupy the territory, to stake out the future.

There are a couple of things to note here. Obviously heroes dominate the American SF story, flamboyant inventive geniuses with calluses who figure in so many of the texts we still find ourselves reading; but there is also a sense of community, a sense that heroes are part of a larger enterprise. That heroes can come home. American SF is community SF. And even though it presents its underlying ethos in terms which tend to obliterate the difference of the Other, it does invite us in. For many of us — Canadians and others — that invitation to join the fable of community is like catnip.

Moreover, there is a trust in reason, too. American SF generates a sense that — even though almost every single story ultimately solves its problems through action — the ethos underlying that action is sustained by arguments no reasonable person can ultimately deny. These arguments — cleanly and clearly conveyed by the hero, or by his uncle, the garrulous but wise scientist/entrepreneur who scorns the bureaucrats back East — are not simply undeniable: in the final analysis, they are *clean*. They bind their readers into futures whose contours are unsullied by blood-guilt or sophistry, without side-effects, and without any lasting resentment on the part of the aliens whose frontier has been smashed, whose culture has been obliterated, whose own future has been canceled. A cynic might suggest that the logic of empire always abides with the victors, but once again a comment like this fails to capture the *allure* of the fable, the generosity of American SF's assumption that reasonable suasion, promulgated by heroes, will bring us all together, even redskins.

Which brings us to a pressing question. Why should the patriotic populist positivism of a literature designed to generate affirmative (and even triumphal) feelings in the citizens of the United States be so successful in other parts of the world? Why (for instance) should Canadian children (in the 1940s and 1950s I was one) find this alien corn so tasty? Like Disney. Like Coca-Cola. Why should we swallow this nonsense? Well, partly because it's not exactly nonsense. Or if it *is* nonsense, then the whole history of the Western world is nonsense. Partly it's because triumph is contagious. When you read American sf you're on the right side. You are going to win. There will be no side effects. And partly because it makes for awfully good storytelling.

So it is hard to escape the allure of the classic American sf myth; and even nowadays — long after many Americans have ceased promulgating it — its characteristic story-types continue to have an almost hypnotic effect on non-American writers and readers and viewers. Both *Star Trek* and *Star Wars* — in TV, film and book form — obsessively continue to present the world as conquerable if you have the Force behind you.

Is there any room for Canadian sf? Has there ever been?

There are two answers. One: we can restrict ourselves to texts like Grove's *Consider Her Ways*, which is a satire in Utopian Discourse mode; or Hugh MacLennan's *Voices in Time* (1980), which is an anatomy of post-holocaust cultural breakdown, without a vestige of the opportunity-loaded flavor of American sf; or Margaret Atwood's *The Handmaid's Tale* (1985), which is a dystopia; or any of the novels of Phyllis Gotlieb or Élizabeth Vonarburg. Though they are certainly speculative fictions, texts like these have little to do with the dominant tone or subject matter or plot-structure of twentieth-century sf, and they tend not to be read as sf by fans. Or Two: we can see if Canadian writers attempting to write within terms of the dominant version of sf have managed — consciously or unconsciously — to convey a dissident sense of the nature of things.

Under One, there seems relatively little to say. Good books have been written and constitute a respectable contribution to the world stock of speculative fiction; and a Canadian concern for the fragility of political and cultural institutions can be seen informing most of them. Under Two, it may be possible to make a suggestion or two, and it might be an idea to glance here at the career of the most prominent single sf writer of Canadian birth.

A.E. Van Vogt has been active from 1939; he is a writer whose prominence from 1940 to 1950 was so marked that most American sf readers thought of him as an unquestionably central figure in American sf, along with Asimov, Heinlein, Clarke (who was British, of course), and very few others. After 1950 he faded from the front rank, partly because of his involvement in Scientology, partly because (as it seems) he burned out, after writing millions of words. In about 1970, he returned to active writing, and enjoyed something of a revival — though he did not regain sufficient fame to be invited to the Science Fiction World Convention held in Winnipeg (his home town) in 1994.

It is the decade of the 1940s, therefore, that must concern us, the period when most American readers of SF thought he was one of them. In retrospect, it is a strange assumption to make, if we actually look carefully at his novels, or novel-like fixups. The most important of these — all at least partly written before he left Canada in 1944, and mostly published in *Astounding Science Fiction* long before they reached book form — are *Slan* (1946), *The Weapon Makers* (1947), *The World of A* (1948), *The Voyage of the Space Beagle* (1950), *The Weapon Shops of Isher* (1951), and *The Pawns of Null-A* (1956). They are all profoundly un-American, as we'll point out. Do they also help define something we might call Canadian SF?

Van Vogt's tales are un-American, to begin with, in their almost total disregard for the details of human community. Their protagonists live in neighborhoods or cities which are generally unnamed, and which are essentially featureless. Countries are also nameless. The planet is probably Earth, but it is not a *special* part of Earth. It is not a promised land. It is, rather, a tabula rasa, a wilderness to be imprinted. But the protagonists who must leave some mark are themselves either without family or have lost their notional families at the moment the tale begins. The destinies they forge (in reality, there is normally only one character who ultimately counts in any of these books) are solitary destinies; though they may ostensibly bear the world on their shoulders, Van Vogt's protagonists are not, in fact, leaders at all, because there is no one in the wilderness to lead. A.E. Van Vogt novels are solitudes; and the fingerprints of passage left by their protagonists constitute not a message to the folk but an indecipherable rune.

These novels are also un-American in the nature of the heroism exhibited or grown into by the protagonist. His heroism — as we have already indicated — cannot be that of the leader of the community who shapes his folk into conquerors of unexplored territories, because of an absence of folk. His heroism is not that of the leader who progresses through the worlds at the head of a folk, but that of the solitary imago-magus who becomes a full-blown superman *through transcendence*. Because there is no intervening tangle of world or community to encumber him, the Van Vogt hero *leaps* into what he is going to become.

Let us put it more positively.

Van Vogt novels pay no attention to ethnicity or nationality, race or color or creed. They pay no attention to civic prides, nation states, or any of the imperial special pleading typical of literatures — like American SF — which plump for the winning side, which treat the cod Social Darwinism to which they're prone as an affirmation of Manifest Destiny to the stars. Moreover, Van Vogt novels — though they are obsessed by supermen — express absolutely no interest in how these super beings affect the details of human discourse. There is no mythopoesis of the culture hero, and there are no prolonged harangues designed to change the mind of the folk — unlike the habitual browbeatings inflicted by Heinlein's typical heroes upon their communities. There is nothing left-wing in Van Vogt; there is nothing fascist.

And finally, Van Vogt novels show an astonishing lack of interest in matters of science or technology, both of which are treated as magic buttons. There is no reverence for senatorial reason.

Canadian SF — in the hands of someone like Van Vogt — is clearly not much like American SF. It is not community based; it is not about the penetration of frontiers; it is not triumphalist about the nation state; it ignores the culture heroes who marshall the folk or who save the world; and it ignores the details of the science and technology which are used by culture heroes to weld the community together and to arm it for conquest. Canadian SF — if A.E. Van Vogt is one of its central founders — can therefore be defined as a genre which translates the fable of survival so central to the Canadian psyche into a fable of lonely transcendence.

Van Vogt is not alone. Gordon R. Dickson was born in Canada, but though he left by the age of twelve or so, there remains something ineluctably Canadian about the solitary take of his heroes on the universe. William Gibson and Robert Charles Wilson were born in the United States, but both have lived in Canada for many years. The protagonist of Gibson's *Neuromancer* is a cyberspace cowboy, a solipsistic hacker in a vast world of owners. He is street-wise — but being streetwise means you know how to survive in the street (or wilderness). It does not mean you understand the street. And Wilson's novels tend to feature transcendental migrations of displaced persons into blank terrains.

For more than half a century, SF has been a literature of culture heroes, conceptual breakthroughs, manifest destiny, and imperial reasonings. Over that period, Canadian SF has been a wainscot halfling, murmuring a more bleak tune. Perhaps it has come time to treat it as the theme.

John (Frederick) Clute is a Canadian novelist and SF critic who lives in the U.K. His first professional publication, a long SF-tinged poem called "Carajou Lament," appeared in Triquarterly *in 1959. He began publishing SF proper with "A Man Must Die" for NW (1966), where much of his earlier criticism also appeared. A selection from this work appears in* Strokes: Essays and Reviews 1966-1986. *In 1960 he was Associate Editor of* Collage, *an ill fated Chicago-based "slick" magazine which in its two issues did manage to publish early work by Harlan Ellison and R.A. Lafferty. He served as Reviews Editors of* Foundation *(1980-1990), and was a founder of* Interzone *in 1982, where he remains Advisory Editor. John Clute is co-editor of* The Encyclopedia of Science Fiction.

FOUR HUNDRED YEARS OF FANTASTIC LITERATURE IN CANADA

by John Robert Colombo

I T REQUIRES *hubris* or *chutzpah* or imagination (ideally the latter) to refer to "four hundred years of fantastic literature in Canada" when the country is little more than a century and a quarter old. As well, to make any sense of the subject it requires some agreement on what constitutes "four hundred years," "fantastic literature," and even the Dominion of Canada. With general agreement in short supply, I am going to offer the patient reader some capsule definitions and leave it at that.

But before I do so, I want to point out that Canada is twice distinguished in the world of the literary fantastic. The most widely quoted fantastic verse in the English-speaking world was written by a poetaster from Manitoba. I am referring to "Relativity," which first appeared in Punch on December 19, 1923. It goes like this:

There was a young lady named Bright
Whose speed was far faster than light;
>   She set out one day
>   In a relative way
And returned on the previous night.

The limerick — the best-known "clean" limerick — was composed by A.H. Reginald Buller, botanist at the University of Manitoba, and it deals classically with the paradox of time travel. Canada is also the sole country in the world with a community that bears the nickname of a fantasy hero. The mining community of Flin Flon in Manitoba was so named in 1913 by a group of miners following their accidental discovery near the future town site of a ragged copy of *The Sunless City* (1905). This dime novel was written by the once-popular English writer J.E. Preston Muddock who set the action on — and beneath — the Canadian prairies. Flin Flon is the nickname of Professor Josiah Fintabbatey Flonatin who develops a remarkable submarine that takes him to the bottom of a Prairie lake, where in the interior of the earth he finds a gold-rich "sunless city" populated by beautiful women. The exploits of Flin Flon so entertained the miners that they remembered the nickname when they registered the site. There is now a fiber-glass likeness of Fintabbatey Flonatin on the outskirts of the town, the work of the cartoonist Al Capp. Flin Flon's nearest rival for civic honors is Tarzana, California.

This inquiry into the tradition of fantastic literature will be a personal one, one limited to the work of imaginative writers, to their fiction and poetry; no art, no film, and no folklore will be examined. The contributors may be a Canadian (including a *Québécois*), a New Canadian (a landed immigrant, what used to be called a resident alien), a Pre Canadian (someone who resided here before Confederation), an Ex Canadian (someone born here who moved elsewhere), and a Non Canadian (a foreigner who wrote about life here). Someone once quipped that anyone who ever flew over Canada in a rocket ship may be considered an honorary Canadian. By this token, anyone, anywhere, may contribute to the development of this literature. Indeed, I have long felt that the most memorable Canadian science-fiction novel is *Roadside Picnic*, which was written in Russian in Russia by the Strugatsky Brothers, Boris and Arkadi Strugatsky, Soviet scientists who were never allowed to visit North America except in the spaceships of their imaginations. *Roadside Picnic* is set in the vicinity of a city like Sudbury, Ontario. It describes in ambiguous terms the effects on humankind of the application of the gift of alien technology, a national preoccupation as well as an international problem.

"Fantastic literature" is short for "the literature of the fantastic." I have in mind three literary genres: Science Fiction, Fantasy Fiction, and Weird Fiction. The three genres are more distinct in theory than in practice, but they do represent different approaches to storytelling. Science Fiction is writing that is realistic and deals with reasonable change that follows the introduction of a scientific discovery or a technological invention or application. Fantasy Fiction is writing that seems closer to legend and myth than to realism; it describes heroic action in a world that is not our own. Weird Fiction, often described as "horror fiction," "occult fiction," or "supernatural fiction," offers the reader a realistic world that lies somewhere between the workaday world informed by science and the world charged with imaginative values; in Weird Fiction, the society and world are recognizably our own, except for the fact that someone finds a miraculous object or develops a strange talent, unexpected and non-scientific in nature. Within Weird Fiction, the difference between the literature of horror and the literature of terror is that in the former the accent is on physical menace, whereas in the latter it is on psychological menace, roughly equivalent to the difference between the physical horror of Frankenstein and the psychical terror of Dracula.

The three genres are easily distinguished, as a consideration of modes of transportation suggests. In Science Fiction, the given mode of transportation may be a rocket ship, spaceship, or starship, perhaps even a flying saucer, depending on the period and the sophistication of the writing. In Fantasy Fiction, the mode of transportation might be a flying carpet or a steed that is the descendant of Pegasus, based on the setting of the work. In Weird Fiction, there might be levitation or sudden appearances and disappearances without rationale. In any prose narrative, the mode of transportation is accepted as the norm, and the reader does not expect to encounter in a given novel or story both sleek spaceships and winged steeds, as consistency and appropriateness are required. Is interchangeability possible or impossible? C.S. Lewis thought it possible, for he once wrote, "I took a hero once to Mars in a space-ship, but when I knew better I had angels convey him to Venus."

Common to the three genres is the working of what could loosely be called the Fantastic Imagination. This imagination, as distinguished from the Realistic Imagination, presents human beings, society, the world, and the cosmos as transformed by change (Science Fiction), as foreign to our own world (Fantasy Fiction), or as menaced by powers from secret or hidden worlds (Weird Fiction). Writers of fantastic literature tend to specialize in one or other of the three genres, but not always. For instance, Brian Moore is considered a mainstream novelist, but there is no way to predict the category of his novel. Here are three instances: *Catholics*, set in the future, is Science Fiction; *The Great Victorian Collection*, which deals with how a "wild talent" transforms the present world, is Fantasy Fiction; *Cold Comfort*, a novel of terror in which the dead do not lie down and die, is Weird Fiction. Yet all three novels are accepted as mainstream fiction. Many of the world's finest novels are novels of the fantastic imagination that have entered into the mainstream — *Gulliver's Travels, 1984,*

Animal Farm, The Fifth Child, The Turn of the Screw, etc.

The notion of "four hundred years" requires some clarification. Four centuries from when to when? I am going to suggest that fantastic literature in Canada began in 1657 and extends to 1995, the year the National Library of Canada conferred official recognition on the contributions made by Canadians to the literature of the fantastic. But the arithmetically minded reader will appreciate the fact that the time-span comes to only 338 years, 62 years short of four centuries. Not to worry: contributions will continue on to the year 2057 and beyond, as they extend backwards into the past, well before the symbolic year 1657. The future will take care of itself. As for the contributions of the past, they emerge from the realms of myth, legend, and lore of the Native Peoples. So let the missing sixty-two years be representative of age-old Indian and Inuit storytelling. Some of the traditional tales recited by the native people are hundreds of years old and may even be thousands of years old. The stories, rooted in native oratory and shamanistic practice, sound to contemporary ears rather like Magic Realism, a division of Weird Fiction.

Augmenting the tale-telling tradition of the Native Peoples are the non-native, imaginative reconfigurations of the Near and Far North. There is a discussion of the enduring and dynamic imagery of the vastness of the Arctic with respect to seven eras of prehistory in *Mysterious Canada* (1988). A succession of Arctics has been imagined in terms of the so-called Imperishable Sacred Land, Arctic Eden, Arctic Atlantis, Mount Meru (original home of the Aryan people), Hyperborea (or Ultima Thule), Polar Opening to the Hollow Earth, and the legend of the Tropical Valley. Lost Race and other novels set in the polar regions of the world offer glimpses of some of the possibilities available to Canadian and other writers. To date, the prospectors of this mother lode of imagery have been foreign writers. One of them, Nicholas Monsarrat, wrote a novel, *The Time Before This* (1962), a parable-like survivor's account, which considers the ramifications of the discovery of a stockpile of advanced alien artifacts in a vast cavern on Baffin Island.

The first prose narrative of a fantastic nature with a chapter set in early Canada appeared in Paris in 1657. I am referring to the initial publication of the first part of *Voyages to the Moon and Sun,* the famous "imaginary voyage" written by the seventeenth-century French writer with a familiar name: Cyrano de Bergerac. The playwright Edmund Rostand celebrated Cyrano's prowess with sword and verse in his 1897 poetic drama. Scholar Sam Moscowitz neatly characterized Cyrano as a "Swordsman in Space." In *Voyages,* Cyrano makes the world's first trip to the moon through the agency of "dew-power." Observing that the dew "rises" in the morning, Cyrano collects the dew in vials, fastens the vials to his wrists and ankles, and takes off from Paris en route to the lunar orb. When the dew expands, the vials explode, and the "early astronaut" crashlands. Forgetting about the rotation of the earth, he assumes that he has crashlanded in the Midi area of France. Instead, the earth's rotation has taken him to the woods of New France. Here he complains about the quality of the French that is spoken by the *habitants* who flock to greet him. When they take him to the Intendant, he remonstrates against the official's narrow views and arbitrary rule. Finding New France not to his liking, he constructs a cherrywood rocket that launches him in the direction of the moon. Needless to add, Cyrano effects a lunar landing and then a solar landing, returning to Old France a sadder but wiser "early astronaut." Whether *Voyages* marks an auspicious or an inauspicious inauguration of fantastic literature in Canada is moot, but it does mark a beginning and it does highlight some themes that have become common: lack of technology, fear of the foreign, and the alienated outsider.

Cyrano de Bergerac wrote in French; so did the next contributor to the anecdotal history of fantastic literature in Canada. Jules Verne is internationally known for his such "fantastic voyages" as *20,000 Leagues under the Sea,* which features the exploits of Captain Nemo, who in his submarine *Nautilus* became the discoverer of the South Pole. Verne's hero Captain Hatteras is less well known. The son of a London brewer, Hatteras heads his own Arctic expedition and is the first person to "attain" the North Pole. All this happens in Verne's novel *The Adventures of Captain Hatteras.* First published in 1866, the novel follows the expedition to the polar region and then across the frozen surface of the Arctic Ocean until Hatteras and his men arrive at the foothills of the North Pole. They discover that the northernmost region of the world corresponds to a mountain on an island in the middle of the otherwise frozen Arctic Ocean. There is no difference between the North Geographic Pole and the North Magnetic Pole. To his dismay, Hatteras learns that the mountain is really a volcano on the verge of erupting. Nevertheless, at great personal risk, he climbs the volcano, "attains" the Pole, plants the Union Jack on its highest ridge, just as the volcano begins to spew forth its lava! Excitement and invention are characteristics of Verne's work. Hatteras flees the scene amid a shower of lava that is not only scorchingly hot but also peculiarly "magnetized." In the last chapter of the novel, there is a description of Hatteras at rest in a convalescent home outside London. Captain Hatteras's brain has been "magnetized," it seems. When he walks across the grounds, he paces in only two directions: north-south, south-north.

In all, Jules Verne set five of his novels in Canada. They illustrate two themes that take on special meaning in the Canadian context: the importance of isolation and the unrivaled opportunity for adventure in the Arctic. For the imaginative use that Verne — and Cyrano — have made of Canadian locales, the two geniuses should be granted honorary dual, French-Canadian citizenship.

The first native-born Canadian author to tackle a fantastic theme in a literary way is James De Mille, professor of classics at Dalhousie University in Halifax. Among his numerous popular novels is one of enduring interest, his fantastic voyage titled *A Strange Manuscript Found in a Copper Cylinder* (1888). It is a survivor's tale of a one-way voyage to the South Pole, through the Polar Opening, into the interior of the Hollow Earth. Here the sailor Adam More discovers that the horizon rises rather than falls, and that its inhabitants, the Koseken, have an appropriate inversion of values. They value death over life and sacrifice over love. Perhaps De Mille saw the Koseken as the Canadians of the day, hewers of traditions not their own, drawers of other people's values. Anyway, De Mille's dystopian novel offers a consistent set of moral reactions and an ethical critique of social values, as well as the richly drawn model of an inner-Earth world.

Algernon Blackwood, one of the greatest writers of the fiction of horror and terror in the English language, lived as a young remittance man in Toronto (1890-92). He served as secretary to the political essayist Goldwin Smith, became part owner in a public house, summered in Muskoka, moved on to New York, and then returned to London where he began to write the weird fiction for which he is remembered. The Canadian woods are the settling for six of his stories, and he used Canadian protagonists in two more stories that are set in Europe. These eight stories are among Blackwood's earliest and most powerful works of fiction. Notable among them are "A Haunted Island" from *The Empty House* (1906) and "The Wendigo" from *The Lost Valley* (1910).

Despite the fact that Blackwood's stories were popular with Prime Minister Mackenzie King, Blackwood's work has yet to be collected and published in this country. One reason for the neglect is that his stories frighten Canadian readers; we are happy with the notion that the Canadian woods have restorative powers; we balk at the suggestion that nature is malign or alien and that the woods are routes to other, darker worlds. The "animal stories" of Ernest Thompson Seton and Sir Charles G.D. Roberts have convinced generations of readers that the natural world may be harsh but it is morally neutral. At the same time these stories have anthropomorphised, essentially sanitized, the wildlife. Blackwood is the sole writer to suggest otherwise, maintaining that nature is not neutral but allied to alien, extra-human powers, and that flora and fauna may be morally malignant. Tracts of earth are "unearthly" and attempts to create clearings are doomed to fail. This is what is most characteristic of Blackwood's weird fiction, especially of his Canadian tales of horror and terror. No wonder he goes unpublished here.

The most outrageous work of the Canadian fantastic imagination is the so-called "Ant-Book." This is Frederick Philip Grove's way of referring to his novel *Consider Her Ways* (1947). Grove is principally remembered as a chronicler of pioneer prairie life; yet in 1919-20 he conceived the notion of writing a book about the migration of 10,000 worker ants across North America. He would follow their trek from the rain forests of Venezuela, across the Panama Canal and the American Plains, to the East Coast, where those ants that survived wintered in the New York Public Library.

In the stacks they particularly relished the glue in the bindings of the books of poetry. Then they returned (by train) to the rain forests of Venezuela. Out of this astonishing material, Grove fashioned a thorough-going critique of modern Western values a quarter-century after the vision that engendered it. Reading the novel one has the feeling that it is too much of a good thing. Had the "Ant-Book" been written by Franz Kafka, it would be a thirty-page masterpiece. In Grove's hands it is an ungainly work, some 300 pages in length. Yet it is also an audacious novel, one too frequently overlooked.

The Golden Age of Science Fiction would lack in energy but for the vigorous prose of A.E. van Vogt, who is the genre's greatest "living master" of Canadian origin. Raised in rural Manitoba, he was doubtless affected by the vision of the prairies and the never-ending horizon when he turned his hand to depicting the far reaches of Outer Space. He wrote his earliest and finest fiction in Winnipeg, Ottawa, and Toronto, before settling permanently in Los Angeles in 1944. He once estimated that he wrote 600,000 words of fantastic literature on native soil, including such classic tales as "Black Destroyer" (inspired by Seton's *The Biography of a Grizzly*) and the perennially popular novel *Slan* (1940). He went on to write millions of words in Los Angeles, though little of the California fiction caught the "fine, careless rapture" (as one critic expressed it) of the early years.

Van Vogt's incredible creative outburst, marked by vivid accounts of planetary destruction, corresponded to the cataclysm of the Second World War. The war marked a watershed in Canadian history and hence in its literature. In the pre-War period, serious writers were few and far between; in the post-War period, serious writers were found right across the country. Donald A. Wollheim, the New York editor and writer, was asked to contribute an article on Canadian writing to one of the so-called CanPulps, pulp magazines printed in Toronto and Montreal to replace the American pulps that were embargoed "for the duration." He called the article "Whither Canadian Fantasy?" and it appeared in *Uncanny Tales*, December 1942. Despite the title, it mentions the name of not one Canadian writer — or British or American writer for that matter! Wollheim stated that Canada's "fantasy" lies in its future and that "Canada's future is in the north."

Wollheim named no Canadian writers. The problem facing the commentator on the writing of the post-War period is that there are too many writers to name. Yet the writers made their impact outside the country, publishing in science-fiction and fantasy publications south of the border, there being no Canadian little magazines or pulp magazines to encourage their writings. By the 1970s, writers came into their own in Quebec and then in the rest of Canada. Here there is the opportunity to take a cursory look at some interesting writers and important works that are of general interest to anglophone students of the literature of the fantastic.

"From the sixties to the early eighties Phyllis Gotlieb *was* Canadian SF. From a purist point of view, she may still be." So wrote the critic David Ketterer in *Canadian Science Fiction and Fantasy* (1992). He had in mind Gotlieb's record of publication in the United States and elsewhere, the quality of her well-constructed stories and novels, the sympathy she shows for human beings, notably youths and mutants, and the empathy she has for animals and other alien beings, especially those that display PSI powers. Gotlieb remains best known for her poetry and for first novel, *Sunburst* (1964). There are many reasons for the fact that she has more successes than readers. Regular readers of science fiction are somewhat resistant to the complex characters and complicated situations found in Gotlieb's GalFed novels, the Starcats series, and books set on Dhalgren's world. Gotlieb is a far voyager; Canadian readers hug the shore. Editors of the larger publishing houses here are by and large fans of mainstream fiction.

Any attempt to date the advent of an indigenous Canadian fantastic literature — as distinct from the continuing tradition of fantastic literature in Canada — should begin with the year 1970. That year Judith Merril established the Spaced Out Library as a special collection within the Toronto Public Library System. What began as the donation of her personal library of paperback and clothbound books has since become one of the genre's great collections. In the early days of the Merril Collection, as it is now called, there was a shelf of Canadian titles. Now bookcases are necessary to hold these titles.

Merril is one of the major "science-fiction personalities," a fine storywriter, and an influential anthologist. In her writing, editing, and teaching, she focuses one eye on the mainstream, another eye on the genre, and her third, intuitive eye on up-and-coming writers and social thinkers and activists. She has inspired, schooled, and critiqued a generation of writers, editors, teachers, and readers across the country. At the Space Out Library, for instance, I was able to compile *Other Canadas*, the world's first anthology of Canadian fantastic literature, in 1979. Nowhere else could it have been edited. Here, in 1985, Merril herself found time to compile the founding volume in the ongoing *Tesseracts* series of anthologies.

Some outstanding novels of the contemporary period that are overlooked by the specialist reader are William Weintraub's brilliant dystopia *The Underdogs* (1979), set in the newly independent State of Quebec; Hugh MacLennan's *Voices in Time* (1980), set in a post-nuclear holocaust Quebec; Gwendolyn MacEwen's poems of "lucid dreaming" in *The Armies of the Moon* (1972); Margaret Atwood's *The Handmaid's Tale* (1985); William Gibson *Neuromancer* (1984); as well as the six novels written by Edward Llewellyn that begin with *The Douglas Convolution* (1979) and end with the posthumously published *Word-Bringer* (1986). There is no room to do more than mention the names of such widely respected writers of high fantasy fiction as Charles de Lint and Guy Gavriel Kay.

Since the 1980s commentators have extolled the virtues of literary regionalism. In practice this amounts to featuring writers who live in Vancouver, the Gulf Islands, Edmonton, Ottawa, Montreal, or Halifax, but not those who live in Toronto for reasons never articulated. Perhaps a Torontonian may be forgiven for singling out prose fiction by three writers of quality active in the country's largest city: Terence M. Green's *The Woman Who Is the Midnight Wind* (1987), Robert J. Sawyer's *Golden Fleece* (1990), and Andrew Weiner's *Distant Signals* (1990). In the 1980s Toronto served as the nexus for the group of talented writers who called themselves the Bunch of Seven, later the Bunch of Nine.

A sign that literary regionalism has not completely displaced literary nationalism was the formation of the Speculative Writers Association of Canada and the appearance of its quarterly journal

On Spec. Yet no Canadian publishing house was interested in publishing David Ketterer's *Canadian Science Fiction and Fantasy* (1992); the first sustained study in the field bears the imprint of an American university press. It is Ketterer's view that only Canadians contribute to the country's fantastic literature. I have tried to show in this personal account that many germane and powerful works that reveal the psychic depths of the land and its inhabitants were written not by natives but by such foreign writers as Verne, Blackwood, and the Strugatsky Brothers.

It is possible to offer a few generalizations that may or may not be apparent from this anecdotal account. Canadian writers have published more fantasy fiction than science fiction; this may illustrate the low priority given innovation in the country. Mainstream writers rather than genre writers account for the most powerfully imagined novels and stories; one reason for this is that there is little market for the work of genre writers (whose contributions to the American pulp magazines and the CanPulps have yet to be collected and assessed). Two characteristic Canadian themes have been identified: Polar Worlds and National Disaster Scenario. In the former, strange events are occurring in the Arctic that may affect the world. In the latter, natural or political disaster strikes; here are some scenarios: the U.S.A. or the U.S.S.R. or both contaminate Canada with nuclear fallout; the U.S. delivers ultimata that cripple Canada economically; Quebec secedes from Confederation; and Alberta and British Columbia conspire to join the American Union. National disintegration is the avowed theme of writers like Richard Rohmer and William Weintraub (in his neglected, prophetic novel *The Underdogs*). It has been said that English Canadians are the only people in the world who more fear an attack from Hull than an attack from Mars.

Do such themes reflect characteristics of the Canadian temperament? If not, it may be possible to find such characteristics through an extended comparison of the Canadian experience with a popular TV series. If *Star Trek* had been conceived in Canada, William Shatner would continue as Captain Kirk, being "Canadian content" by reason of birth. The name of the Star Ship *Enterprise* would be changed to reflect the bilingual and multicultural heritage of all Canadians; an Inuit word would be chosen, probably

Nuna (Earth) of *Krilak* (Sky). Exploration would not be the starship's mission; it would be peacekeeping in Deep Space. Entire episodes would be related from the point of view of a member of an endangered species. The administration of the ship would be military, with Captain Kirk's rank that of Lieutenant-Governor or Governor General. The operation would be a joint undertaking of private enterprise and public regulation — in other words, a Crown Corporation. Continuing concerns would be wrangles over whether the specific interventions were a federal or a provincial responsibility. Compromise rather than coercion would inform the decision-making process, with the occasional Royal Commission to justify delayed action. To respect the national commitment to bilingualism and multiculturalism, officers and crew members would be selected from qualified members of minority groups: Ukrainians, Caribbeans, Poles, Pakistanis, Newfoundlanders, etc. In each episode the Québeckers on board would threaten to "go it alone." Half the episodes, or half of each episode, would be produced in French, with English subs or dubs. Finally, *Star Trek's* option would not have been renewed ... the series would not have lasted beyond its first season.

John Robert Colombo is nationally known as the Master Gatherer for his compilations of Canadiana. He has written, compiled, and translated over eighty books. Among them are five quote books, six anthologies of Canadian fantastic literature, and seven books about the paranormal in Canada. As a bibliographer and editor he contributed to one of the grandest science-fiction anthologies of all time: The Planetary Society's selection of Mars-related SF which has been encoded on a specially engineered CD-ROM that will be an integral part of the Mars Lander spacecraft when it leaves Earth in fall 1995 and lands on the surface of the Red Planet in Spring 1996 — the first anthology of literature to leave the bounds of Earth.

THE NORTHERN COSMOS
Distinctive Themes
in Canadian SF
by Robert Runté and Christine Kulyk

OUT OF THIS WORLD grows out of the recent realization that there is indeed a distinct body of Canadian SF, that it differs from what has gone before, and that — in spite of Canadians' traditional inferiority complex — it is actually pretty good. Since the early 1980s Canadian SF writers have gone from near invisibility in a genre dominated by American publishers, editors, and writers to a growing movement that is helping to redefine, and thereby revitalize, SF. Just as British writers in the late 1960s suddenly found themselves at the forefront of the New Wave which invaded and enriched the genre of Gernsbach and Campbell, Canadian writers today are coalescing into a distinctive voice which is taking SF in new directions. In this article, then, we propose to identify the chief characteristics that distinguish Canadian SF from the traditional British and American varieties.[1]

Any such analysis must begin by acknowledging the pioneering work of John Robert Colombo. In the preface to his 1979 anthology of Canadian SF, *Other Canadas* , he identified four themes as typically Canadian: (1) the "Polar World"; (2) the "National Disaster Scenario"; (3) the "Alienated Outsider"; and (4) the "prevalence of Fantasy over Science Fiction."[2] Of these, only the "Alienated Outsider" is still accepted as valid, but the other categories live on in modified form.

The "Polar World" theme may be dismissed as an example of circular reasoning, since Colombo *defined* as "Canadian" anything set in the Canadian North. Few of the current generation of writers show any interest in the polar world, however, so most critics today talk instead about "an awareness of the environment." In some cases this is manifest as an explicit concern with environmental issues. Wayland Drew's Erthring Cycle, for example, was one of the first post-holocaust series where the fall of civilization was brought about by environmental collapse rather than by nuclear war. More commonly, this "awareness of the environment" refers to an emphasis on the setting itself and an acceptance that we are shaped by our physical environment. As Candas Jane Dorsey has stated during a panel discussion at ConText '89, "in some cases, the protagonist's relationship to the environment *is* the story, more so than the tendency in American SF for characters to collect plot coupons to get out of the story."[3]

From this perspective, even William Gibson's cyberpunk novels may be seen as dealing with environmental themes because they represent the urban environment in a new way. Canadians live in a country climatically and geographically diverse, so Canadian writers tend to understand the importance of the environment in shaping the regional cultures and the individuals that participate in them.[4] Dave Duncan's *West of January* and Donald Kingsbury's *Courtship Rite*, in which humans have adapted both culturally and *physiologically* to their ecological niches, are good examples of the Canadian view that humankind is subordinate to nature. Where American protagonists tend to be larger than life and dominate their worlds, Canadian protagonists tend to be overwhelmed by their surroundings. In Canadian SF, when one goes forth to challenge the elements (as in H. A. Hargreaves' "Protected Environment"[5]), one generally loses.

Colombo was closer to the mark with his second category. Canadians have never really believed that this improbable country could work, so the "National Disaster Scenario" is almost second nature: pieces of the country are always threatening to separate, on the brink of losing their primary resource, or otherwise falling apart. The problem is that these themes are not so much speculative fiction as they are a recap of the CBC nightly news. John Bell, for example, has identified over 40 English-language SF works on Québec separatism, but given the recent election of the Parti Québécois in Québec and the Bloc Québécois in the federal parliament, future stories in this vein may have to be classed as "historical fiction" rather than SF.[6] Indeed, from the francophone writers' view, the "national disaster scenario" refers to a future in which Québec is still *part* of Canada.[7]

Similarly, a significant proportion of Canadians still maintain strong ties to the other nations and cultural heritages from which we came. Whereas the American melting pot attempts to assimilate everyone into a single dynamic culture, the official Canadian policy of multiculturalism attempts to preserve a mosaic of interacting but distinctive cultures. With practically every Canadian belonging to a minority group different from that of their neighbors, and with a national population too small to achieve a very powerful voice in international affairs, the "Alienated Outsider" is every Canadian. Sometimes it seems as if the only thing Canadians have in common is the vague feeling that whatever is important in the world, it isn't to be found here. Culturally, politically, and economically, Canadians feel especially overwhelmed by our American neighbors, but this alienation from the mainstream is conditioned by the desire to *remain* outsiders.

Of course, alienation is a common enough theme in modern mainstream literature. What distinguishes the treatment of this theme in Canadian fiction, however, is this desire to *maintain* one's isolation. Take H. A. Hargreaves' classic short story, "Dead to the World."[8] A computer error lists the protagonist as dead, effectively cutting him off from access to the vast bureaucracy that society has become. After a series of unsuccessful attempts to re-establish his identity and re-enter the community, he eventually accommodates to his situation and achieves an inner peace which would have been impossible in his former role as participating citizen. In the end, he prefers to remain 'dead'. Similarly, in two of Edward Llewellyn's novels — *Salvage and Destroy* and *Fugitive in Transit* — the characters are all so alienated from their own societies that they find it easier to relate to each other than to their own species; and the protagonists ultimately defect to join their former enemies.

The "prevalence of fantasy over science fiction" in Canadian SF (though less pronounced than in Colombo's day) is similarly explained by the fact that, unlike the nation of pragmatic technocrats to the south, Canadians tend to be more concerned with preserving our past — our separate cultural ties and heritages — than with speculating on our somewhat dubious future. Most "hard" science fiction to date has been essentially the literature of expanding economic and technocratic empires, the outgrowth of an America confident that the future belongs to them. It is more difficult for an author from Québec, for example, seriously to believe the people staffing the space station 50 years from now will be named Jacques-Yves and Marie-Claude.[9]

Similarly, Canadians live in a country that is physically overwhelming. Large areas are virtually uninhabitable and population centers are separated by vast distances. Flying up north or driving across the prairies at night may not be a perfect parallel to space travel, but it reminds us what *distance* really means. Perhaps one reason Canadians tend *not* to write about vast interstellar empires is because we know how hard it is for someone in Ottawa to relate to conditions in Halifax or Victoria, let alone to someone on a planet circling Alpha Centauri.

Furthermore, Canadian attitudes towards technology, even now that more Canadians are turning to 'hard' SF, differ from those of the Americans. The quintessential story in John W. Campbell's *Analog* had an engineer land on a planet, be confronted with a technological problem, solve it, and thus make space safe for America. Canadians, on the other hand, are often distrustful of technology, and are more likely to complain about what the engineers are doing to us than laud them. Candas Jane Dorsey's award-winning story "Sleeping in a Box" is a typical example of Canadian hard SF, where people come to hate the space environment. This attitude can be related back to the concern with environmental themes prevalent in Canadian SF — technological progress seen as an enemy of the environment.

In addition to these thematic characteristics, it is also interesting to note that Canadian authors have always moved easily from the mainstream to SF and back again. Practically every significant Canadian author has written at least one speculative fiction story. In contrast, few American mainstream authors attempt to write SF, and American SF authors often find it impossible to break out of the SF ghetto and into the mainstream. This sort of stereotyping has never been a problem for Canadian authors, perhaps because being Canadian is itself a marketing category. Isolated in the Canadiana section, there simply wasn't room for a separate SF shelf. Then, too, with most Canadians convinced that SF was an American genre, Canadian mainstream writers could happily proceed to write their vision of the future, secure in the knowledge that it had nothing to do with that "Buck Rogers stuff."

The downside of this was that few SF readers were aware of the existence of Canadian SF since it was seldom marketed as such. Until the publication of *Other Canadas* in 1979 brought several of these stories together in one volume, they languished in various Canadian small press literary magazines and on dusty library shelves. The upside was that Canadian SF included a higher proportion of what might be termed respectable literature, written by the likes of Margaret Atwood, Frederick P. Grove, Phyllis Gotlieb, William Kinsella, Margaret Laurence, Hugh MacLennan, Leon Rooke, Robin Skelton, Steven Scobie, Michel Tremblay, and Michael Yates.

This literary tradition is also reflected in the stylistic elements characteristic of Canadian speculative fiction. Whereas American science fiction can be characterized as generally having happy endings, and the British New Wave SF of the late 1960s as having unhappy endings, Canadian endings are almost always ambiguous. As Lorna Toolis notes,

> American stories tend to be very problem-oriented. The viewpoint character is presented with a clearly defined problem and he solves it. American readers have been brought up on television, which packages stories in fifty-four-minute-plus-commercials format, complete with happy ending. . . . [In] Canadian literature . . . problems are vaguely perceived, messily resolved, and one is left with the impression that the characters' lives keep going even after the curtain comes down on this particular scene.[10]

In Canadian literature, change does not inevitably equal growth, and the major character is likely no better off, and sometimes worse off, at the end of the story than at the beginning.

Indeed, even the concept of "hero" in Canadian literature is different from the traditional image of heroism in SF. Canadian books tend to concentrate more on ordinary people muddling through ordinary lives, rather than on heroes of the all-capable, aggressive, and conquering type. This may be because Canadians are accustomed to feeling like the underdog, whether in international politics, the world of art, or international athletic competition. Canadians tend to see our heroes as victims, or losers with occasional wins; any victories that these characters achieve will be hard won and indecisive since they are always at the mercy of time, the elements, and other such universal foes, as well as the specific enemies in the individual stories. Even in the rare examples of heroic adventure, such as Dave Duncan's *West of January*, the hero's self-image remains one of cowardice and inadequacy, even though he ends up conquering or saving the world.[11]

Consequently, Canadian SF tends towards introspective character studies rather than action-adventure. This approach tends to give a rather bleak aspect to much Canadian fiction, an aspect which is enhanced by the tendency to slow-paced action and thought-oriented stories. The rip-roaring, supercharged fun of Star Wars style "space opera" is primarily an American motif derived from the stories of the Old West. Even when Canadians attempt to write space opera, it often acquires a uniquely Canadian spin. Leslie Gadallah's *Cat's Pawn*, for example, appears at first glance to be a typical space opera, complete with spacer bars and pirates, but on closer analysis one recognizes the typically Canadian traits of a bungling hero and an ambiguous ending: our hero has been manipulated the whole time by the real protagonist (who has remained offstage for most of the book); and while both of them win all their individual battles, these turn out to have been the *wrong* struggles, and the war is lost. Both protagonists survive, but are forced to live out their lives in dreary exile, knowing that the next generation of their species is doomed.[12]

Similarly, in Gadallah's *Loremasters* our hero-the-spy is arrested almost as soon as he arrives in town; his girlfriend back home gets so caught up in mobilizing the bureaucracy to send a rescue party that she eventually gives him up for a life in politics; the rescue party, when it finally arrives, breaks into the wrong jail; our hero's one bungled attempt at escape proves his guilt just when his jailers were about to let him go; the local woman who falls in love with him finds herself marrying somebody else in the end; and while the bad guys are even more incompetent than our side — thus providing us with a happy ending — nobody ends up with what they thought they wanted at the beginning.[13]

Thus, even in these lightweight actioners written for the American mass market, one can detect typically Canadian themes and styles. Perhaps journalist Francine Pelletier best captured the essence of the Canadian mythos (and therefore of our literature) when she said, "I like the idea that this country is something of a tribute to the underdog and the underbrush . . . . Let's face it, sheer adversity and diversity are what make this country worthwhile, not historical exploits."[14]

Canadian speculative fiction, then, constitutes a distinct sub-genre because it arises out of a distinct Canadian culture. Beyond the broad generalizations outlined above are any number of specific historical and cultural references which, extrapolated into outer space or the future, skew traditional SF projections in unexpected ways. Where an American writing about the colonization of space starts from the Wild West assumptions of a frontier mythos dominated by gunslingers and wars against the natives, a Canadian is likely to draw on a mythos in which stable government and the North-West Mounted Police smoothed colonial settlement. Where Americans project an assimilationist view in which nationalism is a barrier to the emergence of a unified human civilization, Canadians write about the importance of cultural preservation and national identity, as in Guy Gavriel Kay's masterpiece, *Tigana*. Who but a Canadian, steeped in the ideology of "multiculturalism", the theories of Marshall McLuhan, and a distrust of (but nevertheless reliance on) bureaucratic intervention, could have come up with David Kirkpatrick's hilarious "The Effect of Terminal Cancer on Potential Astronauts" (included in the first *Tesseracts* anthology)?

We can only scratch the surface of these cultural differences in this brief overview, but once the question has been asked, the influence of the Canadian experience on the emerging body of Canadian SF quickly becomes obvious to even the most casual reader. The large and still rapidly growing Canadian contribution to the SF genre comprises a literature that also reflects our unique culture and experiences, addresses our specific issues, questions, and concerns, speaks to our hopes and dreams for the future, and therefore serves our particular needs as Canadian readers.

NOTES

[1] This paper combines portions of articles previously published in ConAdian Progress Report #4 (for the 52nd World Science Fiction Convention, Winnipeg, September 1-5, 1994), and the *NCF Guide to Canadian Science Fiction and Fandom*, 3rd Edition (1988); and a presentation at WRITING: The Future, the Saskatchewan Writers Guild Conference, May 31, June 1-3, 1990.

2 John Robert Colombo, *Other Canadas: An Anthology of Science Fiction and Fantasy* (Toronto: McGraw-Hill Ryerson, 1979).

3 Candas Jane Dorsey, "Canadian SF: Differences in the Tradition North of the Border," Panel Discussion at *ConText '89*, July 1, 1989, as reported by Steve Pikov in *SubText* No. 1:1-2.

4 Michael Skeet, "Canadian SF: Differences in the Tradition North of the Border," *SubText*, No. 1:1.

5 H.A. Hargreaves, "Protected Environment," in *North by 2000* (Toronto: Peter Martin Associates, 1975).

6 See "Uneasy Union: A Checklist of English-Language SF Concerning Canadian Separatist Conflicts," *Science Fiction Studies*, Vol. 1, No. 1 (March, 1982).

7 Jean-Louis Trudel, "Science Fiction in Francophone Canada, 1938-1989," *SOL Rising*, 1992.

8 Hargreaves, "Dead to the World," in *North by 2000*.

9 Élisabeth Vonarburg, "Francophone SF," Panel Discussion, *PineKone II/Canvention 9* (Oct. 15, 1989), as reported by Robert Runté in *I'm Not Boring You, Am I?* Vol. 1, No. 7, p. 18.

10 Lorna Toolis, "Francophone SF," Panel Discussion, *PineKone II/Canvention 9*, (Oct. 15, 1989), quoted in *I'm Not Boring You, Am I?* Vol. 1, No. 7, p. 17.

11 Both Michael Skeet and H.A. Hargreaves have commented "that Canadian male protagonists are rarely 'alpha males'; they bumble more, are self-effacing ['like the writers', said Hargreaves], and are traumatically affected by their actions when they behave as alpha males." See "Canadian SF: Differences in the Tradition North of the Border," *Subtext* No. 1:2.

12 In the sequel, *Cat's Gambit,* their descendants finally win the war, but the protagonists in that book all die in the process.

13 *Loremasters* was not well received by most American critics because they found the mismatch between goals and outcomes confused and confusing; but for Canadian readers, that's just life, and the book made perfect sense.

14 Francine Pelletier, *Faces of Canada*, Photo Exhibit, 1993.

Robert Runté *is an assistant professor in the Faculty of Education at the University of Lethbridge where he teaches sociology. He has been actively promoting Canadian SF for nearly twenty years, serving as editor of* Neology, The Monthly Monthly, *and* New Canadian Fandom. *He is also the editor and publisher of* The NCF Guide to

Canadian Science Fiction and Fandom, *which won a Canadian Science Fiction and Fantasy Achievement Award (Aurora) in 1989; he won a second Aurora in 1990 for his promotion of Canadian SF. In 1994 he was honored as Fan Guest at ConAdian, the 52nd World Science Fiction Convention (WorldCon). He is currently on the Advisory Board of Tesseract Books and a founding Director of the Speculative Fiction Foundation of Canada.*

Christine L. Kulyk *is a freelance editor, writer, and researcher whose love affair with science fiction dates back to the 1960s. She has been an enthusiastic reader and supporter of Canadian science fiction, in particular, since 1980, which saw the first publication of her speculative essay on Canadian SF, entitled ". . . And the Canadian Way?" A resident of Kingston, Ontario, she is a former member of Edmonton fandom, former editor of the well-known Canadian fanzine* The Monthly Monthly/The Bimonthly Monthly, *and author of a number of critical essays and reviews dealing with science fiction.*

SCIENCE FICTION IN FRANCOPHONE CANADA (1839-1989)
by Jean-Louis Trudel

Any discussion of French-language science fiction in Canada should start with definitions. As Jean-Marc Gouanvic has pointed out, the usefulness of listing works as science fiction before the concept was even fully developed is dubious.[1] Science fiction now encompasses a whole range of themes, stories, and treatments, some of which hardly existed in the past.

Although the term most widely used in Québec's "milieu" of writers and critics is SFQ: *Science-Fiction Québécoise*, it will not be used here. Many writers of French-language science fiction in Canada were not natives of the province of Québec or did not reside there when they wrote. Even today, its descriptive value remains doubtful, though it has a powerfully prescriptive one.

Though anachronistic, at least for half of the period considered, the term science fiction (abbreviated as SF) will be used and will designate here stories which present situations and plot devices integral to modern SF, such as future societies, fantastic voyages, or superhuman characters. Science fiction will be understood as involving an unavoidable rational component, often but not always appealing to the authority of science. As a result, the bounds of this essay will be time-dependent: the more recent the story, the more rigorous it will need to be to avoid being set aside as fantasy.

This essay surveys most of the history of French-language SF in this country. It is as complete as its sources for the period up to 1945, but only summarizes the situation after 1945. Therefore, it is clearly unbalanced since almost half is devoted to the dozen books or so predating 1945, while the remainder can only provide an overview of the nearly 150 books and intense activity of the postwar decades.

THE PRECURSORS

The earliest known Canadian SF story in French dates back to 1839. A Swiss immigrant, Aimé-Nicolas Aubin, published it under the name of Napoléon Aubin as an unfinished serial, *Mon Voyage à la lune*. The first six episodes appeared irregularly in the newspaper *Le Fantasque*, edited and published by Aubin himself in Québec City, coming out on July 9 and 21, August 3, September 2 and 17, and October 1 of 1839.

Aimé-Nicolas Aubin himself is a fascinating study. Born in 1812, in Chêne-Bougeries, Switzerland, he emigrated to the United States at the age of seventeen. After a stay of six years, he moved to Montréal and then to Québec City, where he founded *Le Fantasque* in August 1837. The irreverent tone of his articles once netted him two months in jail. After *Le Fantasque* died, Aubin became a chemistry teacher, published the first two volumes of the *Histoire du Canada* of Francois-Xavier Garneau, and invented a gas-lighting device. Before dying in Montréal in 1890, he also helped to establish the Société Saint-Jean-Baptiste, the Société canadienne d'études littéraires et scientifiques, and the Institut canadien.[2]

The science fiction component of the serial, whose title translates as *My Trip to the Moon*, is most evident in the first episode. The hero's means of travel to the Moon is more whimsical than ingenious, reminiscent of Cyrano de Bergerac's solutions. Though humbler in scope than Voltaire's "Micromégas" (1752), the serial does offer a broad critique of Earthly prejudices. After the first episode, *Mon Voyage à la lune* veers from social criticism to a Swiftian satire of the mores and customs of Québec's society in particular. Despite the closeness in dates and subject, as well as Aubin's links with the United States, there seems to be no connection between Edgar Allan Poe's "The Unparalleled Adventure of One Hans Pfall" (1835) — which in fact offers much more interesting SF speculations — and Aubin's serial. However, the author does describe green-skinned Lunatics, which is an early occurrence of the green alien motif in SF.[3]

Other characteristics of the work and of its author may be noted. First of all, Napoléon Aubin was still a newcomer when he wrote it: French-language Canadian SF has continued to be influenced by immigrants from abroad — and, arguably, this is also true for English-language Canadian SF. Second, *Mon Voyage à la lune* was an artefact of a small press manned by Aubin himself: again, small presses have been a natural haven for native SF in Québec throughout history. Finally, the story's content itself is typical of another enduring trend. After Aubin, SF in francophone Canada was used again and again as a literary device that allowed a present society to be criticized, either by pointing out its shortcomings through future improvements or by proposing a different and better society.

Two nineteenth-century short stories unequivocally belong to the genre of SF: "Le Carnaval à Québec en 1996 (Écrit à distance d'un siècle, en février 1896)" (1896), by Nazaire Levasseur, and "La tête de saint Jean-Baptiste ou Légende pour nos arrières-petits-neveux, en 1980" (1880), by Wenceslas-Eugène Dick. These translate respectively as *The Carnival in Québec in 1996 (Written at a Remove of a Century, in February 1896)* and *The Head of Saint John the Baptist or Legend for our Great-Grand-Nephews, in 1980*. Both stories reveal "decimal futurism": the tendency to look ahead by a decade, a century, or a millenium.

The stories' themes are not vastly different. In both cases, the twentieth century belongs to Québec. Québec's newfound prosperity is symbolized by new railways and bridges, an increased population, the cultivation of new lands, an unshaken Catholic faith . . . Independence is at most alluded to, however. In "La tête de saint Jean-Baptiste ou Légende pour nos arrières-petits-neveux, en 1980," Lake St-Jean has been drained, and the Province of Saguenay has a population of three million out of seven million French Canadians. Québec owes its new wealth to a gift from Saint John the Baptist who came down to Earth in order to reward the province's piety. In "Le Carnaval à Québec en 1996 (Écrit à distance d'un siècle, en février 1896)," a railway circles the Île d'Orléans and a new bridge crosses the Saint-Lawrence upstream from Québec City.[4]

In these texts, it is of course not so much the stories that are interesting as the speculation about the future, which reflects a society torn between its religious past and the allure of a technological future. This is even more evident in the last known SF work of the nineteenth century.

Canada's first French-language SF novel, *Pour la patrie* (1895), by Jules-Paul Tardivel, builds on the same patriotic and religious themes, and also starts its narrative in the twentieth century. It was published in English as *For My Country* (1975). The founding of a reborn New France, with the mission of extending in North America a French and Catholic civilization, is advocated. Ironically, this landmark novel in French-Canadian letters was written by a Franco-American, for Tardivel was born in Covington, Kentucky, which goes a long way towards explaining the radicalism of his vision, considering the role of the church in the survival — and later the assimilation — of the Franco-American diaspora.[5] The novel bears the imprint of Tardivel's ardent Catholic faith and ultramontane beliefs, and might be classified as fantasy, despite the political speculation, if the author did not believe as firmly in the reality of his religion as any modern *hard sf* writer believes in the truth of science. Nevertheless, it makes for a bizarre contemporary of H. G. Wells' novels.

Another work partially intended as propaganda is *Similia Similibus ou La Guerre au Canada* (1916), by Ulric Barthe, with the French portion of the title translating as *The War in Canada*. In it, Québec City is conquered by the Prussian army. This may be the first alternative history novel of Québec, though it is finally revealed as a mere dream. The author defends the pro-British cause and Canada's participation in the war that is going on in Europe.

Much lighter in tone, *Les Aventures extraordinaires de deux Canayens* (1918) [*The Extraordinary Adventures of Two Canucks*], by Jules Jéhin, has no polemical intent. Two French Canadians use a superior flying machine to set up a short-lived Empire of Space (not of Outer Space, but actually of the Airs). Two elements lighter than hydrogen are introduced to justify the flying machine, which harks back to Jules Verne's *Robur le Conquérant* and *Maître du monde*, but it's all a simple excuse for a humorous jaunt. The son of a famous Belgian violinist who worked with Calixa Lavallée, doctor Jules Jéhin de Prome seems to have spent much of his life in New York.

However, *La Cité dans les fers* (1926) [*The City in Chains*], by Ubald Paquin, is a grim anticipation of a bid for Québec independence, perhaps inspired by the 1916 Easter uprising in Ireland. It features a full-scale revolt bankrolled by a Franco-American multimillionaire, defeated by British might and treason from within. Strictly speaking, it has no science fictional elements and is more properly termed a political thriller.

Also intended as popular entertainment, *L'Impératrice de l'Ungava* (1927) [*The Empress of Ungava*], by Alexandre Huot, tells of an undiscovered city in the Ungava. The tincture of sf is extremely dilute and it is much more in the line of the traditional adventure stories of the time. It does offer the amusing twist that in this tale Québec nationalism is answered by Amerindian pride and self-determination.

In 1931, *La Fin de la Terre* [*The End of the Earth*], by Emmanuel Desrosiers, is more modern in its conception. Earth's agony, caused by overpopulation, famine, lack of fertile soil, natural catastrophes, and exhaustion of non-renewable resources, is described, but the ending is optimistic about the technological (and ethical) progress of mankind: with the consent of the Martians, the survivors remove themselves to the Red Planet. The grandeur of the ideas is noteworthy and the like was not seen again for a few more years. The author also managed to write a full-length novel without a single female character.

Siraf, Étranges révélations, ce qu'on pense de nous par-delà la lune (1934) [*Siraf, Strange Revelations, What They Think of Us beyond the Moon*] was written by a Frenchman who had emigrated to Alberta, Georges Bugnet. Here, SF is a literary device that allows an astral entity to converse with a human about various philosophical problems of interest to the author. Unlike a rare but hardy strain of modern Québec pseudo-SF novels, the author was not half-postulating that this entity really existed, but merely using it as his mouthpiece.

Armand Grenier's novels, on the other hand, tried to uphold Québec's 'race', religion, and language. *Erres boréales* (1944) [*Northern Impetus*] was published by the Éditions Laurin under Grenier's first pseudonym of Florent Laurin. It takes place in 1968. A new invention has warmed the sea off the costs of Labrador and the Eastern Arctic, the French-Canadian race has colonized and exploited the northern territories chock-full of precious ore deposits. Nationalist feeling is exalted, the courage and spirit of the pioneers is glorified. A map of the new lands with their French names is glued inside the book's cover and drawings are included. *Défricheur de hammada* (1953) [*Hammada Pioneer*] was published under Grenier's pseudonym of Guy René de Plour.[6] The ideal Québec society is transplanted in the middle of the Sahara, under domes where Christian and family values are fully adhered to. Grenier announced that he was preparing to write, presumably in English, a work called *The Future laid out in the Unknown*, but it never seems to have materialized.

In the same tradition of proof by science fiction, *Eutopia* (1944), written under the pseudonym Jean Berthos, and improbably attributed to Thomas-Alfred Bernier (1844-1908) instead of plain Thomas Bernier, combines technological inventions and a strange socialism that protects order, justice, and Christian virtue. Some have seen "fascism" in this strange mix.[7]

Other books are sometimes added to exhaustive lists for this period: *L'Île du savoir* (1947), a possible juvenile by Victor Boisson and Jean Conterno — who is mistakenly called Canteno by Daniel Sernine,[8] *Lipha: Ses étapes* (1931), by J.-O. Léger, and *Marcel Faure* (1922), by Jean-Charles Harvey.[9] The title of the first translates as *The Island of Knowledge*. Printed in Canada soon after the end of the war but written in Lyons, France, between 1941 and 1942, it is not mentioned in the *Dictionnaire des œuvres littéraires du Québec*, which is not that significant since the *Dictionnaire* does not include other juvenile novels. Neither was it ever acquired by the National Library in Ottawa. Furthermore, it is among the first of several books published by Victor A. Boisson, whose later ones were released in France, some of them in the Lyons area. Conterno's only claim to literary fame rests on the part-authorship of this book, while all evidence points to Victor A. Boisson being French and probably from Southern France. It has been suggested, rather plausibly, that the book was printed in Canada because the Second World War cast its authors (very) temporarily on our shores. All in all, it seems that it cannot be included as a genuine part of the corpus.

The second book, *Lipha: Ses étapes* [*Lipha's Progress*], must have been mistaken for SF because of its weird-sounding title. In fact, it is a reprint collection of articles on political and agricultural matters, written under the *nom de plume* of Lipha, the persona of an imaginary journalist. It simply has nothing to do with SF.

The third is a mix of the utopian novel and of the future tense political thriller, with a dash of star-crossed love. It is less dramatic in its extrapolation than Ubald Paquin's work, but can still be considered borderline SF like Alexandre Huot's Amerindian utopia. Thus, at the end of this first period, French-language Canadian SF can be divided between the broadly utopian (from Tardivel to Grenier), the philosophical (Aubin, Bugnet, Desrosiers), the propagandistic (Barthe, most others to some degree), and the adventure tale (Jéhin, Huot, Paquin).

In several cases, a considerable reluctance to get to the speculative part of the story is noticeable. Tardivel's novel does start right away forty years into the future, but Jéhin, Huot, Harvey, and Paquin incorporate long build-ups that stay on the safe side of the unknown. In Huot's case especially, the payoff is in the very last few chapters alone.

YESTERDAY

An era ended with *Defricheur de hammada*. Exhaustiveness becomes chimerical in the ensuing years. The new popular serials of post-war Québec used SF to entertain. In *Les Aventures futuristes de deux savants canadiens-français* (1949) [*The Futuristic Adventures of Two French-Canadian Scientists*], by Louis Champagne, the pseudonym of a series of forgotten hacks, the adventures of the heroes are reminiscent of the early pulp science fiction in the United States. In the 1960s, the first blooms of a renewed science fiction were probably not unrelated to the *Révolution tranquille* that had begun to modify the old rules. SF has always been the literature of change . . .

Between 1960 and 1973, several writers were the first to publish more than one or two SF stories, mostly because they shared in the surge of SF in juvenile literature. In 1960, Guy Bouchard was among the first, publishing *Vénus via via Atlantide*. Suzanne Martel followed, with her juvenile classic *Surréal 3000 (Quatre Montréalais en l'an 3000)* (1963), translated as *The Underground City* (1964), with its still very readable account of life underground centuries after a nuclear war. From 1965 to 1968, Maurice Gagnon then published the Unipax series of novels describing a worldwide organization devoted to peace and equipped with fabulous machines. Even Yves Thériault tried his hand at SF, between 1966 and 1967, with the Volpek series starring a secret agent in the James Bond mould who uses a lot of nifty gadgets and tangles a few times with extra-terrestrials.

While these short novels had aimed for a younger readership, Monique Corriveau's *Les Compagnons du Soleil* (1976) [*The Companions of the Sun*] was a trilogy meant for more mature adolescents. It dealt with repression and revolt, totalitarianism and freedom. It still stood in 1989 as the only French-language SF trilogy in Canada. During the 1970s, the "Jeunesse-Pop" imprint of the Éditions Paulines started to include regular SF offerings for its young readers. Normand Côté, writing under the pseudonym of Louis Sutal, and Jean-Pierre Charland were among the more prominent names. The decade also saw the first work by Charles Montpetit and later by Daniel Sernine.

On the adult side, Ronald Després published in 1962 *Le scalpel ininterrompu* [*The Uninterrupted Scalpel*], in which the whole of humanity is vivisected within twenty years. In spirit, it's closer to some surrealists and their predecessors, Lautréamont or Forneret. Yves Thériault also wrote SF for adults: a collection of nuclear war short stories *Si la bombe m'était contée* (1962) [*If the Bomb Was Told to Me*], and a novel *Le Haut Pays* (1973) [*The High Country*], occupying the borderlands of SF — since it talks of parallel worlds — and esoterism — since it mentions Knowledge, Initiates, and Great Ones. Classification can be hard.[10]

Jacques Benoit specialized in a more flamboyant style, sometimes funny, sometimes cruel, producing a kind of skewed SF. His first novel, *Jos Carbone* (1967), has occasionally been classified as speculative fiction: it is certainly not science fiction, and it is hard even to justify the label of speculative fiction. The story does take place in an imaginary wood and the mood is surreal, but the place-names and the general atmosphere are not really distinct from Québec's old storytelling tradition and saint-laden toponymy. The setting is as real and as imaginary as Mariposa, Manawaka, or Yoknapatawpha County, only differing from them in degree: it is a conceivable extension of Québec geography. Benoit's next novel, *Patience et Firlipon* (1970), was definitely SF: it spices a wonderful love story with futuristic gadgets in a Montréal of tomorrow. Finally, *Les Princes* (1973), which translates as *The Princes*, describes a city that cannot fit on the known globe or in the known past, but where no overt magic intervenes. Call it speculative fiction. More somber, it echoes the October Crisis, dealing with repression and discrimination.

Emmanuel Cocke was born in France, moved to Québec, and died in India in 1973, but his novels *Va voir au ciel si j'y suis* (1971) [*Go to Heaven to See if I'm There*] and *L'Emmanuscrit de la mère morte* (1972), which only approximately translates as *The Emmanuscript of the Dead Mother*, portray twenty-first century

Montreal.[11] His hero presents himself as the savior of humanity, who will prevent Earth's end. References to Québec's self-determination underscore the political nature of the hero's project. The rediscovery of human dignity and the transformation of society lead to a new Québec.[12] Cocke's writing is deliriously pedantic, characterized by acidic puns and an often boring psychedelic self-centeredness. As in the novels of Tardivel, Grenier, and Berthos, science fiction is used to invent tomorrow's Québec.

In 1972, Maurice Gagnon returned to SF with a somewhat traditional novel, *Les Tours de Babylone* [*The Towers of Babylon*]. The choice the protagonist has to make between two kinds of societies could be read as an allegory of Québec's situation . . . or perhaps not.

At the end of this second age of French-language Canadian SF, what common traits link the stories listed here? John Robert Colombo found polar lands, catastrophe scenarios, alienation, and more fantasy than hard SF in his survey of English-language Canadian speculative fiction. The last does not apply to this SF overview, though it is noticeable that most of the stories included here are stronger on political or social speculation than hard science. Alienation is of course a central theme. Catastrophe scenarios are actually rare, apart from the novels of Paquin, Desrosiers, or Després. However, Colombo included in his catastrophe scenarios the separation of Québec. In French-language SF, a disaster only occurs if Québec fails to separate successfully, as in Paquin's novel. Several stories and novels deal with a more powerful, if not fully independent, Québec. They are the obverse of John Robert Colombo's catastrophe scenario: the national redemption scenario. As for Colombo's polar lands, Huot's work and *Erres boréales* would be the main examples of the same affinity in French-language SF.

TODAY

The year 1974 marks the beginning of a new phase that has not yet ended. Authors like Jacques Benoit, Yves Thériault, and Maurice Gagnon abandoned the field. Jacques Brossard's pre-1974 incursion into modern fantasy was only followed by a science fiction work in 1989. Cocke was dead.

A new generation of writers who are still active today appeared. In 1974, Esther Rochon published *En hommage aux araignées* [*In Homage to Spiders*]: its revised version as a juvenile novel, *L'Étranger sous la ville* [*The Stranger Under the City*], was published in 1986 and translated into Dutch. The sequel, *L'Épuisement du soleil* (1985) [*The Exhaustion of the Sun*], is a minor classic in the field.

Also in 1974, *Requiem*, a small science fiction and fantastique magazine, was launched in Longueuil. Apart from one lonely attempt to produce a high-school fanzine in the late 1960s, *Requiem*, under Frenchman Norbert Spehner, was the first periodical to focus on science fiction, fantasy, and *fantastique* in francophone Canada. The reason for the choice of the name remains obscure. It may or may not be a reference to Heinlein's famous short story. Legend has it that the name was the suggestion of the original staff's only woman. In 1975, *Requiem* published Daniel Sernine's first short story, as well as Jean-Pierre April's in 1977 and those of René Beaulieu, Denis Côté, and French-born Élisabeth Vonarburg in 1978.

After 1974, books with a more audacious outlook and a more mature style appeared, such as *La manufacture de machines* (1976) [*The Machine Factory*], by Louis-Philippe Hébert, and *Un Été de Jessica* (1978) [*A Jessica Summer*], by Alain Bergeron.

In 1979, several events combined to launch the most remarkable decade yet of francophone SF in Canada. The second lasting SF magazine, *imagine ...*, was born in the fall, with Jean-Marc Gouanvic, another Frenchman, as fiction editor: it eventually published the first works of Jean Pettigrew and Agnès Guitard, among others. Also in 1979, *Requiem* changed its name to *Solaris*, as an homage to Stanislaw Lem. The first Boréal convention of French-language science fiction and fantasy took place in Chicoutumi, adding impetus to the nascent SF community in Québec. In following years, the convention launched the literary careers of young writers like Francine Pelletier, in 1981, and Yves Meynard, in 1986. (Since 1979, four Boréals have been held in Québec City, two more in Chicoutimi, two in Montreal, one in Longueuil, and two in Ottawa.) Daniel Sernine also published his first novel, a juvenile, in 1979.

In 1980, the publications of *L'Œil de la nuit* [*The Eye of the Night*], by Élisabeth Vonarburg, and *La Machine à explorer la fiction*

[*The Machine for Exploring Fiction*], by Jean-Pierre April, launched the first serious SF line in Québec, known as "Chroniques du futur" [*Chronicles of the Future*], by the Éditions Le Préambule. In 1983 appeared the first three French-language Canadian SF anthologies. *Aurores boréales 1* [*Northern Lights 1*] was edited by Norbert Spehner, also in charge of the "Chroniques du futur" imprint. *Espaces imaginaires 1*, which roughly translates as *Imaginary Spaces 1*, was edited by Jean-Marc Gouanvic and Stéphane Nicot from France: it included stories by authors from both Canada and France. Finally, *Les Années-lumière* [*Light-Years*], was also the work of Jean-Marc Gouanvic, who reserved the book to Canadian stories in French. Since then, several more anthologies have come out.

The decade of the 1980s also saw new signs of recognition of French-language Canadian SF in France, English-speaking Canada, and elsewhere. In 1982, the Grand Prix de la Science-Fiction Française was awarded to an Élisabeth Vonarburg novel, *Le Silence de la Cité*, published in English as *The Silent City* (1988), in Canada, England, and the United States. In 1983, the same award was won by a Swiss residing in Ottawa, Pierre Billon, for his novel *L'Enfant du cinquième nord* [*The Child from the Fifth North*]. In 1988, *Les Visiteurs du Pôle Nord* [*The North Pole Visitors*], by a Paris-born Ottawa writer, Jean-François Somcynsky, who now writes as Somain, won the 1987 Prix Louis-Hémon from the Académie du Languedoc, in France.

At the decade's end, French-language Canadian SF seemed healthy. An annual review of the science fiction and *fantastique* published during the previous year in francophone Canada started appearing in 1985. In fact, using the numbers given by *L'Année de la Science-Fiction et du Fantastique Québécois* for the years from 1984 to 1989, it is possible to estimate by extrapolating linearly backwards that about 75 SF novels and 750 SF short stories may have been published between 1980 and 1989. Thus, the number of SF novels published in the 1980s is roughly double that published in the 1970s, and maybe triple that of the 1960s. In 1989, an anthology of Québec SF and fantastique was reportedly among the three favorite books of a certain publisher in Québec high schools.

On the other hand, the "Chroniques du futur" imprint died in 1988 after publishing an eleventh book, a short story collection by Francine Pelletier, *Le Temps des migrations* [*The Time of Migrations*]. The Éditions Les Imaginoïdes, specializing in SF, also stopped publishing SF after their fourth anthology.

In the 1980s, French-language Canadian SF could be clearly divided into two currents sharing the same stream. On one side flowed the 'milieu', consisting of faithful readers of *imagine...* and *Solaris*, regular attendees of the Boréal conventions, fanzine publishers, survivors of the *Requiem* era, and writers for the juvenile market like Daniel Sernine, Denis Côté, or Francine Pelletier. The 'milieu' was distinguished not only by its more professional approach to its subject matter, but also by the fact that many of the people involved, and especially the writers, were at least casual acquaintances. It was characterized by sales to the specialized markets and seemed to comprise people who actually read SF, from here and elsewhere, before trying to write or review it. It was also dominated by writers who had made SF their preferred writing genre. Most of the names quoted here after 1974 belonged to this current.

The second current was dominated by novelists who tried SF for a couple of books and then passed on. Their novels were published outside the specialized small presses or collections. Their science-fiction culture often appeared to be limited to a few SF blockbuster movies or to juvenile adventure novels.[13] The plots were derivative, or messianic, starring Atlantis or wise extraterrestrials. However, in many ways, this was the native Québec current, while the 'milieu' could be viewed as a transplanted European or American product, beating strongly inside the Québec breast. Has the transplant taken? Has the SF literature of the 'milieu' attained the critical publication mass necessary to sustain it? Considering the privileged access of the 'milieu' to the juvenile markets, it does seem that rejection will not occur.

Listen to the heartbeat of French-language SF in Canada. Read its stories.

NOTES

1 Jean-Marc Gouanvic, "La SFQ dans son histoire: quelques remarques rétrospectives et prospective," *imagine* . . . 49: 52-53.

2 Jean-Paul Tremblay, *Napoléon Aubin* (Montréal: Éditions Fides, 1972), 7-14.

3 Napoléon Aubin, "Mon Voyage à la lune," *imagine* . . . 8-9: 26-45.

4 Michel Bélil, "La science-fiction canadienne française," *imagine* . . . 19: 8.

5 The hundreds of thousands of Québecers who emigrated to the United States are known as Franco-Americans; the most notable of them may be another Franco-American writer, Jack Kerouac.

6 The pseudonym "Guy René de Plour" reflects both Grenier's name and that of his mother, who was called Plourde. See Jean-Louis Trudel, "Les pseudonymes dans la SFQ," *Temps Tôt* 8: 42.

7 Monique Genuist, "Eutopia," *Dictionnaire des œuvres littéraires du Québec*, 3, 1978, 35.

8 Daniel Sernine, "Historique de la SFQ," *Solaris* 79: 41.

9 Claude Janelle, "La Science-fiction au Québec," *Solaris* 50: 6.

10 The novel *La Cité dans l'œuf* (1969), by Michel Tremblay, is sometimes called SF, but it is much closer to traditional fantasy, though pleasantly original in its fusion of folklore, Greek myths, and original ideas.

11 While Québec City dominated the future of Québec in the science fiction of the nineteenth century and early twentieth century, at least until Ubald Paquin's work, in which Montréal and Québec City share equal billing, Montréal has come to be the center of Québec's future in its science fiction. If Ubald Paquin marked a turning point, then Suzanne Martel probably marked the beginning of Montréal's ascendancy.

12 Claude Janelle, "La Science-fiction au Québec," *Solaris* 50: 6.

13 I interviewed one writer, Carol Boily, who actually stated this in so many words.

REFERENCES

L'Année de la Science-Fiction et du Fantastique Québécois 1984, 1985, 1986, 1987, 1988, 1989. Beauport: Éditions Le Passeur.

Aubin, Napoléon. "Mon Voyage à la Lune." *imagine* . . . 8-9: 25-45.

Bélil, Michel. "La science-fiction canadienne française." *imagine* . . . 19: 8-9.

Dick, Wenceslas-Eugène. "La tête de saint Jean-Baptiste ou Légende pour nos arrières-petits-neveux, en 1980." *imagine* . . . . 19: 9-12.

Dictionnaire des œuvres littéraires du Québec. Montréal: Éditions Fides, 1978.

Gouanvic, Jean-Marc. "*La tête de saint Jean-Baptiste* entre la science-fiction et le mythe." *imagine* . . . 19: 12-14.

Gouanvic, Jean-Marc. "Rational Speculations in French Canada 1839-1974." *Science Fiction Studies*, 15, 44 (March 1988): 71-81.

Gouanvic, Jean-Marc. "La sfq dans son histoire: quelques remarques rétrospectives et prospectives." *imagine* . . . 49: 51-56.

Janelle, Claude. "La Science-fiction au Québec." *Solaris* 50: 6-10.

Sernine, Daniel. "Historique de la sfq." *Solaris* 79: 41-47.

Tremblay, Jean-Paul. *Napoléon Aubin.* Montréal: Éditions Fides, 1972.

Trudel, Jean-Louis. "Les pseudonymes dans la sfq." *Temps Tôt* 8 (1990): 40-48.

Vonarburg, Élisabeth, and Norbert Spehner. *Science Fiction Studies* 21 (July 1980): 191-199.

Jean-Louis Trudel *has degrees in physics and astronomy, and is presently studying the history and philosophy of science in Toronto, where he lives. He is the author of a couple of novels in French and three books for young adults published in Canada over the past year. His short stories in French have appeared in magazines like* imagine . . . *and* Solaris, *and in various other venues. In English his short fiction has been published in several Canadian and American anthologies, but also in magazines like* On Spec *and* Prairie Fire. *When time allows, he also does translation and science fiction criticism.*

A PAST, A FUTURE ...
Québec Science Fiction
by Jean-Marc Gouanvic

"No past, no future ..."
Starmania

There are two histories to "Québec science fiction": the one that precedes the creation of a science fiction subculture in Québec in the 1970s, and the one that is based on the existence of this subculture, its editorial structures, and its particular logic. The creation of an SF subculture in Québec, as in the United States and France, is the key phenomenon of the genre's history. Adapted from the American model but influenced by the French one (which was itself imported from the United States), the model that was established in Québec in the 1970s imposed certain aesthetic/ideological standards with which all those involved would henceforth have to conform in order to be recognized as working in SF. The Québec science fiction community gradually developed as a network of literary communication (magazines and fanzines, specialized collections, special conventions) which ultimately served to prescribe that which would be deemed legitimate in SF.

The subculture was initially organized around the fanzine *Requiem*, which issued from the Édouard Montpetit CEGEP in Longueuil. *Requiem* laid down the canons of Québec SF (abbreviated here as SFQ) and determined what was possible in the genre in Québec until the appearance of other structures such as *Pour ta belle gueule d'ahuri* (1979) and *imagine . . .* (1979), which strove to take their place in the field and move it forward so as to impose new norms. Next, the editor of *Requiem* created the first specialized SFQ collection, *Chroniques du futur* (1980). This collection was to some extent the culmination of a process of development begun in 1974, in that amateurism had evolved into professionalism in the case of certain authors, most notably Jean-Pierre April and Élisabeth Vonarburg, the first two to be published.

Before the establishment of the SFQ subculture in 1974 and afterward, there were a fair number of novels that could be called proto-science fiction, although they owed nothing to the American strain of the 1920s (the one that was to be imitated in Québec in the 1970s). Here are some of the significant texts of French Canadian proto-SF:

1839: "Mon voyage à la lune" by Napoléon Aubin, a philosophical and satirical tale in the tradition of Cyrano de Bergerac and

Voltaire. This is the first work that can be associated with all categories of science fiction.

1895: *Pour la patrie, roman du 20e siècle* by Jules-Paul Tardivel, an ultramontane novel of the future at the opposite pole from "Mon voyage à la lune" and the Enlightenment: French Canada separates from the rest of the country and sets up Catholicism as the State religion.

1916: *Similia similibus* (subtitle: *La Guerre au Canada: Essai romantique sur un sujet d'actualité*) by Ulric Barthe, a novel of future warfare featuring an invasion of Canada by Germany.

1918: *Les aventures extraordinaires de deux Canayens* by Jules Jéhin, a scientific adventure novel in the Jules Verne tradition: well written, intelligent, light, and respectful of the populace. This exceptional novel proves that, even at the beginning of this century, there existed in French Canada social aspirations comparable to those which would bring about the Quiet Revolution after World War II.

1922: *Marcel Faure* by Jean-Charles Harvey (the author of the *Demi-civilisés*), part of the trend of progressive utopianism founded on industrialization and the science and technology boom.

1925: *La cité dans les fers* by Ubald Paquin, a "separatist" novel like *Pour la patrie*, although the Laurentian Republic never comes to pass, for London and Ottawa call in their armies.

1944: *Erres boréales* by Florent Laurin (pseudonym of Armand Grenier), a utopia of colonization of the Far North by French Canadians. A heavily didactic novel which promotes the prevailing providentialist ideology, the most extreme illustration of which will be *Eutopia*.

1946: *Eutopia* (subtitle: *Le monde qu'on attend. Pour les jeunes qui veulent. Pour les adultes qui pensent*) by Jean Berthos, without question the most didactic, most narrow, most dogmatic utopia in all of French Canadian literature. The author constantly strives to demonstrate the excellence of "Michelism," whose sole objective is to set up a monolithic theocracy in French Canada.

1952: *Défricheur de hammada* (subtitle: *Le roman d'un misanthrope évadé de l'Amérique*) by Guy-René de Plour (pseudonym of Armand Grenier), which recounts the building of a utopian city in the middle of the Sahara by a Canadian ("the symbol of a Canada in a turmoil of excitement"); this city is based on science and technology, "disinterested capitalism," and a Catholic faith in which the priests are elected by the faithful.

These are some of the most significant novels from 1839 to 1960. Paradoxically, they are characterized on the one hand by the constancy of their political and religious utopianism, and on the other by their completely unrelated focal points. The history of SF in French Canada and Québec must recognize this essential fact: by virtue of certain thematic features (these tales are neither realistic nor fantastic), these narratives can be associated with what was to be christened SF in the United States, but historically they have absolutely nothing in common with American SF. Their existence proves how highly non-realistic themes were regarded by those taking a stand on the social future of French Canada: militant Catholics such as Tardivel or Berthos, journalists such as Barthe, etc. All of these titles are therefore not relevant to the history of the SF that was recognized as a distinct entity starting in the late 1920s in the United States. The situation of Québec science fiction was to undergo a sea change in the 1970s, which shall be described very briefly below. But first, we must identify the social and literary issues at the time of the emergence of SFQ by examining the content of such pivotal works as *Les nomades*.

The publication of *Les nomades* by Jean Tétreau in 1967 is one of those turning points (along with *Les tours de Babylone* by Maurice Gagnon in 1972) that contain all the essential elements of modern science fiction, even though they antedate the creation of the SFQ subculture. These novels combine the imaginary adventure based on SF themes (nuclear holocaust, post-catastrophe tales, future societies, space adventures) with ethical and political reflection. With these stories, one has the impression that all that is needed is the turn of a page in the history of the genre in Québec, and that these are the best agents of change. But this was not to be the way things worked out. These books were to have but very little direct influence on the construction of Québec science fiction; no place was provided for Maurice Gagnon (any more than for other talented writers of the 1970s, such as Suzanne Martel). The subculture of SFQ was created on the basis of other priorities than the literature itself: it was as if nothing had existed beforehand, as if, where the writing of SF was concerned, everything was still to be done.

Certainly, American SF did not wait until the 1970s to make its influence felt. In 1949, for example, there were *Les aventures futuristes de deux savants canadiens-français* and some fifteen science fiction episodes among the several thousand in the *IXE-13* series published in the postwar Québec pulp magazines, notably *Police-journal*. These serials were all very short-lived. In fact, Québec science fiction was not ready for professional publication of novels and short stories until the late 1970s. Even *Un été de Jessica* (1978) by Alain Bergeron, the novel closest to the American strain at the time, arrived a little too early for publication in a specialized collection which was to appear only two years later (*Chroniques du futur*).

With *Chroniques du futur*, we move into the current stream of Québec science fiction, insofar as it would feature several of the major SF authors of the period, whether they originated in the science fiction subculture or the field of general literature. Those who made their debut in SFQ were Élisabeth Vonarburg, Jean-Pierre April, Daniel Sernine, René Beaulieu, and Esther Rochon. There were few writers from the mainstream early in the decade: one thinks mainly of Jean-François Somcynsky. It should be noted that an author such as Michel Bélil, a product of the new subculture, published mainly fantasy and had yet to find a natural niche in the specialized SF collections. Concurrently with *Chroniques du futur*, authors such as Agnès Guitard and Pierre Billon published in non-specialized collections. The case of Pierre Billon is most indicative of the image that Québec science fiction holds for the adherents of mainstream literature: Billon was totally opposed to having his novel *L'enfant du 5e nord* (1982) associated in any way with science fiction, even though he was awarded the grand prize for French science fiction the same year. *Chroniques du futur* expired in 1987, leaving the field open for other publishing initiatives, such as the collection *Autres mers, autres mondes* from Logiques (Montreal), which was itself terminated in 1992.

What is the present structure of SFQ? The major authors of the seventies and eighties are still working: Rochon, April, Vonarburg, Bélil, Sernine. Among the promising young or new writers — Beaulieu, Provencher, Dion, Pelletier, Champetier, Prévost,

Bouchard (Guy), Perrot-Bishop — only Pelletier and Champetier continue to publish regularly, mainly literature for young people, while Bouchard, Montambault, and Perrot-Bishop, each with a novel ready for publication, saw their momentum interrupted with the halt of the *Autres mers, autres mondes* collection. Incidentally, it may well be that the characteristic trait of the late 1980s and early 1990s is this attraction of most SFQ writers to literature for young people, this being the only publishing context in which they seem able to survive.

Certain attempts to publish outside the subculture have met with success. Esther Rochon publishes with La Pleine Lune in a collection of general literature, while J-P April, dissatisfied with the lot of his SF works both within the subculture and outside it in the mainstream, has temporarily abandoned the field in favor of the realistic novel. The other first-generation SFQ authors, such as Vonarburg, are turning more resolutely toward light or even serious fantasy, in the manner of Sernine or Bélil, who were very quick to adopt these other non-realistic genres. It is too early for a detailed review of the first half of this decade, especially since the new Québec-Amérique collection has as yet published little SF.

Because of the small market and the limited number of readers, as well as the bitterness of the power struggles in SFQ, the future still seems to be in danger, in spite of the field's subsidized magazines (but for how long?), in spite of the publishers' relay race among Le Préambule, Éditions Logiques, Pierre Tisseyre, and Québec-Amérique, which affords some degree of continuity, and in spite of its talented authors (even though one may wonder whether it isn't literature for young people that is keeping them alive).

We must face the facts: SFQ was born, grew up, and today exists solely thanks to the tireless and disinterested work (that is, financially disinterested, for the power struggles in the field of science fiction presuppose interests of another kind, just as potent as the lure of gain) of its participants, starting with its authors. When an author (such as Rochon or Vonarburg) acquires a reputation in the general popular culture, the issue more than ever in Québec is the immediate recognition of the author *as an SF writer*. However, all indications are that the "SF" label remains as much of a major handicap today as it was yesterday (witness the hostile attitude of Pierre Billon). The authors are therefore facing a dilemma which is the more difficult because the SF market in Québec is a small one: either try for recognition by publishing outside the specialized collections and so betray, in a way, their SF allegiance, or publish in a specialized collection and risk not being taken seriously in Québec culture. Each professional SFQ writer has found a different solution. One of the most recent is that of Élisabeth Vonarburg, who is making a breakthrough in translation on the U.S. market. Let us hope that this American recognition will run its full course and reflect its benefits back upon the whole of Québec science fiction.

HISTORIC BIBLIOGRAPHY (1839-1994)

Note: Despite the historic importance of the establishment of the science fiction field in Québec (SFQ) towards the end of the 1970s, this bibliography does not distinguish between works published before the consolidation of SFQ or those published outside the field and those works that belong to the SFQ genre that emerged in 1980. A great distinction can be made only after a careful analysis of newly instituted components of the field.

1837   *L'Influence d'un livre*, Philippe-Aubert de Gaspé fils *(first French-Canadian novel, fantasy themes)*

1839   "Mon voyage à la lune", Napoléon Aubin.

1895   *Pour la Patrie, Roman du 20e siècle*, Jules-Paul Tardivel.

1916   *Similia Similibus ou La Guerre au Canada*, Ulric Barthe.

1918   *Les Aventures extraordinaires de deux Canayens*, Jules Jéhin.

1922   *Marcel Faure*, Jean-Charles Harvey.

1925   *La Cité dans les fers*, Ubald Paquin.

1931   *La Fin de la terre*, Emmanuel Desrosiers.

1934   *Siraf. Étranges révélations*, Georges Bugnet.

1944   *Erres boréales*, Florent Laurin.

1946   *Eutopia*, Jean Berthos.

1949   *Les Aventures futuristes de deux savants canadiens-français* (collective authorship.)

1952   *Défricheur de hammada*, Guy-René de Plour.

1962   *Si la bombe m'était contée*, Yves Thériault.

1962   *Le Scalpel ininterrompu*, Ronald Després.

1964   *Ségoldiah !*, André Ber.

1966   *Api or not Api*, theater piece, Robert Gurik.

1967   *Les Nomades*, Jean Tétreau.

1967   *Jos Carbone*, Jacques Benoît.

1968   *Le Soleil des profondeurs*, Rolande Lacerte.

1972   *Les Tours de Babylone*, Maurice Gagnon.

1972   *L'Emmanuscrit de la mère morte*, Emmanuel Cocke.

1973   *Les Princes*, Jacques Benoît.

1974   *Reliefs de l'arsenal*, Roger Des Roches.

1974   *Le Métamorfaux*, Jacques Brossard.

1974   *Les Patenteux*, Marcel Moussette.

1974   *En hommage aux araignées*, Esther Rochon.

1974   *Loona ou Autrefois le ciel était bleu*, André-Jean Bonelli.

1974   *Contes ardents du mays mauve*, collection, Jean Ferguson.

1974   Foundation of *Requiem*.

1975   *Grimaces*, collection, Jean-François Somcynsky.

1976   *Compagnons du soleil*, Monique Corriveau.

1977   *Les Anthropoïdes*, Gérard Bessette.

1977   *La Manufacture de machines*, Louis-Philippe Hébert.

1978   *Le Diable du Mahani*, Jean-François Somcynsky.

1978   *Les Hommes-taupes*, Négovan Rajic.

1978   *Un été de Jessica*, Alain Bergeron.

1978   *Québec banana state*, Jean-Michel Wyl.

1979   *La Mort . . . de toutes façons*, Claude MacDuff.

1979   *Un Ambassadeur-macoute à Montréal*, Gérard Étienne.

1979   Foundation of the magazine *imagine* . . .

1979   First Québec Conference on Science Fiction and Fantasy in Chicoutimi.

1979   Foundation of *Pour ta belle gueule d'ahuri*.

1980   *1986, mission fantastique*, Claude MacDuff.

1980   *À l'aube du Verseau*, Henri La France.

1980   *Agénor, Agénor, Agénor et Agénor*, François Barcelo.

1980   *La Filière du temps*, Jacqueline Aubry-Morin.

1980   Creation of the collection "Chroniques du futur" (Éditions Le Préambule, Lungueuil); titles marked CF were published in this collection; ceased publication with No. 11.

1980   *L'oeil de la nuit*, collection, Élisabeth Vonarburg (CF 1).

1980   *La Machine à explorer la fiction*, collection, Jean-Pierre April (CF 2).

1981   *Les Corps communicants*, Agnès Guitard.

1981   *Le Silence de la cité*, Élisabeth Vonarburg.

1981   *Greenwich*, Michel Bélil.

1981   *Légendes de Virnie*, collection, René Beaulieu (CF 3).

1981   *Le Vieil homme et l'espace*, collection, Daniel Sernine (CF 4).

1982   *L'Enfant du cinquième nord*, Pierre Billon.

1982   *Les Capsules du temps*, Henri La France.

1982   *La Planète amoureuse*, Jean-François Somcynsky (CF 5).

1983   *Les Méandres du temps*, Daniel Sernine (CF 6).

1983   *Les Années-lumière*, anthology.

1983   First Publication of four volumes of francophone science fiction *Espaces Imaginaires*.

1983   *Aurores boréales I*, anthology (CF 7).

1984   *TéléToTaliTé*, collection, Jean-Pierre April.

1984   *Janus*, collection, Élisabeth Vonarburg.

1984   Creation of the Grand prix de la science-fiction et du fantastique québécois (First winner: Denis Côté).

1985   *Dix nouvelles de science-fiction*, anthology.

1985   First publication of *L'Année de la science-fiction et du fantastique québécois*.

1985   *L'Épuisement du soleil*, Esther Rochon (CF 8).

1985   *Aurores boréales II*, anthology (CF 9)

1985   *Le Nord électrique*, Jean-Pierre April (CF 10).

1986   *Coquillage*, Esther Rochon.

1986   *L'Étrange monument du désert libyque*, Claude d'Astous.

1987   *Le Temps des migrations*, Francine Pelletier (CF 11).

1987   *Les Visiteurs du pôle nord*, Jean-François Somcynsky.

1988   Creation of the collection "Autres mers, Autres mondes" (Éditions Logiques, Montréal); titles marked AMAM were published in this collection; ceased publication with No. 11.

1988   *Dérives 5*, anthology (AMAM 1).

1988   *Gélules utopiques*, Guy Bouchard (AMAM 2).

1988   *SF: Dix années de science-fiction québécoise*, anthology (AMAM 3).

1988   *Les montres sont molles, mais les temps sont durs*, Nando Michaud.

1989   *C.I.N.Q.*, anthology (AMAM 4).

1989   *Berlin-Bangkok*, Jean-Pierre April (AMAM 5).

1989   *Vivre en beauté*, collection, Jean-François Somain (AMAM 6).

1989   *Dernier départ*, Jean-François Somain.
1989   *L'Oiseau de feu* (first volume in the series), Jacques Brossard.
1990   *La Ville oasis*, Michel Bélil (AMAM 7).
1990   *Les Maisons de cristal*, Annick Perrot-Bishop (AMAM 8).
1990   *Demain l'avenir*, anthology (AMAM 9).
1990   *Le Canissimus*, Pierre Desrochers.
1990   *La République de Monte-Carlo*, Louis-Bernard Robitaille.
1991   *Étrangers!* André Montambault (AMAM 10).
1991   *SOL*, anthology (AMAM 11).
1991   *Chocs baroques*, collection, Jean-Pierre April.
1991   *La Taupe et le dragon*, Joël Champetier.
1991   *Boulevard des étoiles*, collection, Daniel Sernine.
1991   *Le piège à souvenirs*, collection, Esther Rochon.
1991   *Ailleurs et au Japon*, collection, Élisabeth Vonarburg.
1991   *A la recherche de monsieur Goodtheim*, collection, Daniel Sernine.
1991   *L'espace du diamant*, Esther Rochon.
1992   *Chronoreg*, Daniel Sernine.
1992   *Chroniques du pays des mères*, Élisabeth Vonarburg.
1993   *Berlin-Bangkok* (new edition), Jean-Pierre April.
1994   *Les Voyageurs malgré eux*, Élisabeth Vonarburg.

Jean-Marc Gouanvic *is an associate professor in the French department at Concordia University. He founded the Québec science fiction review* imagine . . . *in 1979 and served as its literary editor until 1989. He has published a number of articles on SF in general and Québec SF in particular, and in 1994, he published a book on French SF,* La Science-fiction française au XXe siècle (1900-1968); essai de socio-poétique d'un genre en émergence. *He has edited several collections:* Les Année-lumière *(VLV, 1983), the four volumes of* Espaces imaginaires *(SF stories from Québec, France, Belgium and Switzerland) with Stéphane Nicot, and the series "Autres Mer, Autres Mondes" (Éditions Logiques). He founded a review on the theory and history of translation,* TTR — Études sur le texte et ses transformations, *in 1987.*

QUÉBEC SF AND ITS RECEPTION IN FRANCE

by Stéphane Nicot

I s there such a thing as Canadian science fiction for SF readers and professionals in France? Can such a thing exist in the collective imagination when, in France, everything that is translated from English is more or less considered to be 'made in the U.S.A.'? Yet another example of the whole problem of Canadian identity . . . With a few rare exceptions, Anglophone Canadian authors are regarded as Americans, and their work is lumped in with that of all the other English-language writers. This is obviously not the case for Québec SF, which has the benefit of a common language, a fact which should have facilitated its reception in France. And yet it did not, at least not up until the last ten years. Hence the question posed by Joëlle Wintrebert, author, TV script writer, critic and anthologist, in the *Univers 1985* (J'ai lu) editorial: "Who knows anything about Québec SF?"

QUÉBEC SF: A RECENT DISCOVERY

I t would be wrong to claim that Québec SF writers were completely ignored in France before the mid-1980s. Indeed, this would be an insult to all those on both sides of the Atlantic who have worked since the early 1970s to promote contacts between these two Francophone branches of speculative literature. Numerous fanzines, both amateur and professional, were very quick to open their pages to Francophone Canadian authors and critics. This phenomenon has stepped up considerably since what one might call the turning point of 1984-85. It is thought to be good form among professionals to take an ironic view of fandom and fans, who certainly have their faults (in particular a propensity for bitter feuds and sterile polemics); however, the best of them have a real passion for science fiction and help to open up the field, being less respectful of established hierarchies and often more curious and dynamic than their elders. The fairly recent recognition of Québec SF was born in the pages of the fanzines and fan anthologies. To our knowledge, credit for publishing the first Québec text in France, in the late 1970s, must go to the fanzine *Espace-Temps*, edited by Marcel Becker. In February 1983, in collaboration with Jean-Pierre April, this determined publisher coordinated a "Spécial Québec" (*Clair d'Ozone* No. 4), with short stories by some of the great names in Québec SF literature, starting with Élisabeth Vonarburg and Jean-Pierre April, and publicity for the two magazines which were already providing a structure for the emerging field of Québec SF, *imagine...* and *Solaris.*

Other precursors were Pierre Billon and Élisabeth Vonarburg. Certainly these two cases were very different, since Billon and his French publisher Le Seuil, denying the obvious, adamantly refused to accept the derogatory label of SF, to the point of making no mention of the awarding of the Grand Prix de la SF française 1983 to *L'enfant du cinquième nord*! The previous year, Élisabeth Vonarburg had won the Grand Prix 1982 for *Le silence de la cité* (Denoël, "Présence du futur"), published in one of the best known specialized collections of the time. Her work had first appeared professionally in France with "Marée haute," a short story published in 1979 in *Vingt maisons du Zodiaque*, an anthology by Maxim Jakubowski (Denoël, "Présence du futur"). These two Québec authors helped to attract the attention of a few French specialists.

The 1980s had begun auspiciously with the publication of a *Lettre du Québec* by Norbert Spehner, the founder of *Solaris*, in *L'année 1979-1980 de la Science-Fiction et du Fantastique* (Julliard). There the French public could discover some names which are still current in SFQ: Élisabeth Vonarburg, Jean-Pierre April, Esther Rochon, Daniel Sernine, Alain Bergeron, Joël Champetier, Michel Bélil, and Jean-Marc Gouanvic. Spehner noted: "Not a lot of work was published in 1979, but for the first time in Québec's literary history, we saw the emergence of writers who *specialized* in SF/Fantasy (previously, works of Québec SF had been written by mainstream authors such as Yves Thériault, Jacques Brossard, Jacques Benoit, Monique Corriveau)." And the Québec critic concluded: "1979 will prove to have been an important year for Québec SF — perhaps, even, the year it was born." How perceptive he was! *L'année 1980-1981 de la Science-Fiction et du Fantastique* was more laconic, providing just a few brief items of information, but referred to 1980 as an "active year for Québec SF."

THE YEARS OF RECOGNITION

While the 1970s were the decade of maturation for Québec writers and of the formation of a specialized field, the 1980s were the decade of recognition by French specialized literature.

Some exchanges went on during this period, although as yet in limited and disorganized fashion. *Solaris* published critics from *Fiction* in its pages, and in March 1981 *imagine* . . . introduced "À l'est du Québec," a column devoted to French publications, which affirmed that "the development of a Québec school of science fiction does not run counter to integration within a Francophone corpus — quite the contrary." At the same time, the Paris magazine *Change* (Laffont/Seghers) published an article by Jean-Marc Gouanvic in its fortieth issue (*"Science-fiction et histoires"*).

To Jean-Marc Gouanvic also goes the credit for venturing to launch, as an extension of *imagine* . . . , a series of annual anthologies, *Espaces imaginaires*, designed to provide a meeting place for Québec and French writers within one publication. This initiative arrived at the right time, and Alain Dorémieux, in the editorial for No. 350 of *Fiction* (April 1984), eagerly spoke of an "excellent Franco-Québec anthology," a view shared by Jean-Pierre Andrevon, who expressed his enthusiasm about the second volume of this predominantly Franco-Québec collaboration (there were a few offerings from French-speaking Belgian and Swiss authors as well) as follows in No. 358 of *Fiction*: "Francophone? The word is out, a word which in future will increasingly guarantee expansion through renewal." Without this growing interest, without this quite warm reception devoid of all Franco-French chauvinism, the author of these lines would have been unable to bring off his Francophone anthology project. *Futurs intérieurs* (Nouvelles éditions OPTA) thus came into being, with contributions in September 1984 of excellent texts from Jean-Pierre April, Esther Rochon and Jean-François Somain, alongside nine other Francophone short stories (by authors from France, Switzerland, and Belgium). Here too, the reception was excellent, and French specialists of the genre acknowledged that Québec SF was poised to achieve a level of quality on a par with that of French SF. This view was echoed by French critic and translator Jean-Daniel Brèque in the United States, in *Fantasy Review*: "Canadian SF writing is astonishingly original and may offer a new direction to French authors (the reverse is also true, I would suppose). Logically, the next stage would be for publishers to pave the way for real transatlantic collaboration between writers."

THE GOLDEN AGE OF SFQ IN FRANCE

The reception for Québec SF was no doubt most promising at the turn of the 1980s. Élisabeth Vonarburg, already fully recognized as a writer, independently of the subsequent movement to recognize SFQ, published *Janus* in November 1984 (Denoël, "Présence du futur"), a short story collection which confirmed a talent now unquestioned in France.

The critical reception for the level of quality that had now been attained by SFQ was enthusiastic. When No. 193 (May-June 1985) of *Français dans le monde* (Hachette/Larousse), the journal of the Bureau pour l'Enseignement de la Langue et de la Civilisation Française à l'Étranger, published a report entirely devoted to science fiction, SFQ was allotted two pages entitled "À travers les horizons: destination Québec" by Sophie Beaulé, critic for *imagine* ..., "Nuit Blanche," and then "L'année de la SF et du Fantastique québécois" (Le Passeur). Referring to the *Espaces imaginaires* anthology series launched on the initiative of Jean-Marc Gouanvic, Beaulé stated: "This new collection (in existence since 1983) marks the sudden breakthrough of Québec SF overseas. While SFQ had been known to French fandom (exchange of fanzines, collaborations), it was totally unknown to the general public. Yet it has managed to achieve recognition. . . . The clash of different cultures and fictional approaches will surely have beneficial effects upon Francophone science fiction." SFQ did not escape the vigilant attention of Dominique Warfa, the estimable writer and critic from Liège, who began to highlight it in 1984, notably in a column he wrote for *Séries B*. In No. 6, he cited the literary strength of such Québec writers as Agnès Guitard (calling *Coineraine*, for example, a "superb reflection on alien biology") or Jean-Pierre April (*Canadian Dream*, he said, was a "superb alternate history on the discovery of the St Lawrence by Jacques Cartier"). In No. 10, he saluted the work of *imagine* . . . and then closed with the statement that it was necessary to discuss the "veritable phenomenon that is Québec SF." He added: "Québec, long turned toward the U.S.A., is discovering that sensibilities — and also a certain publication *strategy* — are directing it toward creative activity that is interlinked with all of La Francophonie." There is that word: *Francophonie*!

The notion of French SF, as opposed to the predominant Anglophone SF (predominant as well in French SF publishing), was giving way to the broader notion of Francophone SF. Exchanges became more common: French critics in Québec magazines and Québec critics in France, interviews with French anthologists and authors in *Solaris* and *imagine* . . . but also in the excellent monthly *Québec français* which, under the impetus of Vital Gadbois, took an interest in the matter of SFQ's reception in France (No. 55, October 1984), and then published an article (No. 59, October 1985) on the emergence of Québec authors on the French scene. Joëlle Wintrebert joined the chorus (in *À Suivre*) in February 1985: "Was there really room (and subject matter) for several Franco-Québec anthologies? Here is your proof." Wintrebert then went on to publish in *Univers 1985* (J'ai lu), the annual anthology she was editing at the time, "La machine à explorer la fiction," a short story by Jean-Pierre April, together with a long article on Québec SF. Better yet, Jean-Pierre April reappeared in *Univers 1986* (J'ai lu) with "Il pleut des astronefs," a satirical tale of which Wintrebert wrote in her preface: "Last year you had the opportunity to appreciate the grating humour of Jean-Pierre April; here is our formidable Québecker back again, still in brilliant form, offering us a ferocious farce that spotlights those aspects of capitalism and its twin teats, overproduction and overconsumption, which are particularly hard to swallow." Faithful to Québec SF, Wintrebert's successor, Pierre K. Rey, published a third story by April, "Coma-B.2, biofiction," in *Univers 1988* (J'ai lu). This anthologist as well salutes the talent of the writer to whom he amiably refers in his introduction as our "Francophone Québecker."

The initiatives increased in number: ever more frequent invitations and visits by personalities in the field on both sides of the Atlantic, regular information on Francophone SF, and so on. The *Solaris* award was open for a number of years to French, Belgian, and Swiss writers, and in 1984 *imagine* . . . introduced the Prix Septième continent for Francophone authors, which is still being awarded and has gone to French and Québec writers and one Belgian author. During this period, many Québeckers were increasingly regular contributors to fanzines, anthologies (professional and amateur) and magazines. *Proxima*, an extremely well-made fan quarterly (photocomposed and printed) which attempted for some years to transform itself into a magazine, allotted six pages to Luc Pomerleau, the head of *Solaris* (No. 8, Fall 1985), for a section entitled "Côté Québec." Early in 1986, *Proxima* devoted an issue to SFQ: Élisabeth Vonarburg published a short story, "Les yeux ouverts", as well as an article conveying her view of the condition of Québec SF, while Stéphane Nicot interviewed Jean-Pierre April, Jean-Marc Gouanvic, and Esther Rochon. The next issue featured Daniel Sernine with "Monsieur Olier devient ministre," an excellent story that was supposed to appear in an anthology exclusively dedicated to Québec SF; however, this anthology never came to pass. Éditions La Découverte, which had a specialized collection at that time, had decided at the beginning of 1985 to bring out such a volume; unfortunately, this was not to be, for the collection was suddenly aborted. This particular missed opportunity was no mere historical detail, for it heralded one of the worst crises that French SF has ever faced, a crisis from which it has still not emerged and which was to handicap, or more accurately limit, the breakthrough that SFQ was beginning to make in French publishing.

But this decline was not immediately obvious. For example, Esther Rochon published "Dans la forêt de vitrail" in No. 2058 of the weekly *La Vie du Rail* (September 1986), which had a circulation of 275,000! Everything still seemed to be possible. Alas, such was not the case, as Québec authors were gradually to discover.

THE CRISIS OF FRENCH SF AND ITS REPERCUSSIONS ON QUÉBEC SF

Paradoxically, it was just when Québec SF became accredited in France that French SF began to suffer the first phase of a publishing crisis which, by a sort of boomerang effect, constricted and then disabled the fine mechanism that the creators of sfq and its French defenders had hoped would allow it to become established in France.

The September 1984 publication of *Futurs intérieurs*, whose shortcomings are evident today (in particular, a preface of limited interest) but which was all the same the first professional anthology devoted to Francophone SF in France; the recognized quality of the stories of Rochon, April, and Somain; and the existence since the fall of 1983 of the *Espaces imaginaires* anthology, with its Québec selection handled by Jean-Marc Gouanvic, were supposed to culminate in a collaboration between *Fiction*, the monthly French SF magazine since 1953, and *imagine* . . . . Alain Dorémieux, the editor-in-chief of the time, had in fact agreed to the regular publication of Québec short stories in the magazine, starting with the joint organization of the Prix Septième continent. The winner was to be published jointly in *Fiction* and *imagine* . . .: short story, interview and bibliography. Unfortunately, Dorémieux resigned and left *Fiction* in October 1984. Through good times and bad, this magazine had been the binding force of French SF for over three decades: when Dorémieux left, it basically fell back on translations of the U.S. magazine *F and SF*, and then began what one might discreetly call a process of slow and painful death. *Fiction* ended ingloriously in February 1992 with No. 412.

This missed opportunity for Québec SF was a foretaste of others, equally damaging. *Proxima*, whose interest for SFQ we have seen, disappeared in late 1988. The *Univers* anthology, a powerful vehicle for the recognition of SFQ in France by virtue of its healthy circulation (25,000), good distribution network (including in Québec), and excellent critical reputation, published its final volume in 1989. One after another, publishers stopped the collections, and Québec writers saw their hopes of wide publication in France collapse. Some became discouraged, seeing this as Franco-French protectionism at work. But the reality was more disturbing: the restrictions affected *all* of Francophone SF.

SFQ, AT THE HEART OF FRANCOPHONE SF

The lack of publishing outlets that was so strongly felt in France in the second half of the 1980s has become further accentuated in the 1990s, and is now at a critical juncture. But it is precisely this extremely difficult context that explains in a definite paradox — science fiction is fond of paradoxes — why Québec SF has now succeeded in penetrating the French market, and beyond it, the European one, since SF in Belgium and Switzerland is also open to Francophone exchanges. Today, even if the drastic constraints on French SF publishing are limiting its practical scope,

Québec sf writers are increasingly integrated in the Francophone forum that has been constructed over the past ten years. Since its creation in 1984, INFINI, the professional SF association, has defined itself as Francophone and not French; Québec authors and critics are regularly published in the fanzines or prozines that continue in France, as their French, Belgian, or Swiss colleagues are in Québec.

With a few rare exceptions, SFQ cannot be avoided: Québec authors are to be found in the quarterly *Antarès* (including Somain and Sernine), and in various fan volumes such as *Les enfants d'Enéïde* (Éditions Phénix), which is totally devoted to Québec writers, or *Au nord de nulle part* (Groupe Phi éditeur), a Francophone anthology by Dominique Warfa published in 1992 on the occasion of the nineteenth French sf convention, which features a text by Jean-Louis Trudel. Daniel Walther does not fail to mention Québec production, albeit somewhat summarily, of course, in *La science-fiction* (MA éditions), an encyclopedia by Denis Gulot, Jean-Pierre Andrevon, and G W Barlow. These days, it is rare to see a French convention — officially Francophone for some years — without its guest from Québec: Jean-Pierre April in 1991, Esther Rochon in 1992, Élisabeth Vonarburg in 1993, Élisabeth Vonarburg and Joël Champetier in 1995, and Jean-Marc Gouanvic announced for 1996. Numerous Québec writers were also invited to the sixth Semaine de la sf et de l'imaginaire de Roanne in 1989: Daniel Sernine, Francine Pelletier, Esther Rochon, Jean-Pierre April, Élisabeth Vonarburg, and Luc Pomerleau. Neither have we been outdone in terms of fandom. *Yellow Submarine*, to mention just the fanzine of André-François Ruaud, the most regular (he has surpassed 110 issues!) and most tireless supporter of SFQ, offers information, criticism, and short stories, unpublished or previously published in Québec (Yves Meynard or Joël Champetier). In fact, Ruaud is impatient on this score: "Québeckers are extremely talented and it's a disgrace that they are not published on this side of the Atlantic." Despite the unfavorable context, however, the first successes have been recorded. In 1989, *La frontière éclatée* (Livre de Poche), the third volume of a series of four anthologies dedicated to French sf, opened itself to Québec sf with stories by Élisabeth Vonarburg and Agnès Guitard. Then Jean-Pierre April broke into the most popular and best distributed of the French sf collections with the 1993 publication of a slightly reworked and updated version of *Berlin-Bangkok* (J'ai lu). In 1994 it was the turn of Jean-Louis Trudel to make his entry on the French SF publishing scene with *Pour des soleils froids* and then *Le ressuscité de l'Atlantide* (Fleuve Noir, "Anticipation"). Despite the distances involved, which do not facilitate communication or information, Québec authors are today recognized as full players on the Francophone stage. April and Trudel have begun to establish a niche for themselves in this market: it will be quite surprising if others do not follow them.

The place that Québec SF will assume in future in Francophone Europe, particularly in France, now depends more on the state of French publishing than on the dynamism of SFQ itself. Québec science fiction is now well integrated in this complementary movement of and exchange that is known as La Francophonie. We might also point out that, until its suspension in 1994, it was the Belgian fanzine *Magie rouge* that announced the winner of the Prix Septième continent, and that the publication in No. 83 of *imagine* ... of a report on Swiss SF has encouraged the establishment of ties with our Swiss friends, and in particular with La Maison d'Ailleurs, the only SF museum *in the world*!

We could provide no better conclusion than this comment by Jean-Marc Gouanvic, which appeared in the SF special issue of *Séries B*, No. 14/15: "Québec science fiction has successfully completed takeoff, and . . . is now a force to be reckoned with."

Stéphane Nicot, *literature and history professor, critic, essayist and anthologist, is a specialist in French-language SF. He has written a number of well-received articles on the subject, including* Une SF étrange venue d'falleurs: la SF québécoise *and* Splendeurs et misères de la SF française. *He has published seven anthologies, including* Futurs intérieurs, *which helped introduce France to Québec SF, and the series* Espaces imaginaires, *which he co-edited with Jean-Marc Gouanvic. He has also worked for the paper* L'écho du centre *and, since 1981, for the Québec review* imagine . . . .

THE SCIENCE FICTION NOVEL FOR YOUNG PEOPLE IN QUÉBEC
From the 1960s to the 1990s
by Claire Le Brun

Science fiction for young people stands at the interface of two literary genres: science fiction, from which it draws its themes, and literature for young people, which imposes certain formal models, notably the educational tale and novel. The breakdown of those who write this literature in Québec is a good reflection of the meeting of two worlds. From the 1960s to the 1990s, two types of writers have crossed paths: authors of young people's literature who occasionally write science fiction, and science fiction novelists who by turn address adults and young people. In all, some forty authors have published at least one SF novel for a young audience. Naturally, their commitment to the genre is highly variable in nature, ranging from modernization of the fairy tale using robots or extraterrestrials to the construction of universes remote in time or space.

What would be the best way of giving an account of these thirty-five years of science fiction for young people in Québec publishing? Chronological division, by decade for example? Thematic organization highlighting certain constant subjects? The two solutions seem compatible to us. Therefore we will precede our analysis of major themes with an overview situating the SF narratives in terms of the evolution of literature for young people in Québec.

AUTHORS, PUBLISHERS, COLLECTIONS: A HISTORICAL OVERVIEW

The 1960s were a bad period in the book market for young people.[1] A few figures will illustrate this: 31 titles in 1961-62, 15 in 1963, 6 in 1969! Given the general slump, SF did not fare so badly. The decade was marked by two series, launched by the Lidec company in 1965: Maurice Gagnon's *Unipax* and Yves Thériault's *Volpek*. *Quatre Montréalais en l'an 3000* (1963, original title of *Surréal 3000*) by Suzanne Martel enjoyed great success, which continued on into the 1980s. In 1960 Fides brought out the first Québec Youth SF novel, *Vénus via Atlantide*, written by a very young Guy Bouchard. All things considered, many of the bestselling novels of the 1960s were SF-related. However, this label was not yet common, and the works just mentioned were presented as adventure novels.

The series by Maurice Gagnon and Yves Thériault came to an end in the 1960s. The *Volpek* series saw an "educational" revival in the early 1980s: it was republished by the Centre Éducatif et Culturel for the purpose of teaching French as a second language. The "Jeunesse-Pop" collection took over in 1971 by publishing space adventures, a project in which Louis Sutal played a very active role (six titles from 1971 to 1977). *En hommage aux araignées* (1974) brought Esther Rochon to notice, but this teenagers' novel, reissued by "Jeunesse-Pop" in 1986 as *L'Étranger sous la ville*, did not originally appear in a youth collection. The adventure novels of the Martel and Corriveau sisters include a few SF titles: *Titralak, cadet de l'espace* (1974) and *Patrick et Sophie en fusée* (1975). Some collections lived long enough to produce a few titles (Espace-Temps, Intermondes). If one had to choose a symbol of this decade, one possibility might be Monique Corriveau's trilogy *Compagnon du soleil* (1976), which was a sort of last testament, since the author died before the book was published.

In the early 1980s, science fiction for young people became established, following in the footsteps of the organized movement on the adult side (magazines, conferences), the history of which is contained in these pages. There was a massive introduction of terms explicitly associated with SF. Robots and extraterrestrials invaded the titles in the story collection *Pour lire avec toi*, published by Héritage. Suzanne Martel launched the *Galaxie* collection with the same publisher. In 1982, *imagine . . .* magazine created the "SF/Jeunesse" column. The early years of the decade saw the appearance of two young men with the dual specialty of science fiction writer for young people: Daniel Sernine and Denis Côté. Daniel Sernine began his career in 1979 with *Organization Argus*, a first sketch of an SF universe that he was never to abandon. The author of SF, fantasy, and occasionally heroic fantasy (*Ludovic*, 1983), Sernine established himself in the 1980s as a promoter/cultural animator in two areas: science fiction/fantasy (*Solaris*) and literature for young people (*Communication Jeunesse*). As for Denis Côté, he made a sensational entry into young people's literature by publishing three novels the same year, on different themes: *Les Parallèles célestes, L'Invisible puissance, Hockeyeurs cybernétiques* (1983). It should be noted that this new writer for young people was the first winner of the Grand Prix de la Science-Fiction Québécoise, created in 1984. This got the movement well and truly under way. Many authors made their debut; some were like shooting stars, while others joined the fairly closed circle of Youth SF writers. Sernine (the *Argus* novels), Côté (the *Maxime* and *Inactifs* books), Pelletier (the Arialde police investigations), and Massé (the Australians' time travels) built their fictional universes using the series concept. But individual titles also made their mark: *Simon Yourm* (Gaétan Leboeuf, 1986), *La Mémoire des hommes* (Jean-Michel Lienhardt, 1988), *Le Domaine des Sans-Yeux* (Jacques Lazure, 1989). Despite the genre's success, there was no collection exclusively devoted to it after the swift demise of *Galaxie*. The *Jeunesse-Pop* collection, which began labeling its titles in 1978 (science fiction, fantasy, detective novel, heroic fantasy, mystery), is still the one that publishes the most SF titles.

The 1990s have seen some degree of tailing off. The 1980s series are continuing, but in the spectacular development of the novel for young people late in the decade, the realistic introspective narrative carved itself the lion's share. Consequently, there has been an especially warm welcome for novels with new tones and new themes and which respond to new collective concerns, such as *Un mal étrange* (Paul de Grosbois, 1991), on genetic engineering. A few authors are engaging in acute social criticism, in sharp contrast to certain navel-gazing excesses of the prevailing realistic novel: for example, Jacques Lazure pondering how to write history, or disinformation (*Pellicules-Cités*, 1992; *Monsieur N'importe Qui*, 1993). While dystopias are predominant, other trends are represented: space opera (Camille Bouchard), heroic fantasy (Philippe Gauthier, Joël Champetier), verbal and thematic fantasy (Gaétan Leboeuf, *Boudin d'air*, 1990). Hindsight will more clearly reveal the strengths of this decade.

Québec Youth SF has therefore gone through two stages. In the 1960s and 1970s, its main creators were young people's writers working in various subgenres, or authors of general literature who also wrote for young people, such as Yves Thériault, and it was not identified as science fiction. In the late 1970s, science fiction became established as a genre in Québec, and this movement had an immediate impact on young people's literature, where an SF current was formed.

THE MAJOR THEMES

Themes and age of the target audience
The choice of themes varies according to the age of the target audience. It therefore seems to us appropriate to introduce a distinction between the themes of novels for children (in academic terms, elementary students) and those for adolescents (secondary level). In recent years, this second category has been tending to expand and subdivide: 'teen', 'teen plus', 'over 14', etc. Since literature for young people is now targeting young adult readers, it is not surprising to see it diversifying its themes and becoming more thoughtful. To give but one example, the short story collection by Jean-Pierre April *N'ajustez pas vos hallucinettes* (14 and over) focuses on themes dear to the author: simulacra, physical and psychic manipulation. We see Westerners buying Asian babies who are orphans of war, and then whitening their skin and widening their eyes, or a teenage girl on a search for her genetic father, who is a universal sperm donor. In the 1990s, there is not much that is off limits in young people's literature!

Fantastic planets, robots and extraterrestrials:
the lure of the different, the return to the familiar
Generally speaking, there are two standard characters in children's SF: the extraterrestrial and the robot. Young readers are transported to paradisiacal planets, true lands of plenty where robots grant their every wish and they are welcomed by picturesque extraterrestrials. But rare are the narratives in which this marvelous landscape is not the pretext for a moral lesson. In the early 1980s, the *Pour lire avec toi* collection published a number of so-called science fiction works which are in fact traditional tales disguised by a technological decor. In *L'Enfant venu d'ailleurs*, Marie Pagé tells of a secret island with advanced technology where humans and robots live together on good terms: to the former go the creative activities and to the latter the repetitive tasks. Henriette Major's *La Ville fabuleuse* presents the same dreamscape, with a hidden trap: to live in the city, you must agree to become a robot, that is, to lose your ability to feel emotion. In Daniel Mativat's *Ram, le robot*, the robots attend to everything, and the

only human worker is the one who maintains the robots — but in the end is he not the happiest of all? *Le Robot concierge* by Mimi Legault shows that a machine cannot replace a human. Although initially attractive, the robots in Québec children's novels are a warning against the alienating machine that deprives humans of their freedoms and values. However, there are a few voices who use humour and imagination to dispel fear of the machine: Francine Loranger (*Chansons pour un ordinateur*) and Bernadette Renaud (*La Dépression de l'ordinateur*).

Robots and extraterrestrials generally play an identical role of friend, helper, and confidant to children and teenagers. Suzanne Martel's hero *Titralak* is the secret friend who is passed off to the parents as a Japanese! In *Nos amis robots* by the same author, Earth is threatened by an interplanetary war, but everything works out thanks to collaboration between some young Earth heroes and their extraterrestrial friends. In certain tales, however, one cannot fail to notice the traditional opposition between the extraterrestrials' technology and our own moral and spiritual values. Novels often deal more with the fascinated discovery of our world by extraterrestrials than with our own attraction for the Other. Nasty extraterrestrials appear mainly in novels for adolescents.

At times, treatment of the theme of the extraterrestrial can be unconventional and non-moralizing. Biological otherness is brilliantly conveyed by Danièle Simpson in *L'Arbre aux tremblements roses*, where she imagines a planet where life is characterized by multiplicity instead of continuity. In Denis Côté's *Les Parallèles célestes*, the suspense intrigue is paired with a discussion of UFOs. *Les Géants de blizzard* and *Les Yeux d'émeraude* by the same author present the UFO phenomenon in a manner unprecedented in young people's literature. In the latter novel, a young extraterrestrial who has taken the form of a stray cat succeeds in winning a little boy's complete affection. Charles Montpetit gives the theme farcical and parodic treatment in *Temps perdu* and *Temps mort*, where an entity that can only move through time collides with a teenage girl. Two other recent successes in the humorous vein are *Le Cosmonaute oublié* (Marie-Andrée and Daniel Mativat) for children, and *Le Secret le mieux gardé* (Jean-François Somain) for teenagers.

Crusades for peace

This theme is typical of production during the 1960s, but it is present throughout the period as well. In *Vénus via Atlantide*, scientific collaboration is a stage towards world peace. The *Unipax* and *Volpek* stories have as their central motif the establishment of international organizations devoted to the prevention of war. These two series postulate utopian future societies, although Thériault's utopia is threatened by the Evil incarnate in the Soviet bloc. Louis Sutal's Err-hêtians roam the universe in the company of their Québec friends with the mission of maintaining peace. Daniel Sernine continues this tradition in the *Argus* series, in which the most brilliant minds on Earth have been fleeing our planet since the eighteenth century to form a pacifist and highly technological society on Érymède. We note in passing that the theme of superior intelligence placed at the service of pacifism is a constant in all authors. The Éryméans have founded the Argus organization, which is responsible for monitoring Earth and preventing the more serious conflicts. Similarly, the search for peace is the main message of *Nos amis robots* and *Les Géants de Blizzard*, mentioned earlier.

Cities of the Future and Remote Societies: Dystopia and Social Criticism

Strange as it may seem in view of the obligation of young people's literature to be optimistic, there is a very strong dystopian current in Quebec Youth SF. *Surréal 3000*, whose success was mentioned earlier, and *Le Soleil des profondeurs* (Rolande Allard-Lacerte) describe underground cities of the future, perfectly regulated by a central authority, where nightmare soon shows through the apparent utopia. The much darker *Compagnon du Soleil* proposes a society similar to *1984*, Ixanor, in which the citizens are drugged into euphoria with a substitute for drinking water, which in its pure form is reserved for the ruling elite. Unlike these three universes situated in a distant future, the urban society described by Denis Côté (*Hockeyeurs cybernétiques* and the *Inactifs* books) is in the near future: 2010. The population is divided into half-starved Inactives, who have no reason to live apart from spectator sports, and Actives, who are more decently housed and fed, at the price of exhausting labor. All the intrigues describe the struggle of a few protagonists against the system, a struggle that is the more difficult in that those who pull the strings are invisible. Incidentally, *L'Invisible Puissance* is the title of another novel by Denis Côté about neo-Nazi sects and movements.

Certain authors prefer a setting on a distant planet to moving far ahead in the future: *Le Domaine des Sans-Yeux* by Jacques Lazure and *La Mer au fond du monde* by Joël Champetier both denounce the oppression and loss of cultural identity suffered by certain communities. Luc Pouliot reflects upon how society operates in an animal fable called *Le Voyage des chats*.

Novels of Female Education

These stories, written by women, consider those aspects peculiar to female life, and show teenagers with charismatic personalities acquiring power. The prototypical tale is *En hommage aux araignées* by Esther Rochon. The heroine is a member of a fallen people to whom she restores a reason to live. As she goes through her learning process, self-discovery and self-affirmation are achieved through the assumption of social duty. In *L'Ombre et le cheval* (1992), the artist-heroine has these same characteristics.

La Cavernale by Marie-Andrée Warnant-Côté and *Le Rendez-vous du désert* by Francine Pelletier are post-cataclysmic narratives in which the convention of the *tabula rasa*, by removing all social pressures, allows the heroines to ponder the real issues of their existence. This type of story, where the emphasis is on interpersonal relations more than social structures, is related to the trend of the female *Bildungsroman* as the vehicle of new models and proposals, as illustrated in science fiction by the American Ursula K. Le Guin.

A Few Other Trends

Occasionally intersecting with these main themes, one finds secondary themes which are present to varying degrees over the years. Some authors are inspired by time travel: Monique Corriveau (*Patrick et Sophie en fusée*), Reynald Lefebvre (*Les Voyageurs du temps*), Denis Côté (*Le Voyage dans le temps*), Johanne Massé (*De l'autre côté de l'avenir, Contre le temps, Le Passé en péril*).

Leading mainly into the past, time travel is a means of revisiting crucial moments in national history (the Irish immigration in 1847 in *Le Passé en péril*) and international history (the Six Days' War in *Contre le temps*). The mad doctor, an important character in fiction of the 1960s and 1970s, reappears in *Les Prisonniers du zoo* by Denis Côté, an interesting variation on the theme of *The Island of Dr. Moreau*, and in *Un Mal étrange* by Paul de Grosbois, in which an American scientist, having slightly botched his son's *in vitro* generation, is constantly performing corrective operations on him.

Certain themes, already present in the dystopias of the 1960s and 1970s, are becoming increasingly significant: environmental degradation and media manipulation of societies. The environmental battle was the theme of many books for children and teenagers at the turn of the 1990s: the *Wondeur* series by Jocelyne Sanschagrin, set in a city that has become a garbage dump, *Les Enfants de l'eau* by Hélène Gagnier, *Le Paradis perdu* by Jean-Pierre Guillet, *Le Chant des Hayats* by Alain Bergeron. The deterioration of natural resources is one of the major causes of the decay of the social fabric in Côté's *Inactifs* series. The theme of disinformation, which has been reserved for adolescents and young adults, has been treated convincingly by Jacques Lazure and Jean-Pierre April.

CONCLUSION

Since 1960 the science fiction narrative, whether it bears that label or not, has held an important place among Québec novels written for young people. The historical overview has shown a period of intense activity in the early 1980s, thanks to the movement in adult fiction, followed by a lull in the early 1990s, when the psychological novel became dominant. Youth SF reflects to a young audience the social, economic, religious, and political concerns of the time: the struggle for world peace; resistance to technological takeover, perceived as a threat to humanist values, and resistance to globalization of the economy; feminist affirmation; environmental struggle; and finally, in recent years, the search for a code of bioethics. Borrowing the classic SF themes, the authors generally lighten their subjects with a touch of optimism, humor, or fantasy. The darkest dystopias of writers like Corriveau,

Côté, and Lazure bear a message of hope. We can only hope that quality SF tales continue to be published alongside the realistic and psychological novels, complementing self-knowledge with discovery of the world.

NOTES

1 See Louise Lemieux, *Pleins feux sur la littérature de jeunesse au Canada français* (Montreal: Leméac, 1972); Édith Madore, *La Littérature pour la jeunesse au Québec* (Montreal: Boréal Express, 1994), ch. 2.

Claire Le Brun *is an associate professor in the French Department at Concordia University. She has worked for several years on Québec and Canadian children's literature, publishing articles in various reviews, notably* Canadian Children's Literature, Voix et images, Revue francophone, *and* TTR — Études sur le texte et ses transformations. *Her main interests in her articles on science fiction for young people are utopian and dystopian narratives and the female Bildungsroman. She founded the column "SF/Jeunesse" in the review* imagine . . . *in 1982 and was its main contributor until 1992. A medievalist by training, she has written articles on the relationship between* uchronie *(the apocryphal history of European civilization, not as it was but as it ought to have been), the* chanson de geste, *and the ancient forms of scientific narrative: eschatological explorations and fabulous and utopian voyages.*

SCIENCE FICTION AND FANTASY FOR THE YOUNG
An Overview of the Planet
by Daniel Sernine

Not counting a few rather quaint early works (nineteenth-century novels, mid-twentieth-century serialized stories), Québec science fiction first came into being in the 1960s. Even then it was clear that science fiction and fantasy for young people would account for a large part of the body of work: rarely less than one third and often more than one half of all books published. The surveys in *L'Année de la Science-Fiction et du Fantastique Québécois*, which are available for nine years (1984-1992) as I write this article, show that 61.5% of the novels or stories published during this period were for young readers. There were even years when novels for young people accounted for 69% (18 novels in 1989), 74% (28 novels in 1992), and as much as 86% (25 novels in 1991) of the annual total.

This predominance of SF for young people applies only to the novel. As far as short stories published in magazines, collections, and anthologies are concerned, it is usually the adult audience that is targeted. The few collections for young people published by Pierre Tisseyre, Québec/Amérique, Héritage, or Fides are not enough to offset the vast numbers of stories for adults. Qualitatively, on the other hand, some excellent stories, both fantasy and science fiction, have been published in collections for teenagers; sometimes these were written specifically for young people, although in other cases authors have taken stories that were originally written and published for a general audience, reorganized them, and adapted them for younger readers.

Like science fiction intended for a general audience, SF for young people was not very common in the 1960s and 1970s. With their Unipax and Volpek series, respectively, Maurice Gagnon and Yves Thériault alone published most of the science fiction in Québec in the 1960s (although only two of the works in the series by Thériault were SF titles). Their science fiction was closer to the spy novel: Thériault's Volpek series was set in the near future and used futuristic gadgets, many of which are now outdated. This series and, to a lesser extent, the Unipax series by Maurice Gagnon depicted with remarkable naivety the struggle between good and bad, the bad guys, of course, being cruel, ugly and communist, the good being the champions of peace and freedom. In the Unipax series this Manicheism was rather more subtle since the good guys were not identified with any country in particular and they were also resolutely non-violent.

To these ten short novels published by Éditions Lidec between 1965 and 1968 we should add those of Suzanne Martel. She published four SF novels between 1963 and 1985, but in their style and themes all four are decidedly novels of the 1960s. The best known is the first, *Surréal 3000*, originally published under another title. This author's fiction, like that of Monique Corriveau, was marked by the values and stereotypes of the times: exemplary, enthusiastic, and naive young heroes with an emphasis on the family and everyday life. In another article I called this "pastel science fiction." It was served more by the quality of the writing than by the scope of the imagination.

I was going to say "the movement continued into the 1970s" but, on reflection, there was hardly a movement or a trend. The names of Monique Corriveau and Louis Sutal stand out, the former for her fame as an author of works for young people and the latter for the number of novels he published. Monique Corriveau published an SF novel for young people, followed by an impressive trilogy, *Compagnons du Soleil*, which, by its writing, themes, and place of publication (Éditions Fides) seemed to be aimed at young people, although it was presented as a work for a general audience. Louis Sutal stood out less for the quality of his fiction than for the fact that he published a series of six novels with Éditions Paulines, which made him the most prolific writer of SF for young people in the 1970s. What is more, Jeunesse-Pop was already at that time the Québec series that contained the most science fiction, although it must be admitted that the quality was very uneven and distribution of the works was limited.

During the 1980s, Québec SF, like literature in the province for young people, was marked by a rapid growth in publishing — in fact, an explosion, just as we talk of the population explosion. Previously, the quality of SF for young people had generally been rather uneven. Novels had often been written by young authors with no literary experience or by experienced authors who knew little about SF. However, beginning in the early 1980s, with works by professional authors who were masters of the genre, SF for young people attained a level of quality that withstands comparison with its French equivalent. (In the strict sense, the quality of the body of science fiction as a whole remains uneven because it includes both virtual masterpieces and real duds; however, the quality of the best is much better than it was.)

With the growth in the number of publishers of novels for young people, similar growth in the number of SF novels might have been expected. However, the number of Québec publishers issuing science fiction identified as such is small. (I shall continue to use the adjective "Québec" to limit my subject; to the best of my knowledge, there is no Francophone publisher of science fiction or fantasy outside Québec.) It is as if most publishers were aware of the contempt in which science fiction is held and preferred to publish such novels "on the quiet" without the label rather than face up to prejudices by offering excellent literature labeled SF. Thus it is possible to read SF (or fantasy) novels or short stories published by Éditions de la Courte Échelle, Éditions du Boréal, Québec/Amérique, Pierre Tisseyre, Hurtubise HMH, Héritage, Coïncidence Jeunesse, and, occasionally, Éditions Fides. However, the only collection openly identified with science fiction, fantasy, and heroic fantasy is Jeunesse-Pop, published by Éditions Mediaspaul (formerly Paulines).

The science fiction put out by non-specialized publishers depends on the quality of a particular author's writing. As a rule, the editors of collections are not familiar with science fiction; even if they are able to judge the writing in a manuscript, the science fiction aspects of a novel nevertheless escape them. Plot construction, internal consistency, questions of probability or improbability, the scientific background, if any — you have to be familiar with this literary genre if you want to appreciate these various aspects of a science fiction novel. This explains why many manuscripts that are blatantly ridiculous have made it to publication, especially when the authors themselves understood nothing about science fiction, for example, confusing science fiction with fantasy, Saturday morning cartoons with literature, science with magic.[1] In works of this kind you often find that technical and scientific jargon is used like magic formulas in witchcraft and science fiction gadgets replace the magic wand: you only need to use the word "computer" for everything to become possible in these stories. On the other hand, a publisher who has no SF culture is fortunate if he receives manuscripts from authors who are masters of the genre or know how to write — or, better still, both. This is true of Denis Côté (who has published with Éditions Paulines, Hurtubise HMH, Québec/Amérique, Pierre Tisseyre and, above all, Éditions de la Courte Echelle).

This distinction between publishers knowledgeable about science fiction and those who are not can also be extended to authors. A number of novels have been published by authors who touched on science fiction and fantasy only by accident — or even without realizing what they were doing in some cases. The figures noted at the beginning of this article taken from *L'Année de la Science-Fiction et du Fantastique Québécois* cover all books classified in these literary genres by the editorial board of that publication. Thus, they include stories whose authors were no doubt unaware of the fact that specialists might see them as containing fantasy (or, less commonly, SF). And they may still be unaware, if the articles and reviews in specialized journals have not been brought to their attention.

Without wishing to pontificate, I would strongly suggest that the best SF for young people is written by authors who "know what they are doing" — in other words, who deliberately write SF or fantasy because these are their favorite genres and because they have assimilated large quantities of this material (from reading, TV, and the movies). A review of the bibliography shows that there are only one or two exceptions to my thesis. The reverse, however, is not necessarily true: mediocre works of SF or fantasy have been published by authors who seemed familiar with the genre but were simply poor writers. The publishing market in Québec is structured in such a way that even poor manuscripts are sometimes published and, it should be noted, not only in science fiction but also in general literature.

This overview would not be complete if I failed to mention the main Québec authors of science fiction and fantasy. The most frequently read and the most prolific author of novels for young people in these genres is, without a doubt, Denis Côté of Québec City. Since 1985, he has been closely identified with the Courte Échelle publishing house. At the time of writing, this publisher has brought out thirteen of his novels that contain at least some science fiction or fantasy, sometimes both together, a risky venture in which Côté is one of the few success stories. Côté has written pure science fiction (*Les Géants de Blizzard* and the Inactifs series, which began with *Les Hockeyeurs Cybernetiques*); horror (*Terminus Cauchemar* and *Aux Portes de L'Horreur*); and adventure novels containing fairly large doses of fantasy or SF (the Maxime series, for example, which includes the moving *Les Yeux D'Émeraude*). The critics have been unanimous in stressing the quality of Côté's writing, his sensitivity, and the close connection between his imaginary world and the social and cultural trends in which young readers are interested. Denis Côté has also published a half-dozen books with other publishers, including two collections of stories with Pierre Tisseyre and the first-class novel *Nocturnes pour Jessie* published by Québec/Amérique.

Those responsible for this anthology insisted that I write an article, even though they knew that I was also a writer of science fiction and fantasy and the literary editor of a series for young people which is dominated by these two genres. Thus, I feel that I am at liberty (although not without some embarassment) to talk a little about my own work, at least that which is directed towards younger readers. As far as SF is concerned, I have to date published four novels in the Argus series. The opening novel, *Organization Argus* (1979), can, I feel, be considered to be the first in the period I earlier assigned to the 1980s, the period that saw young authors destined to become professional writers *deliberately* publishing works of SF fiction or fantasy, mastering these genres and intending to devote all or most of their careers to them. As far as fantasy is concerned, when this series of articles is published I shall be finishing a series of ten novels, the Neubourg and Granverger Cycle, extending over four centuries of this country's history, from 1595 to 1995. The best known of these novels are undoubtedly *Le Cercle Violet* (Éditions Pierre Tisseyre, 1984) and *Le Cercle de Khaleb* (Éditions Héritage, 1991). I also touched on heroic fantasy in my novel *Ludovic* (1983, reissued by Héritage in 1992).

With the dozen or so novels she has published since 1987,

particularly in the Jeunesse-Pop series, Francine Pelletier is certainly the most regular science fiction author in Québec. Some of her novels take place in the narrow border zone between science fiction and mimetic or "realistic" mainstream literature (the Bizarre series), but most are clearly science fiction (the Arialde series). Environmental themes and young people's search for independence dominate this fiction, which often takes the form of the detective novel, so much so that people often speak in Francine Pelletier's case of the "SF Detective" novel.

Besides two novels for adults, Joël Champetier has to date published six books for young people (Jeunesse-Pop collection), two that are science fiction (including the deeply moving *La Mer au Fond du Monde*) and two that are heroic fantasy. Properly speaking, these four books make up two novels, each of which consists of two volumes: *La Requête de Barrad* and *La Prisonière de Barrad*, on the one hand, and *Le Voyage de la Sylvanelle* and *Le Secret des Sylvaneaux*, on the other. Although not an innovator in the genre, Champetier has succeeded in these novels in allowing his inner voice to be heard and in surprising his readers with ingenious plots.

Among other important authors are Jacques Lazure, who has published with Québec/Amérique Jeunesse a collection and two novels, one of which was the remarkable *Le Domaine des Sans-Yeux*, a finalist for various prizes and winner of the Prix Québec/Wallonie-Bruxelles (1993); Charles Montpetit, author of *Copie Carbone* (Québec/Amérique Jeunesse) and the story in two parts *Temps Perdu, Temps Mort* (Jeunesse-Pop; the latter won the Governor General's Award in 1989); and Jean-Louis Trudel, author of serialized novels and many short stories since the mid-1980s, who made an explosive entry into the major leagues by publishing five works of SF in a single year, two novels being published by Fleuve Noir in France and three in the Jeunesse-Pop series.

Although it is not possible in this article to discuss in detail the dominant features of Québec SF for young people, an in-depth article by Simon Dupuis in *Lurelu* and later in *Solaris* can be read with profit; double the length of the present article, it is still relevant despite the novels and collections that have appeared since it came out.[2]

In brief, a number of trends can be noted in Québec SF. Its starting point is often the "here and now" of present-day Québec, but just as often it also moves to worlds that are far removed (in space and time) from Earth and whose links with the Mother Planet are often tenuous, if not non-existent. The near future, as a metaphor for the ills and perils of contemporary civilization, is the somber backdrop and sometimes even the subject of a number of works. Extraterrestrials, symbolizing what is foreign or representing disappearing species, not to mention threatened ethnic groups, often appear in the cast. All the sub-genres of SF can be found, from classical *space opera* (Jean-Louis Trudel, Alain Bergeron) to speculative fiction (Esther Rochon, Jacques Lazure), not to mention the challenges of the temporal paradox (Charles Montpetit, Johanne Massé). Various concerns come to the fore in Québec SF: ecology has a major role as do the dangers of science without a conscience. Electronic recreation, the media and sport as entertainment, major concerns of our times, are at the cutting edge, as are issues of work and unemployment, transposed into a world of robots and androids.

In concluding, I should note that Québec SF for young people cannot be separated from general Québec SF. A number of authors have realized this, and they divide their creative energies between the youth and adult audiences. Besides its quantitative importance, SF for young people holds out the promise of initiating young readers. We can only hope that they will be pleasantly stimulated by the prospects thus offered to them and even as adults will still be prepared to open their minds and imaginations to other ideas, innovative concepts, and different visions — in short, that they will remain open and alert.

NOTES

1   See my article "Les questions de vraisemblance en science-fiction pour jeunes," *Des livres et des jeunes* 37 (Autumn 1990): 2-5.

2   "La science-fiction québécoise pour la jeunesse," *Lurelu* 15, 3 (Winter 1993): 12-17; *Solaris* 104 (Winter 1993): 70-75. See also by the same author, "Le fantastique dans la littérature québécoise pour la jeunesse," *Lurelu* 14, 3 (Winter 1992): 4-10. Both articles contain what I believe are the most extensive bibliographies on these two literary genres.

Daniel Sernine *has a degree in History and Library Science. He has had thirty books published since 1978, and has won several literary awards in Québec, establishing himself as a major French Canadian writer. In 1984, he was awarded the Canada Council Children's Literature Award for his juvenile novel* Le cercle violet.

FAMILY, IDENTITY, AND SPECULATIVE FICTION
by Terence M. Green

In 1950, the American writer William Faulkner spoke with eloquence upon receiving the Nobel Prize for Literature in Stockholm. He said what he believed simply and clearly. His fear was that the young writer had "forgotten the problems of the human heart in conflict with itself which alone can make good writing because only that is worth writing about, worth the agony and the sweat." Every writer should have these words committed to memory.

I suspect, though, that many "young writers" and readers today are hearing these words for the first time — and upon hearing them, evaluating them, either in connection with what they have written or with what they have read. Is this valid? they may ask. Is all writing that fails to treat the "old verities and truths of the heart" doomed and ephemeral, as Faulkner states? I'm not sure myself. Perhaps Faulkner is too all-inclusive, too sweeping. Perhaps he is right on the mark. Whichever way one leans, what he says rings much truer than it does false to anyone who will truly hear it, and certainly goes a long way towards explaining why so much of the literature of SF&F fails to strike a chord in the masses of general readers as being little else than very clever. It is an observation about which the exceptions only tend to prove the rule.

There is nothing wrong with 'clever'. Being clever is often the mark of an excellent entertainer. One can be seduced easily by novelty, verbal pyrotechnics, a convoluted plot, and well-wrought speculation, or extrapolation. Faulkner's words, though, suggest that it is simply not enough, that so much more is possible — in fact, desirable.

For Faulkner's dictum to be applied, a story must be about people, what happens to them, and how they change as a result of their experiences. The writer's task is to make the reader care about the lives of the people they are reading about, to feel, understand, and empathize with the conflicts at the center of their hearts — to identify with them at some profound level.

SF has traditionally been called "The Literature of Ideas," and herein lies the core of the issue. W. Somerset Maugham noted in *The Summing Up* (1938) that "the dramatist of ideas loads the dice against himself." His argument, sensible and well-taken, is that most drama is ephemeral; basing a drama upon ideas, which once exposed and contemplated, "will be stale the day after tomorrow," makes the drama even more ephemeral.

A story written around an idea — no matter how fascinating the idea — runs the risk of being a one-trick pony. A novel written around several ideas runs the risk of being a three-ring circus. I do not mean to diminish ponies or circuses, both of which I happen to enjoy upon occasion. It's just that too often — and I would argue that it is far too often — SF seems content with a whip-snap of an idea, rather than a long chord of understanding and involvement with a character.

Asimov's Robot stories. Black holes, nanotechnology, cloning, cryonics, cybernetics. Generation starships, genetic engineering, overpopulation, time paradoxes. Cyberpunk, anyone? Fascinating stuff, all. But Literature, at its best, as a reflection of what makes us human, goes the extra mile — the mile found too seldom in SF. Too many SF writers don't even bother to give it a try. (Fantasy often fares better; the often-dominant obsession with verisimilar explanation that marks much SF is absent.)

In mainstream drama, consider Arthur Miller's *Death of a Salesman*. It played in China within the last decade and left audiences on the other side of the planet, in a different culture, riveted with emotion. Produced in 1949, the hopes, dreams, and failures of the Loman family clearly has an appeal that is universal, and probably timeless. Tennessee Williams's *A Streetcar Named Desire* (1947) is playing somewhere in the world every day. Audiences are stirred as they witness the passionate byplay between Stella, her husband Stanley, and her sister Blanche.

J.D. Salinger's novel *The Catcher in the Rye* has been captivating people of all ages since 1951. Holden Caulfield is a youth caught in the web of family incident (his young brother has died of leukemia), expectation (his parents are professional and expect him to succeed at exclusive private schools), and responsibility (his little sister Phoebe idolizes him). John Updike has written four "Rabbit" novels: *Rabbit, Run* (1960); *Rabbit Redux* (1971); *Rabbit Is Rich* (1981); and *Rabbit at Rest* (1990). They follow the life of Harry "Rabbit" Angstrom, his wife, Janice, and his son Nelson over a thirty-year span, and represent a great literary achievement by any yardstick one wishes to use. When Rabbit dies, part of all of us dies.

In *Hamlet,* William Shakespeare explores a young man's simultaneous love and anger towards his mother, the powerful feelings he holds for his dead father, and the pangs of his youthful, romantic heart. In *King Lear* we are privy to an old man's foolishness and his daughters' filial ingratitude. *Othello* maps out the green-eyed monster, jealousy, and its consequences. *Macbeth* shows us how ambition and weakness of character can lead to a couple's destruction. Audiences share their passions and confusion and struggles.

Anne Tyler, Margaret Laurence, John Steinbeck, Bernard Malamud, Mordecai Richler, Raymond Carver, even Scott Turow . . . the mainstream list is bountiful. They all understand how to make their stories outlive an idea, how to make them more than diversions and amusements and clever entertainments. Their fictions linger with an emotional resonance.

What is the source of most drama? How can a writer best achieve the aforementioned "emotional resonance?" What have all the above writers, in fact, done? The prime source, the common pool of all drama, from ancient time, is the family; and a theme as universal as it is timeless is the search for identity, both within and without that family unit. Simply put, this is the common pool that all the above writers have explored.

Why have so few SF and fantasy authors learned this lesson? Why do they persist in writing the surface material, developing the background technology, while ignoring the basic stuff of drama? The answer must be either simple market forces, or a lack of any real familiarity with literature beyond the genre in which they are working. If the market shapes the writing, it will seldom be literature; if the writer is ignorant of the vast literary tradition of his own culture, it will seldom be literature either.

The world of modern SF&F film (post-1977) seems to have learned the lesson that the writers of stories and novels in the genre too often ignore. In all the cases that have successfully transcended genre limitations and have achieved the wider, general, mainstream audience, one finds impeccable and intriguing visual pyrotechnics, artfully wedded with a story about people, families, and the search for identity. And the audiences *care* about the characters. These films do achieve their "emotional resonance" as a result.

E.T. (1982) lets the audience identify with the boy and his family, and the emotional bond between the boy and the alien. *Star Wars* (1977) and its sequels (*The Empire Strikes Back,* 1980, and *The Return of the Jedi,* 1983) are visually dazzling, but beneath them all is the eternal, mythic story of the search for identity within and without a family (Luke discovers who his father and sister are; Darth Vader must battle what it means to be a father). Even in *Batman* (1989), the masked protagonist is presented to us as tortured, struggling to determine his true role in life. In many ways, *Batman* is *Hamlet,* as the protagonists try to avenge the murders of their fathers by altering their identities (Batman dons a grotesque costume; Hamlet adopts an "antic disposition" and feigns madness). *Blade Runner* (1982), in the entertaining guise of a SF/Detective Fiction hybrid, is really about the search for identity and what constitutes our humanity. And even *Field of Dreams* (1989) — based on a wonderful story ("Shoeless Joe Jackson Comes to Iowa," 1979, which became the novel *Shoeless Joe,* 1982, written by Canadian W.P. Kinsella) — on the surface a clever baseball fantasy, is all about family and making peace with one's father.

Audiences identify. The film visions achieve a universality. Their audiences are staggering in size. The same is true for all the works of mainstream literature cited above. Two words: emotional resonance.

In written SF&F, quite often the closest thing to this emotional resonance is what we have come to call the "sense of wonder." Arthur C. Clarke achieved it in *Childhood's End* (1953), as well as in such stories as "The Nine Billion Names of God" and "The Star" (collected in *The Nine Billion Names of God,* 1967). The final, haunting image of the Clarke/Kubrick book/film collaboration *2001: A Space Odyssey* (1968) suggests, according to Peter Nichols (*The Encyclopedia of Science Fiction,* 1993), "an unhappy mankind crying out for a lost father."

Asimov published "Nightfall" in 1941 (since collected, literally, in dozens of anthologies). Again: its final image conveys the sense of wonder to many. Perhaps Alfred Bester achieved it in *The Stars My Destination* (1956). I believe Frederik Pohl captured it in *Gateway* (1977). On occasion, Wells, Stapledon, Bradbury, and hosts of others — some substantial names in the field, others less so — have touched it. In each of these cases, what creates the sense of wonder in the reader is the fact that the story suggests some sense of the mystery of life and of humanity's destiny as a race. And what are these but explorations of where we fit into a cosmic family, and who we are as a species? Family and the Search for Identity, on a macro-scale.

The most ambitious of these, such as Pohl's *Gateway* (and the ensuing Heechee saga), deal with both microcosm and macrocosm, with individuals' foibles and personal relationships as well as Mankind's place in the universe — from inner space to outer space. And I would be remiss if I failed to draw attention to a truly wonderful story, a jewel within the field: Dan Simmons's "The River Styx Runs Upstream," published originally in 1982, which can be found in his collection *Prayers to Broken Stones* (1990). Read it for yourself. Simmons truly understands.

But it especially pleases me to note some Canadian writers (besides Kinsella, cited earlier) whose aspirations are moving clearly in this direction. In fact, considering the disparate population sizes between Canada and the United States, it is fair to argue that Canadian SF&F writers are in the vanguard in this area. Robert Charles Wilson's *The Harvest* (1993) is a further twist on the "Childhood's End" theme. In many ways, it is even more mature, since we feel the end of humanity through a father's loss of his daughter when she chooses what he rejects: the next step in evolution. This is precisely the kind of thing I have been suggesting more genre writers should strive to do, and here is one of the most interesting attempts already among us. Robert J. Sawyer's *Golden Fleece* (1990) blends, in its best moments, the inner space of its protagonist with the outer space of its setting. Many of the stories of Andrew Weiner, such as "Going Native" (*Distant Signals and Other Stories*, 1989), and his novel *Station Gehenna* (1987), are vastly underrated, achieving as they do the same synthesis.

And let me, finally and boldly, be personal. Let me endeavor to discuss some of my own work — subjective and fraught with folly as that must necessarily be — for it is probably the work I know best. What I have been describing is what I *try* consciously to do in most of my own fiction. Whether or not I am successful, of course, is for others to determine. But I would like to go on record as saying that I see it as a desirable goal and a viable goal, one that should be pursued consciously, in light of the dramatic works surrounding us that so clearly light the way.

Thus, if, in the midst of the attempted technical dazzle and suspense of *Barking Dogs* (1988), you should spot the protagonist involved with his family, struggling with his love and his anger, it is no accident. (*The Globe and Mail*: "The SF touches of Toronto in the very near future are really nice and the invention of the Barking Dog is terrific, but the truth is that Green doesn't need them. This story of nice people under immense pressure is good enough to deep the reader riveted to the last paragraph.")

If during a reading of *Children of the Rainbow* (1992) you think you may have spotted a theme of both personal and cosmic displacement, and wonder about the final scene in which a man talks to his mother about his need to find his father, neither is it happenstance. (*The Ottawa Citizen*: "The realism in *Children of the Rainbow* connects Green to a growing coterie of science-fiction and fantasy authors who are utilizing their genre's strengths to illuminate the contemporary world and our place in it.")

Nor is it probably an accident that a story like "Ashland, Kentucky" (*The Woman Who Is the Midnight Wind*, 1987), about a man's attempt to find a missing uncle in the past in order to give some sense of family closure to his dying mother, has proven popular for me. (Orson Scott Card in F&SF: "Best of the lot, to me, is the story "Ashland, Kentucky," about a man's bittersweet journey to uncover the mystery of his own family's past." And *Books in Canada*, reviewing *Tesseracts2* (1987): " 'Ashland, Kentucky' . . . That kind of writing is becoming so much a lost art that this story alone is worth the price of the book.")

The reactions to my own work, from literate, widely-read individuals, has been instructive and enlightening. I hear what many sane voices are saying. You can hear them too. And I see by example all about me that they are mostly right.

To return to Maugham, he has summarized it nicely: "in order to give the glow of life to brute fact it must be transmuted by passion" (*A Writer's Notebook,* 1949). The challenge for the writer of SF&F is to utilize the vast potential for thoughtful entertainment inherent in the genre, to blend the intellectual and the emotional, to dazzle with clever ideas while simultaneously telling a truly, universally moving story. The attempt should be made, because the final result is possible, and eminently worthwhile.

Writers: invest yourself in it. Touch your reader.

Readers: be more demanding. Look beyond novelty.

Family. The search for identity. Emotional resonance.

Faulkner, when he stood on the podium in Stockholm, was, as might be expected, far more right than he was wrong. Those of us in the field who fail to heed his words just aren't paying enough attention.

***Terence M. Green** is the author of the short story collection* The Woman Who Is the Midnight Wind *and the novels* Barking Dogs *and* Children of the Rainbow. *His newest novel, written with the support of several Ontario Arts Council grants and a Canada Council Project grant, will be published by Tor Books early in 1996. He teaches English at a secondary school in Toronto.*

CONSIDERING MAGICAL REALISM IN CANADA
by Charles de Lint

Before one can begin to discuss the classification of North American magical realism as it appears in Canadian fiction, it's first necessary to define what we mean by that label, which immediately leads us into problems, for, as with the term science fiction, no one can quite agree on its meaning.

Most people realize that North American magical realism has grown out of its South American cousin, but too many of us are unfamiliar with the work of the South American writers from whom we've borrowed the term and I don't think that the impetus behind the fiction of North American magical realists is quite the same. It's certainly not as focused in its delivery, or drawn from one cultural source. And to complicate matters, most of the practitioners of magical realism will undoubtedly feel as uneasy having their work collected under such an umbrella as the writers who got lumped together under the term cyberpunk did in their time.

It's easy to understand why. Writers involved in a creative endeavor do not like to have their work labeled because they know that such pigeon-holing too often limits the potential audience. But categorizing has become a necessary evil, and while it's easy to blame publishers and booksellers for the proliferation of specifically-labeled sections in today's bookstores, academics and readers are as much to blame. Labeling makes the business of selling books easier, certainly, but academics have made careers out of categorizing, while it's the readers who, when they're in the mood for a certain kind of book, don't want to have to go through the entire store looking for that mystery, romance, western, or science fiction novel; they expect to be able to go right to the section that collects all such books together to make their choice. Booksellers are certainly aware of this and present their goods accordingly. Publishers, in their turn, separate their catalogues by genre because their own customers, the booksellers, are stocking their shelves, and therefore making their orders, section by specific section.

In some instances, labeling actually helps writers — especially when they are beginning to establish themselves. Whereas their science fiction novel might get lost in a plethora of general fiction, it has a good chance of standing out in the more limited shelf space of the science fiction section. But that only works when everyone agrees on what the labels mean. When a book is mislabeled, it's actually detrimental to all concerned. Readers don't get what they're expecting, writers lose their potential audience, while publishers and booksellers lose money.

In 1981 when I first began writing *Moonheart* (Ace, 1984), a novel that's as much a contemporary thriller as it is a fantasy, I didn't really consider what it was that I was working on; I just knew that it didn't fit into any neat pigeon-hole that existed at the time. In many respects, *Moonheart* and many of my subsequent novels, still don't fit into any one tidy category. I started describing the work I was doing as contemporary fantasy, for lack of a better term. But this is too vague as well. Just as discussions defining science fiction usually narrow down to, "I can't describe it; I just know what it is," the term contemporary fantasy can mean many things to many people. It can describe a book of mythic depth and resonance, such as Robert Holdstock's *Mythago Wood* (Gollancz, 1984), as well as any number of slighter novels that are simply standard high fantasy stories disguised in contemporary urban trappings. The term becomes useless when it becomes equally interchangeable for serious, meaty novels and fluff.

I'm somewhat more comfortable with the more recent designation of North American magical realism that is being bandied about these days, but only insofar as it refers to my own work, and the work of other writers situated on this continent. That's because the "North American" aspect of it cuts out such fine practitioners as the aforementioned Holdstock, who is based in England, Jonathan Carroll, who lives in Vienna, and Australian author Margaret Mahy, as well as books by other British authors such as Diana Wynne Jones's *Fire and Hemlock* (Greenwillow, 1985) and Michael Scott Rohan's recent *Chase the Morning* (Morrow, 1991), to name just a few.

Narrowing the consideration simply to Canadian magical realists limits matters even further and still doesn't quite describe what the South American authors such as Borges, Fuentes, and Marquez are doing in a northern context. The South American authors attempt, in the words of SF author and essayist Norman Spinrad, "to illuminate the nature of the Latin American psyche, indeed to evolve it, through the understanding of its past, not so much the past enshrined in history books as the deeper inner reality thereof, the evolution of the collective Latin American unconsciousness, the Latin American soul, if you will." ("North American Magical Realism," in *Asimov's*, February 1991). Spinrad goes on in the same article to discuss how North American magical realism "does much the same thing, but since it arises out of a quite different cultural and psychic matrix, the result is quite different."

I have no disagreement with either of those statements, except to reiterate that the "North American" aspect of the term is limiting. What becomes rapidly clear, when considering the cultural background of North Americans, is just how varied those backgrounds can be. When Spinrad talks of the central North American cultural myth as being "that of filling a supposedly empty frontier with a new society, a society forever in the process of self-creation, a zeitgeist with its eye fixed on the future rather than the past, a culture which at its best seeks to understand its present not so much as the product of its history but as the current stage of its ongoing evolution," he is ignoring the work of French Quebec writers, of Native American writers, of writers whose cultural background is Chinese, African, East Indian, Jamaican, or European. Many such writers live and work in North America. Their voices are tied as much to their own cultural pasts as the voices of the Latin American magical realists are to their cultures, for all that they remain residents of this northern continent. In fact, it's for that very reason that their work can so invigorate the field of North American fiction.

A better description, and one that Spinrad also cites in his article, is a definition offered by Lou Aronica, one-time publisher of Bantam-Spectra-Foundation. When told of a story that would follow an "imagistic line of inner reality rather than a 'realistic' depiction of external phenomenology," Aronica is quoted as replying, "It could work — as long as the emotional story is realistic, whether the events that generate the emotions are realistic or not." This seems to be one of the best working definitions of all, a point on which Spinrad and I both agree, though I would leave the term broadly open, rather than limiting it as Spinrad does later in his article.

All the strange goings-on and beings that can pervade magical realism, all the quirky characters, odd situations, bizarre moments, curious descriptions, serve but one purpose: to reflect the human condition; placing the "magical" elements against the "realism" of contemporary settings helps to exaggerate the dichotomy of our relationships with each other and our environment and so make it more easily understood. Which isn't to say that the "emotional storyline" need be simplistic. The deeper, richer, more resonant the emotional story being told is, the more relevance it will have to its readership.

To this can be added one more element, an exploration of the roots of myth — its origins, its relationship to our world, and especially to our modern age. Myth is more than the Romantic notion of faerie or angels or devils abroad in modern society, more than escapism or primitive explanations as to how the world works. It also provides a metaphorical blueprint which allows us, often subconsciously, to define our spiritual state in context to the rest of the world; it's what gives an underlying sense of vibrance and meaning to the workaday world, to that sense of commonality which can often lead a man or woman to feel that his or her spirit is being stifled.

What happens in such cases is that we lose sight of the greater whole, which starts with our relationship to friends and family and our immediate environment, and then stretches out to encompass eventually the rest of the world. Our vision narrows until all we see is what lies directly before us, and we forget that the world is large and filled with any number of wonders. What inevitably ensues is boredom, depression, a downward spiral from which some people have a great difficulty in extracting themselves.

Sometimes all that can awaken one from such negativity is a mystical experience. It need not be of occult origin; it can be as simple a thing as appreciating the flight of a crow across an afternoon sky. But what happens at such a point is that it allows the person burdened down with commonality or depression to look suddenly beyond his or herself, to understand that they are not alone, but connected to everything.

This is, as Colin Wilson says in *Beyond the Occult* (Bantam Press, 1988), "the most basic assertion that all descriptions of the mystical experience have in common. *Everything is seen to be connected.*

And the word 'seen' deserves to be underlined. This world of infinite relationships, in which everything is connected with everything else, is seen all at once — from a bird's-eye view, as it were. And language instantly becomes useless, because it can only pin down one thing at a time."

But what language can do, in the form of stories and poetry and essays, is be a catalyst. The result will not necessarily be of the intensity of experience as described by Wilson, but it will allow readers to step outside of themselves and look beyond the commonality and bleakness that can so often pervade the contemporary world.

Myth can help us remember as well, whether it be the ancient legends of the gods such as Dionysus, considered by some to be a prototype of Christ, or the more secular exploration of myth's worth and origins as can be found in Robert Holdstock's *Mythago Wood* books, or merely the simple verification of humanity's need to care for one another and their planet. Today it's more important than ever to keep these connections open.

In an interview on Fiona Ritchie's *Whistle and Shamrock* radio show, the Scots storyteller and musician Robin Williamson put it this way: "People before the atom bomb had a profound faith that the world would continue." But that's no longer true, Williamson goes on to say, when "it's obvious that the world can be destroyed at the drop of a hat. In this profoundly pessimistic world that we live in, I think it's very important to magically create a sense of optimism and to make a sense of permanence out of nothing. And that's what these stories do — they're an act of magic, an act of faith and an affirmation of the power of the human soul over its own destiny."

Williamson was speaking of folk tales and myths, but what he had to say is also relevant for what we might call magical realism. The optimism he speaks of does not mean that the stories need to be upbeat, but that they do need to make a connection between ourselves and the world we live in, and those with whom we share that world. The human animal needs to believe that what he or she does has relevance, no matter on how small a scale; that their contribution is part of an ongoing pattern connecting the past to the future.

This is what art can teach us, and something for which magical realism is particularly appropriate. The magical elements found in this fiction, be they an intrusion of faerie or merely a slightly askew take on how we perceive the world, are not escapism. Rather, they put us back in touch with the wonder that actually does exist in the world, the wonder that we have forgotten.

British author Mary Gentle made a good argument for the use of such elements in a recent article in the *ROC SF Advance* newsletter (Vol. 3, Issue 1, 1991). "There is a whole other world that has been censored out by the age of reason," she is quoted as saying. "If you're going to write wide screen, the broad canvas, you have to put everything in. And the world is fantastic. Our universe contains things that are impossible to explain. If you narrow it down to one version congruent with 19th-century realism, you've left out ninety percent of everything."

The "magic" in magical realism is a twist on the world as we know it that allows us to see it and ourselves differently. In *Voice of Our Shadow* (Viking, 1983) Jonathan Carroll wrote, "Somebody's death is like walking down a staircase you're used to going down, but then suddenly there's no step there." That's what magical realism can do as well. Along with remaining truthful to what Aronica called the "emotional storyline," this fiction contains the staircase without the step. "You just keep tripping on it for the rest of your life," Carroll went on to say in an interview in *Weird Book* (Winter 1990-91). Magical realism forces the reader to view the world differently — past, present, and future — and to understand not only the connections, but the relevance of those connections.

One of the best examples of such writing is by a North American who also happens to be a Canadian of mixed Cherokee and European descent: Thomas King. In his *Green Grass, Running Water* (Harper Collins, 1993), King reaches into his mythic subconsciousness and pulls up everything but the kitchen sink in order to tell his story. He doesn't trip all over himself trying to explain his material the way so many genre fantasists do. Instead his novel is true in and of itself and does what all fiction is supposed to do: entertain, certainly, but also broaden our own understanding of history, the world we find ourselves in, and each other. Like his first novel, *Medicine River* (Viking, 1989), *Green Grass, Running Water* deals with the concerns of Native Americans, both on and off the reserve. But unlike the first novel, it immediately ups the ante and takes us into the shadowy world of myth manifesting itself in the real world. It's a very funny book, but it deals with serious concerns as well; like the best Trickster stories, solemnity and buffoonery walk hand in hand through its pages. Besides the real-life Native characters we meet, King has filled his novel with a hodge-podge of figures from history and myth — not only from Native sources, but European as well. So we have Coyote in one section, discussing the making of the world with an unnamed first-person narrator. In another, the head of a mental institution, one Dr. Joseph Hovaugh (think: "Jehovah") is trying to track down four escaped inmates who just happen to be four-hundred-year-old beings from Native creation myths. We visit Hollywood and the sets of old B-westerns where a Native actor has to wear a false nose because his own isn't "Indian enough." We get caught up in the lives of the real-world Native characters, both on the reserve and trying to make their way in the outside world.

The plot and the characters moving through it defy easy summary, but at the heart of the novel is an understanding of how illogical and foreign Natives found Christian religion, while their own beliefs were misinterpreted, derided, and even outlawed. To make his points, King has had to pull off a balancing act akin to those old vaudeville performers trying to keep all those plates spinning in the air on poles. The seriousness of his themes are delivered to the reader in a rich, evocative prose that also carries any number of puns, literary allusions, tongue-in-cheek asides, and comic revisions of European religious beliefs. "I worry about that a little," King is quoted as saying in a profile that ran in *The Ottawa Citizen* (May 2, 1993), "because I think of myself as a serious novelist. And people will see you as a comic. But that's the beauty of novels. . . . A novel you write for yourself, and the wonderful thing is that they take so long, so you can't think about what people are going to think."

King shouldn't worry. His mythic elements convey their messages through humor and a certain ambiguity, and these are tactics that make the best magical realism work so well. Even when the wonders are paraded on stage in the flesh, we're often left with the suspicion that it's all just a play on the idea of consensual reality. The magic exists only because we and the characters have agreed to it. Should we blink, it fades away like mist before the sun. But the experience remains.

As for humor, well, it's a funny old world, isn't it? In an introduction to James P. Blaylock's *Two Views of a Cave Painting* (Axolotl Press, 1987), Dean Koontz made a reference to Blaylock that might well also apply to King and many of the authors whose works can be labeled magical realism. "I suspect Jim was standing in front of a mirror one day," Koontz wrote, "and he said to himself, 'Wait just a minute here! If God insisted on positioning our nose precisely where it could drip into our mouth, then he was clearly having some fun with us!' That revelation, or one like it, caused him to look at the world around him from a far different perspective than that from which most people see it, and he glimpsed a whole new creation. Now he writes about that new place and, though it seems to be the strangest fantasy to [those who aren't admirers of his work], it seems like our very own world to the rest of us."

What King's fiction tells us about magical realism, what the work of his peers tells us, is that more than simply surface story is necessary, more than the characters getting from point A to point B, whether that journey be physical, mental, or spiritual. There must also be an underlying resonance that speaks beyond the words on the page, a subtext that gives meaning to the reading experience beyond what the story itself had to tell in its most prosaic terms.

Some might say this is the *raison d'etre* for all good fiction, and perhaps that's true, but it remains particularly appropriate for magical realism. And if magical realism can be used as a label for such extraordinary, disparate works such as John Crowley's *Aegypt* (Spectra, 1987), Alan Brennert's *Time and Chance* (Tor, 1990), Tom Robbins's *Skinny Legs and All* (Bantam, 1990), O.R. Melling's *Falling Out of Time* (Viking, 1989), Ken Grimwood's *Replay* (Arbor House, 1986), James Morrow's *Only Begotten Daughter* (Morrow, 1990), and Leslie Marmon Silko's *Almanac of the Dead* (Simon & Schuster, 1991); if it can be used to describe the work of the other writers mentioned in this essay and so many others that we don't have space to mention here; if this is the case, then perhaps it will be the first time a label has been coined for a field of writing that is not only accurate, but also places no boundaries upon the imaginations of its practitioners, whether they exercise their craft in Canada, the United States, Africa, or China.

In the end, nationality isn't important. Magical realism deals with the heart and the spirit, and such concerns aren't captured behind arbitrary borders — whether they appear on maps or in publishers' catalogues. No two writers have the same story to tell, just as no two individuals have the exact same life experience. So it seems fitting that a story or novel dealing with the connections between individual hearts and spirits to their environment, whether locally or globally, as well as how they connect to the hearts and spirits of others, should also each be unique unto itself.

Charles de Lint is one of Canada's most successful writers of fantasy. He won the Casper Award in 1988 for his novel Jack the Giant-Killer *and the William I. Crawford Award for Best New Fantasy Author in 1984. He lives in Ottawa and is the writer-in-residence for the Ottawa and Gloucester Public Libraries.*

MY CANADA INCLUDES MAGIC
by Ven Begamudré

Once upon a time a young Canadian studied public administration because he wanted to become a civil servant. It was
an honorable profession in those days. Many of his great
uncles had once been gazetted to the grand, old ICS: the Indian
Civil Service. Soon, though, he decided he also wanted to become
a writer. Not instead. Also. After his second year of university, he
turned down a summer job in the Québec civil service to write
his first novel. It was not a success.

Within months of turning twenty-one, he was a Bachelor of
Arts with honors. He had also finished his second novel. No one
wanted it. His prospects for federal employment were also slim,
but he had the obsession which helps the young prevail: an obsession which never allows them to question their choice of career. In
his case, two careers. That same fall he returned to visit India for
the first time since he had left as a boy. It was not a happy return.
He fell ill. His mother died.

One day, while sorting through her belongings, he found a
horoscope which had been cast shortly after his birth. He had
never seen this horoscope, and his mother had never spoken of it.
There were many pages including one for the effect of each planet, the sun and the moon. Having been raised in the rational West,
he found the horoscope quaint and, after reading it, threw it away.
But in years to come he would never forget two intriguing details.
First, the page describing the sun's effect on his life was missing.
Second, and far more relevant to this story, the horoscope claimed
the (then) child would, as an adult, pursue one of two occupations: he would become either an administrator or a writer.

Is this a true story? Of course it's true. Why wouldn't it be true?
After all, I was born in a country which doesn't distinguish
between magic and reality, so why would I? But even more
important, I was born in a country with a written history which is
five-thousand years old; now I live in a country with a written
history which is only five-hundred years old. So you see, I live
not only at the intersection of two cultures but also at the intersection of two roads in time. One just happens to be shorter than
the other.

Of course, some people do distinguish between magic and reality.

Or the writing of realism and the writing of speculative fiction — which I've heard includes science fiction, fantasy, and horror. Maybe even magic realism. The first summer I taught creative writing, a more senior teacher was going over the applications for our introductory program. Two of the successful applicants wrote sci fi. "I don't want them," this more senior teacher said. "Give them to Ven." Boy, did we have fun.

We workshopped one student's story about a unicorn. It was pretty good. Then we workshopped the second student's story, about an artist who uses holographic paints. If I remember correctly, the painting comes to life. It might even have been a painting of a unicorn. Whatever. It was brilliant. Not because of the premise but because something happens at the end which changes your take. If you go back to the beginning and start reading again, it's as if you're reading a completely different story. A perfect example of blending form with content. To this day I haven't been able to duplicate — by working deliberately — what that student did without even knowing what he was doing. My poet friends call this "possession."

In case you think this is an essay on defending speculative fiction, don't worry. But I'm still surprised by the number of participants I get (it's not cool to call them students anymore) who look sheepish when they admit they write SF. That's why I ask my creative writing groups this question every summer: "What's the difference between genre fiction and so-called literary fiction?" After they discuss this for a while, I suggest, "Maybe the difference is the quality of the writing. Is Edgar Allan Poe considered a genre writer now? Why not? Because he's considered to have been a good writer?"

I say "considered" because I haven't read anything of his for almost twenty years. But my well-read friends tell me he wrote well. Like a modern-day Blanche DuBois, I have always depended on the truthfulness of friends. (Jessica Tandy died last Sunday. She was the original Blanche on Broadway in "A Streetcar Named Desire," so she and the play have been on my mind.) Yes, I depend on the truthfulness of friends because I read even less now than I used to. In fact, everything I've said since the section break was meant to put off telling you I know next to nothing about

Canadian SF. I just do it. And why wouldn't I do it when I come from a country in which horoscopes tell the future?

So what you're going to get from here on are some random thoughts on SF. They're so random, in order to give them structure I'm going to list them alphabetically. In ASCII. (Just kidding.)

Fantasy. Don't read much, unless you count stories from Hindu and other Indian mythologies. I have no idea whether this counts as fantasy. It seems real enough to me. But when you have five-thousand years' worth of reading to catch up on, you can't read everything. It's too bad that when we're reborn we forget things from our previous lives. I think a Greek philosopher said it's the shock of birth which does this. I knew his name, once.

Horror. Don't read much, either. Just got a book from the library called *The Mammoth Book of Short Horror Novels* because I'm trying to write a horror story for my new collection. Do watch the odd horror movie. Loved David Cronenberg's remake of "The Fly." As for *Dead Ringers*, I was so busy watching Jeremy Irons *and* Jeremy Irons, I nearly forgot to swoon over Genvieve Bujold.

Yes, I'm trying to write a horror story, but the Canadian in me needs to separate the horror of real life from the horror of fiction. Is the news horror? Last week, a US Air plane dove nose-first into the ground. Searchers are looking for pieces of the passengers and crew. A passer-by found a thigh bone. And people still ask, "If Jeffrey Dahmer didn't exist, would Hollywood have invented him?" What if Hollywood did invent him?

Magic Realism. Used to read a lot more, the usual stuff like *A Hundred Years of Solitude.* Now I just write it. But maybe what I write isn't really magic realism. Eve Drobot, who used to review small-press books regularly for *The Globe and Mail*, said this on February 13, 1991:

> If the modern writers of Latin America have created a body
> of literature we collectively (if somewhat unfairly) dub
> "magic realism," then the modern writers of the Indian sub-
> continent can be as effectively lumped together in a genre
> I'd call "mystical realism."
> Gabriel Garcia Marquez, Julio Cortazar, Isabel Allende and

Moacyr Scliar have maiden aunts ascending miraculously to heaven, appearances, disappearances, prophecies and wishes coming true. But R.K. Narayan, Ruth Prawer Jhabvala, Salman Rushdie and Nayantara Sahgal have a dozen deities in every leaf of every tree, gods raining from the skies, birth, death, rebirth and the inexorable cycle of never-changing time.

Sounds good to me. My very own genre, and a lot less crowded — at least in Canada — than magic realism. The basic difference, if I caught Drobot's drift, is that Christians from North and South America write magic realism while Hindus and others from Asia write mystic realism. So here's a theory: What if magic realism in general is the bailiwick of four kinds of writers?

1. Writers from religions which embrace mystery, especially Catholicism and the mystic branches of Islam and Judaism: the Sufis, who emerged in the eighth century, and the Hasidim, who emerged in the eighteenth century. I don't think Salman Rushdie is a Sufi, but he was born in Bombay, so he might fit the next category. (That's the nice thing about a theory like this. Everything fits if you try hard enough.)

2. Writers from cultures which are synonymous with religions, especially Hinduism. To this we might as well add anyone born in India since it's such a mishmash of cultures and religions. Good, then we can also fit Rohinton Mistry, even if he is a Parsi.

3. Writers from the regions, as opposed to the centers, of a country. Someone from Vancouver Island might be more likely than someone from southern Ontario to write magic realism. Someone like Jack Hodgins in *The Resurrection of Joseph Bourne*. I tried this part out on a scholar named Janine Falck. She suggested it might be because places like Vancouver Island haven't lost their myths. Yet. Then I thought of Timothy Findley, though I'm not sure *Headhunter*, even with Kurtz stalking Metro Toronto, owes as much to magic realism as, say, *The Telling of Lies*, with that giant iceberg offshore. Besides, unless Findley is Catholic, and I haven't checked, he wouldn't fit this theory. Oh, but wait, yes, he would. He's gay, and there's one category left.

4. Writers, like women, who have had to constantly struggle to be heard. Though women clearly have the upper hand in

Canadian fiction now even if they don't earn more than men. So why doesn't Alice Munro write magic realism? Maybe, Falck suggested, Alice Munro simply isn't interested in writing magic realism. (There are obviously a lot of holes in this theory.)

Science Fiction. Like it. Don't read much, though one of my favorite sci fi stories is E.M. Forster's "The Machine Stops." The same E.M. Forster who wrote *A Passage to India*. No, haven't read it, either. Saw the movie, and that one reviewer was right. Alec Guiness (one of my favorite actors) really did look like a Tootsie Roll in a diaper.

A few years back, I asked another scholar whether anyone has written Hindu sci fi. He referred me to a novel called *Lord of Light*. I gave up after one chapter. All I remember is a talking monkey. Besides, I wanted to write Hindu sci fi, not read it. (Not because I thought I could do better; just because it's what I do. Writing, that is.) The narrator in one of my stories says, "Strange, isn't it: how one person's history and mythology become another person's speculative fiction?" Now there's an essay in itself.

It's also strange the cultural appropriation debate has passed this topic by. But I guess if you don't take sci fi seriously, you won't care if anyone is appropriating history or mythology to write sci fi. Mind you, there have been fine speeches about appropriating mythologies to write realistic or even magically realistic stories. So why do people draw the line? Then again, how would I feel if the captain of the Federation starship "Enterprise" was a francophone from South India — down by Pondicherry — named Jean-Luc Kumar?

And that's all I have to say about SF. Well, not quite. The Parti Québécois won the Québec provincial election last Monday and so, along with Jessica Tandy and that plane crash in the States and even Jeffrey Dahmer, politics has also been on my mind.

It still amazes me: how often history repeats itself. If you were born in my generation on the prairies, you grew up under the shadow of the Depression. Listening to your parents' stories like, "We weren't rich, but we were happy. Even if the outhouse latch did freeze shut in winter." If you were born in my generation in India — which I was, in this lifetime, anyway — you grew up under the shadow of Partition. Listening to stories like the one about Muhammad Ali Jinnah hiding the fact he was dying of lung cancer because he wanted to be the first president of a Pakistan separate from India. Jacques Parizeau smokes, too. Okay, maybe the *Québécois* really will be happier after separating than Indians were after Independence but — and it's a big but — considering history keeps repeating itself, what if history is just another branch of speculative fiction?

Truth is, politics has been on my mind ever since the last federal election. Ever since the battle lines were drawn between Us and Them. And I don't mean anglophone and francophone. I mean Us and Them because I'm obviously one of Them. So here's my last theory: Out of the ashes of the New Democratic Party of Canada will rise an even more glorious age of Canadian SF. I'm serious. Because when any country embraces intolerance (the States during the McCarthy witch hunts) or Big Brother (the Soviet Union at its most banal), artists no longer find realism either a satisfying or a safe genre in which to work.

Proof? Well, there's the popularity of sci fi movies in the States in the 1950s and 1960s. It's true many of them, like "Invaders from Mars," were anti-alien (as in anti-Communist), but there were exceptions. Think of *Farenheit 451*, a story about the beauty of books in a society which fears the printed word, because it fears having to confront the new. Because it fears the intelligence it has to bring to the printed word. Because it fears the intellectual and emotional engagement — that fist in your brain, that fist on your heart — to which the best writing exposes us. As for Eastern Europe, from Poland we have the work of Stanislav Lem, who used sci fi to satirize the mind-numbing bureaucracy of the Soviet Bloc.

And now, in the Canada of the 1990s, we find ourselves embracing intolerance, and our Canadian version of Big Brother is Big Red. As in redneck, and proud of it, too. Big Red sees and hears only what he wants to see and hear. He's the self-pitying Canadian — often male but not always — who's looking for someone to blame so he won't have to look in the mirror. The one who doesn't know art but knows what he likes. And this ain't it. The one who doesn't have a thing against people who are different as long as he doesn't have to fraternize with them, especially over a quiet drink at the you-know-where. And, of course, Big Red doesn't read.

Yes, Preston; yes, even you, Audrey. One day we will salute you as the father and mother of a glorious literary age. Especially you, Preston, for letting Big Red out of his closet at last. Let the phoenix rise! Let the astronauts sing! Magic is here to stay.

September 1994

Ven Begamudré *is the author of the novel* Van de Graaff Days *(1993) and the short story collection* A Planet of Eccentrics *(1990). His work-in-progress includes a collection of realistic and speculative fiction, "Laterna Magika," and a historical fantasy novel, "Echo and the Wise Man." He was the 1994-95 writer-in-residence in the University of Calgary's Markin-Flanagan Distinguished Writers Program.*

THE HAUNTED SILENCES
Canadian Dark Fantasy
by Robert Hadji

earching for Canadian dark fantasy, the initial impression one has is of peering into a dark wood, in which the foreground is clearly visible, but the background is lost to view. Admittedly, most of the undergrowth is scrub, written to please the passing fancies of far-away markets and readers. The true background extends far into the national psyche, and from these recesses emerge the legends and literature in which peculiarly Canadian qualities become apparent, and we glimpse the face of the boreal darkness somewhat revealed. Insights may be gleaned, patterns discerned among a chosen, well chosen, few works of dark fantasy over the past hundred years. This is an inquiry, nothing more or less; it is not a chronology, nor is it a comprehensive overview. It merely guides the reader to some fearful pleasures of a heritage largely unknown, and a present full of bright promise, albeit of dark matter.

Before plunging into the dark wood, however, I shall endeavor to provide the reader with some wilderness tips to recognize the landmarks and not stray too far off the true path, from there to here — if here *is* here. I suspect few of you reading this article will be familiar with the term 'dark fantasy', though you may well recognize some of the works described as such. Not to worry: most professionals in the field simply use it as a nebulous catchall for anything from a good old-fashioned ghost story to Stephen King and Clive Barker. Which is to say, the material mentioned hereafter is dark fantasy by inclusion. A more informative, but still flexible definition would cover fictions in which the fantastic shapes or penetrates the reality presented to the reader, with the primary purpose of inducing a sense of unease, dread even, in the mind of same. In addition to the aforementioned ghost stories and supernatural horror, 'dark fantasy' can include contemporary fantasies such as those of Charles de Lint as well as literary tangents of a grotesque or macabre bent, such as Eric McCormack's post-modern fictions.

"As to ghosts and spirits, they appear totally banished from Canada. This is too matter-of-fact a county for such supernaturals to visit . . . Fancy would starve for lack of marvellous food to keep her alive in the backwoods. We have neither fay nor fairy, ghost nor bogle, satyr nor wood-nymph: our very forests disdain to shelter dryad or hamadryad." With these rueful words, Catherine Parr Traill lamented in *The Backwoods of Canada* (1836) the absence of a Canadian mythology, at least recognizable to European eyes, whilst failing to discern that this absence was, in itself, significant. A place without a past, unsettled and unsettling, Canada's very newness precluded the familiarity of ancient sites, at least recognizable to European eyes. Rather, it unfolded before the immigrant's gaze an unbroken monotony of timeless, trackless wilderness, inhuman in its vast scale — an immense silence unresponsive to human needs, whether for physical or spiritual succor. And the very human response to their awful insignificance in such a landscape? Northrop Frye discerned in our literature "a tone of deep terror in regard to nature. . . . It is not a terror of the dangers or discomforts or even the mysteries of nature, but a terror of the soul at something that these things manifest" (*The Bush Garden*, 1971).

Therein perhaps lies a clue as to why there has been a dearth of dark fantasy in Canada until quite recently, given that the metaphysical terror described does not lend itself to mechanical Gothic formulae or ghost stories told over a bowl of hot punch. Our forbearers, living in a truly *wild* place, set to mapping its mysteries away in good order, and where a civilizing hand could reach and master the landscape, they succeeded. But there were wastes no hand could tame, an outer darkness the light of civilization could not illuminate. In Margaret Atwood's contemporary ghost story, "Death by Landscape" (1989), a young girl walks into the bush and simply vanishes, with a shout "like a cry of surprise, cut off too soon." The devouring wilderness is viewed not as a landscape "in the old, truly European sense. . . . Instead there's a tangle, a receding maze, in which you can become lost almost as soon as you step off the path."

An enduring Canadian fear was that, in entering the wilderness, it entered *you*. Going bush, a body can lose oneself. A remarkable continuity of experience, a Northern sensibility as it were, is revealed in two of our most compelling legends: that of the windigo, which obsessed our Algonkian predecessors; and that of the Franklin Expedition, which has fascinated and haunted their English successors unto our own generation. The former were hunters for game, the others for glory, both wandering wind-swept in the frozen wastes, stripped of their humanity by starvation, until the cannibal emerged to feed on nearest and dearest. Paralyzed by guilt, rather than sustaining life, their transgression left them skeletons of ice — only the hunger endured. Perhaps the most terrible part of these legends, apart from their essential truth, is the utter absence of hope, either for survival or redemption. Few writers have addressed this material directly, though the windigo's near relation the loup-garou is more frequently encountered. It is singularly appropriate, perhaps, that the wind walker is often sensed, but rarely seen, just as the Canadian approach to horror fiction has often been an oblique one.

Morton Teicher's definitive study *Windigo Psychosis* (1962) notes that the outstanding personality trait among the Algonkian peoples of Northeastern Canada was "a powerful pattern of emotional restraint and inhibition . . . and instant repression of any display of emotion." How like those grimly determined Calvinists who came after, whose morbid Celtic imaginations contributed a dark thread of fantasy to the pattern of Canadian literature. Duncan Campbell Scott's "Vengeance Is Mine" (1896) is set on the gray barren shores of James Bay where a Scottish trader, perversely cruel to those he loves, is visited by supernatural retribution, is seized by "the intense and awful cold" until Black Ian turns white with hoar frost, frozen "ice to the core, rigid and unchangeable," the crystalization of his death-in-life.

More recently, the post-modern fictions of Eric McCormack collected in *Inspecting the Vaults* (1982), while at times reminiscent of Kafka or Borges, are by the author's own admission steeped in "the good old Scottish tradition of . . . tales of blood and guts." Grotesque and macabre they are, but not repressed, as violence and sexuality erupt from within these bleak narratives. Such mysteries hold their secrets; in these tales, there's no knowing, only telling. In *Paradise Motel* (1989), a mad doctor murders his wife, then surgically implants her body parts in their children. These things happen. Like many immigrants before him, McCormack arrived unprepared for the reality of Canada. Happily, it delighted him, save for the harsh winter that fractured his good Scottish Mac with paralyzing cold. Some things never change . . .

The Calvinist death-trip invariably arrives at stasis, death or death-in-life, the repression released in an unholy trinity of sin, violence, and guilt, but there are other responses to the conflicts of flesh and spirit, by transformation, as ice melts to water. P.K. Page's *The Sun and the Moon* (1944) is an *avis rara* in Canadian literature, a Symbolist romance with a psychic vampire as its heroine. Born during a lunar eclipse, the adolescent Kristin can spontaneously project her hungry, inchoate soul into "the static reality of inanimate things"; when this involuntary power turns against her artist lover, the effect is devastating, stealing away his talent and vitality. The subtext of her budding sexuality, echoed in turbulent wind and wave, is almost too obvious to mention. The novel becomes a modern variant of the Daphne myth at the climax, as, horrified that her impending marriage will obliterate both personalities, "the moon eclipsing the sun," she passes into a storm-wracked tree, withstanding the gale to greet the morning, "holding her branches up to the sky in the simple, generous gesture of the victor . . . steady in the security of her fibre and bark." Her already damaged husband marries a "waking shell," while outside of "the seed that was herself" has taken root within the landscape, now awash with brilliant colors of "scarlet, vermilion and burnt orange." A sacrifice had been made, but whom?

A direct coupling of sex and death is a recurrent theme in Anne Hébert's literate, if overwrought, Gothic romances. In *Children of the Black Sabbath* (1975), Sister Julie of the Trinity's waking visions recall a traumatic childhood of backwoods diabolism and ritual abuse erupting into the present as demonic possession, her hallucinations infecting the entire convent. Just as the Sabbat inverts the Catholic offices, reality and delusion become confused, culminating, in an immaculate conception, save that the child born is a tumescent monster, "a son of Satan" consigned to snowy death. The triumphant sorceress, having shed her nuns habit like a snake's skin, descends the walls to coin her Master below, satisfied that "Evil is in them now. Mission accomplished."

Héloïse (1980) is elegantly elegiac, and as erotic and blasphemous as the above. A young Québécois couple fall prey to vampires that prowl the underworld of the Paris Métro, albeit Bernard the husband was clearly foredoomed to fall under Héloise's embrace, too romantically enamored of her old world delights and terrors, too lightly bound to his sweet, sensible wife, the present and his homeland termed, "a blank page," like the modern apartment he rejects as "primeval nudity. Limbo. Nothingness. . . . I cannot live in this white box. It has . . . no past! Could you make love here? It would be like trying to do it in a block of ice."

In Canadian culture the conjunction of sex and death as a transforming process culminates in David Cronenberg's films which are germain to this study, as he is not only the auteur, but often the author of his own material. Throughout his early films, from *Shivers* (1975) through *Scanners* (1980), the cold clinical landscape of modern architecture housed these "big science" institutions that, from the most altruistic motives, develop destructive/reverberating mutants, whether bipedal or visceral, that invariably disrupt the safely ordered world without. Cronenberg views the body as in "a state of revolution" — this revolting flesh, as it were, ever seeking to overthrow the tyranny of the mind, or throw off the tyranny of death, much as fantasy and horror deluge the realist paradigm.

Initially, disease, sexually transmitted, is the *agent provocateur* of choice, but *Videodrome* (1982) marks a transition, as the images spawn brain tumors that open physical reality to metaphysical change. "Word begets image and image is virus," as William S. Burroughs puts it in *Naked Lunch*, filmed by David Cronenberg in 1991 as a hallucinatory experience, in which reality and illusion fully interpenetrate until they become indistinguishable. In interviews, Cronenberg envisions mutations where "human beings could swap sexual organs . . . or develop different kinds of organs that would give pleasure. The distinction between male and female would diminish . . . sheer force of will could allow you to rearrange your physical self." Long live the New Flesh: death and transfiguration can be viewed as positive experiences, in the eye of the beholder.

Much as Cronenberg single-handedly created a genre of Canadian horror cinema from his own body of work, so distinctively Canadian voices have contributed dark fantasy of high quality in several genres of popular fiction over the past decade, forging paths for others to follow. Young adult fiction appeals to an adolescent readership, standing at the cusp of maturity, and the novels of Michael Bedard, *A Darker Magic* (1987), its sequel *Painted Devil* (1994), and *Redwork* (1990), explore that borderland between dark and light, death and life where young protagonists and older mentors must confront, and defeat, supernatural evils that threaten body and spirit, the former achieving passage "from a state of innocence to a state of experience" in the process.

Charles de Lint is best known for contemporary fantasies set in the Ottawa valley and the Laurentians, in which magical worlds, usually drawn from Celtic and Amerindian mythologies, interpenetrate with our reality, often though dreams. One notes with some amusement that he has managed to locate in such a quintessentially Canadian setting every creature Traill summarily banished a century and a half ago and quite a few more besides. Supernatural predators cast a darker hue over some of these fantasies: in *Yarrow* (1986) Lysistrakes, "the Thief of Dreams," feeds on creative imagination, while in *Jack the Giant Killer* (1987) and its sequel, *Drink Down the Moon* (1990), the evil Faerie host of the Unseelie Court menace our world with their darkness, threatening to rob it of all wonder and joy.

For de Lint, the worst evils are invoked by human agents who, feeling wronged, summon powers of darkness to encompass the destruction or others, which is in itself a source of spiritual self-destruction. In his best dark fantasy to date, *Mulengro* (1985), a spirit huntsman, "He Who Walks With Ghosts," is summoned by a malicious gypsy to set his ravening *mules* upon his own people. The protagonists of de Lint's pseudonymous horror novels, *Angel of Darkness* (1990) and *From A Whisper to A Scream* (1992), written as Samuel M. Key, both female abuse victims, also come to realize, belatedly in the former case, that empowerment cannot come from employing evil against itself; one can resist the darkness, within and without, by fighting for the good.

The breakthrough Canadian horror writer of recent years has been Nancy Baker, whose vampire novels *The Night Inside* (1993) and *Blood and Chrysanthemums* (1994) juxtapose 1990s 'Goth' *sangfroid* with robust sensuality, while conveying the abiding melancholy of a night that never ends. Her sensible, straight-laced heroine Ardeth is metamorphosed by the vampire

Rozonov's surprisingly tender 'gift' into a formidable, impulsive avenger. Their combined power obliterates their corrupt, corporate captors in an exhilarating orgy of carnage, but after the bloodbath, both must confront the painful dilemma of afterlife, that to live merely as a ravenous predator is to become less than human. "The way of the vampire," as explored over the course of two novels, increasingly becomes a meditation on the moral choices an immortal must make, in the knowledge that humanity is hard won, and too easily surrendered. It is worth mentioning that Garfield Reeves-Stevens, no mean horror writer himself, believes Canadian dark fantasy to have "a stronger moral grounding" that most, "and a clear sense of moral order is something you need in good horror."

Given recent developments, the emergence of a market for original short fiction in the genre was inevitable, and when *Northern Frights* (1992) appeared, the response from readers, and contributors, was enthusiastic enough to merit two sequels in rapid succession, *Northern Frights 2* (1994) and *Northern Frights 3* (1995). Editor Don Hutchison believes "what makes Canadian [dark fantasy] different is a sense of place . . . once you step outside the city . . . you feel all the time like there's something out there, or nothing out there. . . . Canada has this huge untapped vein of darkness running through it." A touch of chill can be felt through many of the stories, a cold wind blowing through our Canadian memory and imagination. But diversity in setting, style, and tone is what most powerfully impresses the reader. From the lonely anguish of Karen Wehrstein's "Cold," to the rustic grue of Nancy Kirkpatrick's "Farm Wife," to the unnerving reality-shift of Andrew Weiner's "The Map," to the menacing metascience of Garfield Reeves-Stevens "The Eddies," to the sheer grotesque weirdness of David Nickle's "The Sloan Men," *Northern Frights* has indeed opened a vein in contemporary Canadian dark fantasy, and established a place where dark imaginings are no longer shunned, but invited.

Having searched so long for that elusive boojum, the Canadian identity, the baffling quarry may well be on the verge of extinction, unless it stands revealed as the one and the many, in a myriad of forms. We possibly face imminent fragmentation, in a limited political sense, but while borders may shift and maps change, the land itself remains constant beneath the feet of whatever dweller chooses to walk here.

Immigration has ever introduced new voices, and fresh responses, to the Canadian environment; Rohinton Mistry's excellent "Ghost of Firosha Baag" (from *Tales of Firosha Baag*) and Mary E. Choo's "Feast of ghosts" (from *Northern Frights* 2) are harbingers of things to come. A world of mythologies has settled a home here, without apologies to Mrs Traill, and with them new dreams and nightmares infuse a landscape perhaps more brightly lit, but not lacking its dark recesses. The outer darkness has given way to an inward one, a sure sign that this new place is no longer so new, or so young. A multitude of voices in many tongues crash in upon those awful absences and silences now, as our very being here continues to shape the landscape of the Canadian imagination.

The modern urban environment may press too close, at times, and the emergence of Canadian Fantasy, light and dark, may signal a dissatisfaction with that rational orderly space, a yearning for something lost, or never found. I suspect those level planes and upright walls will soon yield their own ghosts and demons to our view. Two solitudes are giving way, if not to Cronenberg's polymorphous perversity, then certainly to a cross-cultural, cross-genre community in dark fantasy, the womb of terrors and wonders without boundaries. And without end.

Robert Hadji, *in early youth, first heard, in George Hebert's lovely words, "music at midnight," the desire for and pursuit of beauty in dark places, and has sought those sweet discords ever since. He edited* Borderland, *a small-press periodical devoted to dark fantasy in the mid-1980s, and subsequently was a core contributor to the* Penguin Encyclopedia of Horror and the Supernatural.

CANADIAN URBAN HORROR
It's Not Just Trees and Tundra Anymore
by Tanya Huff

> The City is of Night; perchance of Death,
> But certainly of Night.
> — *James Thomson*
> *"The City of*
> *Dreadful Night"*
> *(1874)*

As everyone who's sat through a Can Lit course in high school or university should know, the landscape is an integral part of Canadian writing and, in the beginning, Canada's vast untamed geography provided sufficient inspiration for early horror. Henry Beaugrand (whose story "The Werewolves" was adapted into a movie in 1913 by Canadian director Henry McCrae), Algernon Blackwood (visiting from England), and John Buchan (Governor-General of Canada 1935-1940) were all touched by the dark potential under the trees and across the tundra. An element of the supernatural was barely necessary given the combined assault of isolation and brutal weather. For many writers, winter became a living, malevolent adversary.

These themes have not been entirely abandoned. In *Northern Frights* and *Northern Frights 2*, new anthologies of Canadian horror edited by Don Hutchinson and published by Mosaic Press (1992 and 1993), fourteen of the thirty-five stories involve isolation or winter, or, as in Steve Rasnic Tem's "Going North" (*Northern Frights*) and Cindie Geddes "Emancipation" (*Northern Frights 2*), both. That said, an increasing number of English Canadian dark fantasy authors have been exploring the untamed geography in the heart of our cities. Some have adapted the old traditional horrors to a new-arena of steel and concrete, others have created specifically urban terrors to roam an urban geography.

On December 30, 1989, in a Toronto *Star* review of current paperbacks, Paul Stuewe wrote, "As old Hogtown bumbles its way toward world-class city status, we're being favored with novels set in our burgeoning metropolis." He went on to point out that although Toronto's recent history had been explored and her meaner streets patroled, "there has been much less activity in fantasy-fiction circles." While there are those who might suggest that the shadowed corners of Toronto need no supernatural additions, in the years since 1989 it has developed a darkly active fantasy life. As Carolyn Clink points out in her poem "Toronto Necropolis" (*Northern Frights*), "There are dead men on Yonge Street."

Not only the dead, but the undead are active in the Toronto of the 1990s as a number of vampires rise to walk the strip at night. Considering that the pale, black clad denizens of Queen Street West appear to have wandered off the set of an old horror film, this sudden infestation could easily be a case of art imitating life. From a literary standpoint, this urban plague should come as no surprise, for the events in Stoker's Dracula were, after all, precipitated by the count's desire to relocate in London.

Tanya Huff's series *Blood Price, Blood Trail, Blood Lines, Blood Pact* (DAW Books) puts vampire Henry Fitzroy in a condo at Bloor and Jarvis: " . . . it had been centuries since he'd had a home that had suited him as well." Nancy Baker's *The Night Inside* resurrects vampire Dimitri Rozokov "to run through jungles of mortar and wood" and creates for him a dark companion, Ardeth Alexander. Her latest book, *Blood and Chrysanthemums*, moves both vampires across the country to Banff, returns one of them to Toronto, and then reunites them back in the mountains.

It's important to note that for both authors, an obvious Toronto, rather than a bland could-be-anywhere kind of city, is an integral part of the story. While mentioning no names, Huff accurately describes the most colorful of the three city newspapers — "On Tuesday morning, the front page of the tabloid screamed 'SLASHER STRIKES AGAIN.' A photograph of the coach of the Toronto Maple Leafs stared out from under it, the cutline asking, not for the first time, if he should be fired. It was the kind of weird layout the paper excelled at" (*Blood Price*). In turn, Baker walks the reader down Queen Street West, "where appearance became a statement of purpose and graffiti had a decidedly political bent. It was home to some of the city's coolest clubs and to a number of musicians, artists, and designers. Or those with aspirations — or pretensions — to any of those callings" (*The Night Inside*).

In "Tear Down" (*Northern Frights*) by Garfield Reeves-Stevens, vampires stalk through those Toronto neighborhoods where large and modern houses fracture the landscape and disrupt old patterns: "Taken one by one at street level, they were minor interruptions in a once orderly plan. But taken together, seen from the vantage given by wings that beat against the night, they coalesced like grains of dark silver, drawing shadows on X-rays of healthy tissue in the first warning sign of worse things to come." This unique look at urban renewal should be considered mandatory reading in the city planning department. Although David Lyle Hardwick, the vampire protagonist of Nancy Kilpatrick's *Near*

Death (Pocket), travels over the course of the book from Montreal to Vancouver, even he stops over in Toronto.

Nor are vampires the only undead to stroll the Yonge Street strip after dark; Huff has added a demon (*Blood Price*) and a mummy (*Blood Lines*) to the mix. The demon is using death to write the name of a more powerful demon on Toronto and open a gate to Hell. The mummy stalks out of the Royal Ontario Museum, in the best monster movie tradition, and attempts to take over the souls of the city for his dark god. He chooses a particularly soulless venue for a temple — the disco at the top of the CN tower: " 'and any god that feeds off hopelessness and despair' observes another character, 'should find itself right at home in that meat market.' " The CN Tower makes an even darker appearance in Garfield Reeves-Steven's terrifying "The Eddies" (*Northern Frights 2*). When a storm traps a father and son at the top of the tower with a young woman they've only just met, all three learn how the physical properties of the structure can have metaphysical and deadly results. Hundreds of pictures have been taken of the CN Tower being struck by lightening, and, after reading this story, there's an overwhelming urge to check each of them for faces in the background. Twenty-seven lost souls . . .

Perhaps the most evocative use of Toronto occurs in Andrew Weiner's "The Map" (*Northern Frights*). Weiner uses *only* the streets: no vampires, no mummies, no demons, no things that swirl out of the storm or go bump in the night. By layering one Toronto on top of another and mapping the way between them, he touches the very real terror of the urban Canadian displaced in the city they thought they knew. Has that building always been there? When did they tear down that block? "Did Heath Street always dead-end at the ravine?"

The biggest difference between the old wilderness and the new is the speed with which it changes. The forest, the prairies, the tundra changed only seasonally from year to year. The cities change from moment to moment. And change is . . . unsettling.

Most Canadians, east to west, would agree that Ottawa doesn't really need visits from the supernatural — as the country's capital, it has enough to endure. But, besides the government, a topic too terrifying to deal with here, Ottawa also has Charles de Lint,

Canada's premier fantasist, a writer who has not only found the wilderness at the heart of the city, but who brilliantly is able to adapt the old terrors of the hearth to nights lit by photo sensitive, quartz halogen bulbs. The wild hunt is an archetype common to a number of European cultures; in *Jack the Giant Killer* (Ace) de Lint updates it for a hunt through Windsor Park: "One by one the Harleys came into view until there were nine of the big chopped down machines moving down the concrete walkway that followed the river. . . . As she reached out to grab the black leather-clad arm, the man turned. She looked for his face under his helmet but there seemed to be nothing there. Only shadow, hidden by the smoked glass of a visor."

The vampire that de Lint brings to Ottawa is not the blood sucker suddenly so prevalent in Toronto — the observation that Ottawa has bloodsuckers enough is unavoidable — but a parasite who feeds on dreams: "He took his bulk nourishment from those who didn't dream so true. The dreams of creative beings were more of a delicacy . . ." (*Yarrow*, Ace). The police, of course, are far out of their depth, and it takes the courage of one young woman, one young writer as it happens, to defeat the darkness. The police are, if no less helpless, at least less out of their depth in *Moonheart* (Ace) and its sequel *Spiritwalk* (Tor), for de Lint has given Ottawa (and the country) a "special branch of the RCMP that investigates the paranormal," beating out Fox TV's popular *X-Files* with its similar special branch of the FBI by about ten years. Unfortunately, de Lint also gives Ottawa the tragg: "It was one thing to be sitting in a theatre and watching the wonders of modern special effects technology make the impossible real, but quite another to be confronted by these things in the middle of an Ottawa Street" (*Moonheart*).

If urban horror seems to have more sharp edges than the horrors found outside city limits, more claws that slash and teeth that bite, perhaps that's because shadows cast in concrete canyons are sharper edged than those in the murky depths of the forest or flickering ill defined over seemingly endless expanses of snow.

In the vast American market, Canadian cities are considered exotic locals. Unfortunately, although Huff puts werewolves outside London, Ontario (*Blood Trail*) and a high tech Dr. Frankenstein in Kingston (*Blood Pact*), Toronto and Ottawa are almost alone in their attraction for the dark fantasist. London makes a reappearance in Charles Grant's ghost story "Sometimes, in the Rain" in (*Northern Frights 2*). Banff is used both in Baker's *Blood and Chrysanthemums* and in "Deer Season" by Lucy Taylor (*Northern Frights*), but with the glory of the mountains right on the main street, it can be argued that Banff is hardly an urban environment. Given the difficulty of obtaining translations of French Canadian dark fantasy in English Canada, it is possible that urban horrors lurk in Montréal and Québec City, but what's happening in the rest of the country? Where are the stories creeping out from the Halifax Citadel after dark? What lurks below the polished image Vancouver presents to the world? Can Edmonton have no urban horror besides the West Edmonton Mall? Why does everyone keep picking at Toronto and Ottawa?

Perhaps it's because they're the two Canadian cities the rest of the country loves to hate. Why *not* give them a hard time? Why not visit them with the quick and the dead — or more accurately, the slow and the undead.

In the introduction to *Northern Frights*, Don Hutchinson points out that "70% of Canadians now live in urban settings." They didn't move to the cities alone. Their fears moved with them. Seventy percent of Canadians wouldn't have the faintest idea of what to be afraid of if confronted by trees or tundra, but they have a very good idea of the darkness lurking in the urban jungle. Or at least they think they have.

For there are more things at Cogswell & Brunswick, St Laurent and St Jacques, Sparks and Metcalfe, Yonge and Bloor, Portage and Main, Lorne and Victoria, Centre and 7th, Granville and King Edward than are dreamed of in your philosophy.

Tanya Huff was born in the Maritimes, raised in Ontario, and served three years in the Naval reserve before studying for a degree in Radio and Television Arts. She then moved out to the middle of nowhere with her partner and four cats. With Blood Pact, *she concluded the Vicki/Henry/Celluci books, her vampire series. Her most recent books are* Sing the Four Quarters, *a heroic fantasy, to be followed by another two books* (Fifth Quarter *and* No Quarter) *in the Quarters mythos, and a* TSR *Ravensloft novel,* Scholar of Decay.

FORM=CONTENT=FORM?
Catching the Conscience of the King
by Candas Jane Dorsey

> I think virtual reality is neat because
> it turns everybody into a fish.
> — *P.J. Groeneveldt*

First I must confess that I made up the title long before I had more than a vague idea what I wanted to say about writing/writers and interactive technology, or virtual reality, or hypertext, or any of that stuff.[1] The title dates from a moment of monkey mind, not wild mind, to use Natalie Goldberg's concept. So I warn you I won't be inventing any some new cyberterms here. Not that I didn't try. I sat around the table with my folks and we worked on it for a whole half hour at Ed and Fred's Diner. My mom, who turns seventy-nine this year, was actually best at it, which probably comes from all the Scrabble she's played. Moving those little tiles around on the rack and trying to convince the rest of the players that this ingenious but hitherto unknown combination of letters is a word is good practice for making up jargon. But though we got some great words — like "cyberghett" — they didn't seem to have meanings attached to them — which seems to relate directly to the problem I'm going to address.

At one time I wrote a collection of speculative short fiction called *Machine Sex and Other Stories*, and the title story being a kind of cybersatire, I have been in some quarters assumed to be driving a fast car down the InfoBahn. In fact, I suspect that I'm rather more like the cartoon of the desperate little person pedaling their tricycle like mad down an Info SuperHighway thronged with semis. Me, I just upgraded from a Kaypro in the fall of 1992 and I'm telling you right now that I loved that machine. Like I loved my 1971 SuperBeetle. I don't drive either any more, but it gives you an idea of what a hopeless cybertraditionalist I am.

But I also write and read fiction which looks to the future implications of present trends, which demands a certain attention to what's going on in technoland. There are those who think computers are a great force for evil, others who say they're on the side of good — and some of us who, given those little boxes to check, always want to check both "all of the above" and "none of the above."

To start with, I take issue quite seriously with this idiotic term 'the information superhighway'. For one thing, it's such a cliche that it is vaguely nauseous to hear it yet again. But more seriously, it's wrong. It seems obvious that information is more like an ocean, with a multiplicity of dimensions and directions. Or you could steal the metaphor from Spider and Jeanne Robinson's *Stardance* and recognize that swimming in the infosea is like dancing in free fall. You can be a lot bigger and stay light.

A highway is concrete, linear and marked off in lanes/ruts. It goes through a landscape like a knife, cutting off one place from another. It carries dangerous, single-purpose vehicles which often eliminate small life — and even human life — without their operators even noticing. It leaves pollution. It's authoritarian and controlling. And indeed, computers, technology et all have the potential to be just like that (much like TV has been). Or, they can be individual, idiosyncratic, communal, and subversive.

The CyberSea, the InfoOcean, all that jazz, is the most subversive milieu, or perhaps I should say growth medium, we've had since writing — or perhaps I should say art — was invented. Forget Gutenberg and Underwood. They just provided means of being more efficiently linear. Computers and networks of computers have not taken us back to the stylus, the fingertip dipped in paint, the harp and the quill.

It's true that computers at first seemed like magic typewriters but by now everyone knows they're not. Bill Gibson was telling me about cafés in San Francisco where homeless bicycle messengers, the ones sleeping under bridges and owning nothing but their bikes, go entertain themselves on laptops epoxied onto the tables: for two bucks they're on the InterNet for as long as they need to pick up their e-mail and cruise a bit. In Toronto, the Binary Café offers a hamburger, drink, and InterNet access for $4.99. Everybody within range of the media knows the net is coming into being. Everybody sees it. And everybody's taking the plunge, from the Banff Centre's virtual reality project to my partner's father who's putting together the family history on computer when he can get his wife to quit playing Tetris. Even the homeless have an address on the InfoBahn, if they live in a city with a FreeNet and visit their local library branch to sign on.

(Still, the issue of elitism is not settled until we come to the uncomfortable recognition that computers are a technology of and for the elite, and the world wide computer network is further elitist. Dispute it as you may, you won't win the argument. You may cite the fact that 80% of Canadian homes have cable and 98% have telephones. You may know the increasing level of penetration of personal computers into homes in Canada, the U.S.A., Japan, Britain, Australia, Germany, Norway, France or even Ukraine. You may cite the 60 million in Canada and the U.S.A., growing all the time, who have access to the Internet. You may say, as would-be computer guru Ashley Grayson did recently, that by the turn of the millennium "everyone on the planet will have a cell phone." But there are people in Rwanda who are lucky to have ever seen a telephone, and if your answer, like Grayson's, is, "Well, there'll be a computer in every village, anyway," you are contributing to the myth that what's good for the North is good for the South, and you are heavy into denial, as the jargon has it, about how much platinum is available to bring about the universalisation of the chip, how much environmental damage would be done, how much economic infrastructure would be needed, and to what degree it is unrealistic to expect the elite to give up its privilege.

If we factor in the artist as an intellectual and spiritual elite — not a given, but a least a possibility — albeit not a very privileged one in our culture, and then recognize that we are talking about those artists with a more-than average level of computer literacy, we are looking at a very specialized group of human beings: those with the potential to create with computers and share their creation by computers.

It can be an exciting medium, and it is fraught with potential. But it is also prone to the delusion of universality. Reminds me of my father saying, "Motorcycles are 100% safe — until the moment of impact." The World Wide Web is 100% accessible — to the literate, computer-literate, computer-owning telephone subscriber who can read English.)

This is all the known universe now. People write books about it. Universities and colleges put together conferences about it. And among the cyberliterate there are a few of us wide-eyed ones, the SF writers invited along because everybody knows that people like us to *write* about this stuff and so we must *know* about this stuff.

Hmmm. One of the best-leaked secrets in cyberpunk is that Bill Gibson wrote *Neuromancer* on a 1922 Underwood. "I thought computers were kinda sexy," he said. "If I'd had one, I never would have thought so!" He could invent it because he already existed in the same cyberspace every writer does.

Every artist enters that creative space but writing is special. It is special because it involves symbols which are interactive with the participant in a completely non-physical way. Everything in text is hypothetical, everything is speculative. You can't introduce me, or any writer, to interactive technology, or virtual reality, or hypertext, on any level beyond the naming and the deconstruction of it, because we are there already.

I'm writing this in my living room with cat attempting to supplant the six-pound computer on my lap, and typing. Yeah, I'm writing, doing that archaic, shamefully linear thing, typing it in sentences all in a row, the way I usually if not always write. Still hooked on paper. I publish *books*, for goodness' sake. I make these confessions to remind you where we stand. Right here in the middle of a *text*, not a hypertext. I know more semioterms than cyberterms, when it comes to that, tho I've not made a formal study of what's hip in either semiotics or cybermysticism. Mostly, I read *fiction*. Yikes.

(Oh, yes, and I'm *old*. In computer years, that is. In terms of the youthfully acute degree of facility, inspiration, invention, and intuition which wears off after the hormone storms of adolescence. I know there are guys still walking these virtual halls who are *older than I am* — hey, even in their *mid*-forties! — but none of us are the callow and concentrated youths we used to be. I heard Gregory Rawlins say recently that in all the rooms he goes to where the discussion is about the death of the book, everyone has gray hair. Welcome to the Winnebago convention on the overcrowded tourist-laden InfoBahn.)

Now, the studied ingenuousness I have so far adopted in this text is deliberate. I am being a parable of a certain kind of being. And I am doing it for a better reason than just to work the room. I am doing it to get out of the way any delusions of multisyllabic credential. What qualifies me to address this issue is something much simpler and deeper than making up cyberjargon or knowing how to strip down, oil and reassemble a program in my own garage. I admit, I go the the cyberequivalent of Mr. Lube and

Midas Muffler. But this does not mean I do not know about inter-active media or virtual reality. I am really here because I dedicated myself to virtual reality twenty-five years ago, before any of us called it that. I am one of a long tradition of void-jumpers, people who went off the edge of the world without a hope of rescue.

I am a writer. My workplace is the text. It has no up and down, no structure, no rules besides the ones I make, no landscape but the one I program. There's nowhere to go but the universe I pro-vide, and you only get to bring one suitcase, the one containing your experience. You can plug that into my system if you like, but I won't guarantee compatibility and I won't warrant you'll get out unscathed. You enter my story, my poem, my novel, my essay entirely at your own risk, you jack into a reality you have never experienced, you are wrenched out into the same void where I fall and float — or into your own.

This is a virtual reality which has existed since the first text. Text has a dizzying array of tools available for making close copies of reality and running scenarios in them. Text has infinite interactibility, limited only by the ability of the reader to exer-cise imagination and get access to their own and communal experience.

All technology is doing is catching up.

There is certainly nothing *new* I can tell *you* about the *mechan-ics* of interactive technology, and I'm not even very interested in too much talk about how to use it, unless I have an idea which demands it. I am more interested in why I would use it, to illu-minate what content, and it's to that end that I enter into dis-course such as this, not because I need another hobby. Life is already short enough for all the work waiting to be written.

But if I don't have the hobbyist's wild enthusiasm, I have the professional's focused respect. If I need to know a thing, I learn it, and so it will be with the technology which will help shape and form my texts, just as it has always been. If language is the earliest and still purest of interactive technologies, then the writer's task is managing that technology. I taught myself to type at ten, after a few minute-long lessons on the basics from my sister. That meant learning to think and write in a straight line, not an easy thing for me for more than one reason. Later I learned the way into a computer, one which spoke only English and suited my particular combination of the anarchic and the anal-retentive, and I became quite a CP/M/PerfectWriter expert. Recently it's been the upgrade to MS-DOS, learning to design books on-screen, getting into editing hypertext and critiquing programs. If there is a metaphor, it is certainly me on the tricycle pedaling away, singing along with Ian Matthews' "There's a Diesel on My Tail" and swearing at the bugs on the windshield of my helmet. But the *parable* is rather more serious.

The secret of these toys, for writers, is not the stuff itself. It is the simple and yet easily overlooked reality that it's just *stuff*, after all, just a tool, and that we learn and use our tools in the service of a greater art. It's all very well to get wrapped up in the excitement of what this stuff can do. Hey look at this! But it is best not to forget what it if *for*, and as far as I'm concerned it is *not* just for playing with. Color field painters do that with paint. "Look how he's activated the surface," I heard an admirer say at one gallery, looking at a lime green slab of paint-encrusted canvas which looked like the seven-minute icing in peaks on a birthday cake from 1957. But there was nothing beneath the surface. It was all paint. It was all medium and no message, to reference the Grand Old Man of quotable cyberquotes.

It's the greatest danger for artists, for writers. We might forget that if we're going to *make* with it, we have to make *something*, not just make for making's sake. Cancer is uncontrolled making, immature cells stuck in an amorphous state of undifferentiated *making*. You can't call it *creativity*, however, until it creates. William Gibson made the point, on a panel at W.R.I.T.E.94 in Vancouver, that the great hypertext novel will not be written until the technology is as *transparent* as written and typed text is to us now.

Consider entropy and information. Entropy, my old enemy, the enemy of every creator, is about *unmaking*, about chaos. Progressive differentiation, the heat-death of everything, the closest thing to an integrated field theory we have yet. Information, on the other hand, is an organizing principle as well as a commodity. Linguistically, anyway, it's a self-ordering entity, which is both a thing and the set of conditions which governs that thing

— and the only condition in that set, it seems to me, is the condition of creation.

Like every human, I am intimately familiar with both entropy and information. Because I have studied how things work, the nature of process if you want more syllables, I know how both to destroy and create — and I choose create. The first piece of equipment I use is simple in the extreme: an idea of *how* to communicate. Whatever devices I use to animate that idea might, according to Schrödinger, whom I think should have been busted by the SPCA, influence the nature of what I create, and I'm willing for that to happen.

But in the pursuit of ever better ways to tell the story, let us not lose sight of the story itself. Let us not let the form become the only content possible. That is too dangerous, and we are already living in a dangerous world.

When I talk about danger I am not talking about youth crime (the biggest red herring of the 1990s), lack of gun control (although it's about time we all looked at that, as part of our study of what Germaine Greer and Brian Fawcett call "testosterone as a race poison"), or even the holes in the ozone layer. These are dangers indeed, but we are in spiritual danger as profound as our physical dangers, and writers are imaging (rather than imagining — these poisons are all too real) the toxins which threaten to debase us. I live in Alberta, where provincial politicians are standing up in the legislature to suggest the banning of books and the repealing of human rights and anti-discrimination laws, even suggesting that opting out of the Charter of Rights would be a good way to remove civil liberties from gays, lesbians, and bisexuals. The Kreever enquiry into HIV-tainted blood was told that British Columbia under van der Zalm actually conceived of a plan to put homosexuals in concentration camps, ostensibly to prevent the spread of AIDS. And on the same theme, Colorado and Oregon both ran anti-gay legislation up the flagpole, and one state saluted. I was in New Orleans a few years ago when the democratically-elected Sandinista government in Nicaragua fell to the U.S.-supported contras: the *Times-Picayune* headline said "Miracle in Managua." Everywhere we look there are more examples of the haves scapegoating the have-nots. Social service, education, senior's services, and health care are cut in the interests of deficit reduction, while interest rates are kept low by accepting ever-higher percentages of unemployment (did you know it was once considered unthinkable for unemployment to rise above 2.8 percent?) If there is a decline in our rate of growth, due mainly to the fact that we are running out of room at the top of the graph, it's blamed on too much immigration or not enough spending by the poor.

Further, if we start to feel a little threatened in the fat cat side of the world which can afford interactive technologies, we need only look around the world to see that we are fortunate compared with places where famine, pestilence, political brutality, and war reduce people to statistics, casualties, and estimates. But people are not statistics or estimates. Each statistic is made up of just that many complete lives. A princess is beheaded in Saudi Arabia for having sex with a commoner. The lash is common punishment in Singapore, but when one white teenager gets it, it becomes a world debate, and a surprising number of supercilious, "sophisticated" folk think it's a helluva fine idea. (It always amuses me to remember that "sophisticated" means "adulterated, impure.") Salman Rushdie is sentenced to death, and Taslima Nasreen, placed under similar threat, flees into exile — all for writing a book. These are the token individuals — but every woman in a rape camp, every child with kwashiorkor, every adult trained to shell or be shelled, every refugee and every Disappeared is a person with history, with *story*. Just like us.

Any of these barbarisms, individual or collective could happen here (and some do). Remember, the Nazi government was elected. Ethnic cleansing in Bosnia-Herzegovina is today: ten years ago it was "civilized" Yugoslavia. Here, Sikhs are barred from Legions because they won't take off their turbans. Be worried. Be very worried.

What does this have to do with interactive technologies, with "form=content=form?" It's pretty clear, I think. We have a bunch of toys that not everybody in the world has or has access to. We think they're pretty neat. We play with them. What are they for?

Are they to tell, to retell, the human stories which desperately need to be told to keep us human? Are they to show the depths to which humans can descend, and the possible heights to which we might rather aspire? Are they to educate our children with the myths and metaphors which make the strongest teachings, far stronger than linear didacticism? Are they going to be used, these tools, to illuminate the human condition and liberate our potential? Will they challenge the status quo? Will the stories we tell with these tools be the subversive and necessary ones? Are we willing to risk the life challenge of the void, and the potential death sentence by the threatened (I mentioned Salman Rushdie and Taslima Nasreen for a reason!), in order to tell the most necessary and brilliant stories? Are we going to resist the implicit and explicit censorship of the monied socio-industrial complex which wants these technologies to be normalizing —

Or are we going to accede to mediocrity? Are our stories going to be formed by the technology; elitist, sexist, racist, macho, reactionary, and meaningless in the true sense of the word: without meaning? Do our fancy technologies merely exist to pollute the rivers in their manufacture, use up all the platinum, create an unreasonable energy demand and dehumanize the participants?

("We live in the chinks of your world-machine," wrote James Tiptree Jr. a.k.a. Alice Sheldon in "The Women Men Don't See." It is useful to remember, when considering the Internet, that it began as a strategy by the Pentagon to create a decentralized military computer capability uncrashable in case of nuclear attack.

If swords have now been hammered into ploughshares, it is probably for two reasons, one noble and one commercial: the free flow of information subverts structure, and the market potential has long since overcome the paranoia potential of networked computers. It is not because continued efforts have not been made to control the activity of creators and users of computers and computer networks. In the process, the targets of paranoia have shifted.

It is instructive to read *The Hacker Crackdown*, Bruce Sterling's documentary of the 1991 initiative launched in the U.S.A. to catch computer criminals. Following a telephone network crash cased by a faulty line of code in a software program, but attributed to hackers, the idea of the mad hacker breaking into essential systems like 911 computer fueled a massive investigation. However, the only actions taken were against one hacker (charges unproved) and one creator, Steve Jackson of Steve Jackson Games. Jackson's creative material and computers were seized and although he was not charged, his work was never returned — shades of current customs and court battles here in Canada on censorship issues.

In Canada, high-level meetings have been taking place between government and industry stakeholders — read: those with an interest in control or profit or both — to regulate access to, use of, and direction of the Information SuperHighway. No unaffiliated users, scholars or creators — writers, for example — have been, to my knowledge, part of that regulating group.

Consequent to these and other actions, some users and creators are developing a nice line in paranoia themselves, centered on their fear that the free flow of information, the only "product" of the InfoBahn, will be cut off from common access or subject to surveillance. They cite as examples the American civil-liberties struggle with the encryption chip, a supposedly-benign privacy-protection device to which the government proposes to have duplicate keys: the virtual equivalent of giving them the keys to your hose, safety deposit box, diary — and your Interac password.

Those who believe that technology is inherently evil and dangerous welcome the regulation of the *technology* to protect human culture. Those who think it is a tool ripe for misuse — "Computers don't kill human culture, humans kill human culture" — welcome the regulation of users to protect human culture.

Meanwhile the synthesists — and what else writers? — know that regulating technology and users satisfies the need of authority and the desire of commerce, neither of which are inherently evil either, to restrict and tax the free flow of information — but that there is also a need to protect access to information and to creative potential as a right not of the few but of everyone.

It is a familiar discussion. We have it often in the creative community. The technology may be new but the issues aren't. Remember what happened to Gutenberg?)

We have a choice every time we use a tool to shape the raw power of language, no matter whether that tool be the storyteller's voice or the entire Media Lab at M.I.T. John Gardner said, "Writing is a way of processing reality." We have developed some pretty funky processors: but there's the old rule about garbage in/garbage out to guide us here too.

In the Christian bible somewhere it says, "Where there is no vision the people perish." That need for vision precedes the invention of the virtual reality goggles or glove or suit. Like the Ghost at the Feast, I bring a warning: form must not drive content, especially in this world where there is a great drive politically and economically towards the lowest common denominator of culture, the Box that renders the population docile, Virtual Bread and Circuses.

Jerzy Grotowski talked about a Poor Theatre. He was talking about not poverty of spirit or body, not famine or barrenness, but about removing artifice and hypocrisy, substituting simplicity and honesty. These technologies which have so much potential to bring change come with their responsibilities. An example: what will be the content of interactive cable programming delivered to an Inuit child in Spence Bay? Will it be a sort of push-button Three's Company, where they can decide among a number of equally banal and culturally loaded options for redundant plot wrapups of the middle-class hassles of a bunch of Caucasian bunnywits? Or will they have an opportunity to truly *exchange* cultural material with individuals in the dominant culture down south? And I do mean exchange: ideally, we should learn and change as much from contact with other cultures (and especially I think with aboriginal cultures, for our sins) as they do (often as they are forced to do) from us. That is true interaction, that which goes beyond democracy to a positive and constructive anarchy.

There are far more decisions to be made than what kind of microprocessor, software, or distribution mechanism will give us the snazziest results. And just as those ethical choices have to be made before we start writing, so they will have to be made a long time before we start programing.

The first medium is story. The first challenge is vision. Content demands form, which then shapes content. If we forget that, if we think it works the other way, as in my hastily invented by ultimately apposite title, we are making a fundamental mistake.

NOTES

1 This is a slightly different form of an address presented to, and published in the proceedings of, W.R.I.T.E.94, Writer's Retreat on Interactive Technology and Equipment, June 16-18, 1994, co-organized by UBC/Emily Carr College of Art/Simon Fraser University. Portions of the parenthetical notes were published in a slightly different form as part of a much longer article in ArtsBridge, Fall 1994.

Candas Jane Dorsey *is a writer, editor, and publisher of speculative fiction, fiction, poetry, and non-fiction. Her work has appeared in the* Tesseracts *anthologies, the* Norton Anthology of Science Fiction, *and other anthologies. Her books include* Machine Sex and Other Stories, Dark Earth Dreams *(with composer Roger Doogan),* Leaving Marks, *three other poetry books, and an upcoming novel from Tor Books. She is founding and past president of SFCanada, the Canadian professional sf writer's association, and past-president of the Writers Guild of Alberta. Having seen the wisdom of workers taking over the means of production, she recently headed a group of writers and editors to acquire Tesseract Books, Canada's senior English-language sf publishing imprint. She lives in Edmonton.*

CONSIDER HER WAYS
Canadian Science Fiction and Fantasy by Women
by Christine L. Kulyk

The women who write speculative fiction in Canada today are — like their counterparts in other parts of the world — producing work which challenges the traditional limits and conventions of the genre in both style and thematic content, constantly pushing back the boundaries of what we recognize as science fiction and fantasy literature. As women their work is often refreshingly different from that of their male counterparts and predecessors. As Canadians, their writing reflects in many subtle ways (and sometimes more overtly) the uniqueness of the Canadian cultural environment from which it springs. Perhaps most important, their fiction gives us a glimpse of how women view the past, present, and future of the human race — how we have become what we are, and what we might yet become, whether remaining here on the planet of our evolutionary birth, or going outward to the stars. Here in Canada as elsewhere it is women who are producing most of the most exciting and innovative work in the genre today. There is a world of wonders awaiting anyone who delves into the ever-growing body of works by women writers of SF and fantasy in Canada. This essay attempts to provide an introduction to a representative sampling of those works.

SF AND FANTASY FOR ADULTS

If you couldn't control the diseases, you had to avoid contact, any contact at all. That was when the Houses had begun to build walls and invest in barbed wire, electric fences and broken glass. They had also begun to expel rule-breakers. "These are houses of sanctuary, and this is a state of siege," Sharmayne heard herself saying. She'd had to say it often enough, back then. "We must think of the children."
— Margaret Atwood, "Freeforall,"
in *Tesseracts*[2] (Porcépic Books, 1987)

Many of the finest women writers of mainstream fiction in Canada have turned their hand from time to time to producing SF or fantasy short stories or novels. Writers like Margaret Atwood, Marian Engel, Margaret Laurence, and P.K. Page are known primarily for their mainstream, non-genre fiction, but each has also produced speculative fiction of quality second to none. Indeed, it is only since the late 1970s and early 1980s that a small but steadily growing number of Canadian women writers began to be known primarily for their work in the SF and/or fantasy genres. Those numbers, and their output, have grown since then to such a phenomenal extent, however, that it would be impossible to attempt to include a mention of all of those practitioners here, let alone all of their works. What I will try to do is to give a sampling of some of the best, in the hope that this tantalizing glimpse might ultimately spur readers on to seek out more of the same — and there is a lot more to be found!

One of the best-known SF books by any Canadian writer is surely Margaret Atwood's *The Handmaid's Tale* (McClelland & Stewart, 1985). A powerfully moving, deeply disturbing vision of the near future, Atwood's dystopian epic became a bestseller both in Canada and internationally, receiving the Arthur C. Clarke Award for Best Science Fiction in 1987. Readers who are interested in reading more of Atwood's SF should get hold of a copy of *Good Bones* (Coach House, 1992), a collection of Atwood's short stories that includes several fine examples of her science fiction writing.

Pauline Gedge, of Alberta, a bestselling author of historical fiction, turned her hand to SF with a novel called *Stargate* (Dial Press, 1982; Penguin, 1983), remarkable for its truly unconventional style. More recently, Gedge's *The Scroll of Saqqara* (1990), a blend of dark fantasy/horror and historical fiction (in the setting of ancient Egypt which Gedge handles which such consummate skill here and in her other works), was selected by the Doubleday SF Book Club as one of their feature offerings.

The title novelette in P.K. Page's *The Sun and the Moon and Other Fictions* (House of Anansi, 1973) is an unconventional blend of fantasy and psychological horror, about a strange girl named Kristin, who is born during a lunar eclipse. Described in the story as being "like a dreamchild, fair and ethereal," pale as the moon, Kristin as a child has many "imaginary" playmates — playmates whose existence she takes very seriously — but no real friends. Avoiding people and hating noise, she spends much time lying on a beach trying to emulate the rocks and stones beneath her. Her fixation with the notion of being absorbed by her environment (which includes the people around her) creates a dilemma for her when a man named Carl proposes marriage: "For I am a chameleon, she thought, absorbing the colors about me, and our marriage would submerge us, wipe us out as sun obliterates the markings of water on a stone."

Phyllis Gotlieb, a renowned poet and author who has been publishing SF stories for more than four decades, has produced an impressive body of work outstanding for its literary quality as well as its breadth of imagination and originality. Many SF readers will perhaps know her best for her stunningly original novel *O Master Caliban!* (Harper, 1976), which was followed more recently by a sequel called *Heart of Red Iron* (St. Martin's Press, 1989). *Caliban's* protagonist is a product of genetic engineering gone awry, on a planet where Earth scientists sought to alter humanity to be better able to survive the hostile environment. The book took the SF-reading community in North America by storm when it first appeared, and it has remained so popular and unique that it has since been translated into six languages. Other well-known works by Gotlieb include *Sunburst* (1964; Berkley edition 1978) and *Son of the Morning and Other Stories* (Ace, 1983). In 1987, Gotlieb was co-editor (with Douglas Barbour) of *Tesseracts²* (Press Porcépic), the second volume in the Tesseracts anthologies of Canadian SF.

Judith Merril, who already had a well-established reputation as an SF writer and anthology editor by the time she moved to Canada from the United States in the late 1960s, published a collection of her short fiction called *Daughters of the Earth and Other Stories* (McClelland & Stewart, 1985). In 1985, Merril broke new ground and gave a tremendous boost to the SF-writing scene in Canada by editing the first *Tesseracts* anthology of Canadian SF. A true friend of the SF community in Canada for many years, Merril donated materials from her own collection to found what is now known as the Merril Collection of Science Fiction, Speculation, and Fantasy, a special collection within the Toronto Public Library system that has become an invaluable resource for Canadian researchers, writers, and readers of speculative fiction.

Candas Jane Dorsey of Edmonton has established a considerable reputation with her award-winning short stories, many of which are collected in an impressive volume called *Machine Sex and Other Stories* (Press Porcépic, 1988). In 1990, Dorsey co-edited (with Gerry Truscott), the third *Tesseracts* anthology, and in 1994, she edited *Prairie Fire* magazine's special issue of New Canadian

Speculative Fiction. Very active in working for the benefit of the SF-writing, editing, and publishing community in Canada, Dorsey has recently become a member of the new publishing consortium for Tesseract Books (now published in Edmonton).

Élisabeth Vonarburg, of Chicoutimi, Québec, has written many short stories and novels which English readers are now fortunate to have available in translation from the original French. Her translator, Jane Brierley, was nominated in 1993 for a Governor General's Award for her translation of Vonarburg's epic novel of the future, *The Maerlande Chronicles* (Beach Holme, 1992; originally published in French as *Chroniques du pays des mères*). Vonarburg's previous SF novel, *The Silent City* (Press Porcépic, 1988; originally published in French in 1981 as *Le silence de la cité*), had already drawn considerable attention and admiration for its breadth of vision and its originality, employing a narrative style which departs refreshingly from the strictly chronological, with vibrant characterizations and twists of plot which afford the reader many surprises. For many years a member of the editorial staff of *Solaris* (one of the premier SF magazines of Québec), Vonarburg has been very active in the SF-writing and fan communities in both Québec and English Canada. In 1987, Vonarburg was awarded a Canadian Science Fiction and Fantasy Achievement Award for her work with *Solaris* and her continuing contributions to "improving francophone/anglophone communications." In 1994, she became a member of the new publishing consortium for Tesseract Books.

Of all the women writing SF in Canada today, Leslie Gadallah, of Alberta, is among the few that have chosen to do something approaching traditional "hard" SF and "space opera" adventure. Gadallah's *Cat's Pawn* (Ballantine, 1987), which was later followed by a sequel called *Cat's Gambit,* is a novel of interstellar intrigue that explores the issues of communication — and misunderstandings — between life forms (and personalities) that are alien to each other. In *The Loremasters* (Ballantine, 1988), Earth is divided into two separatist classes, Phobes and Philes, based upon their attitudes towards (and use of) high-tech or low-tech, in a post-holocaust future. The political conflicts explored in the fictional world of this book will sound very familiar to all Canadians:

... the political systems of the world were breaking down. World trade was in chaos. The Bush Wars had been going on for about 80 years. Continental North America was beginning to feel the direct effects with self-rule movements in Puerto Rico, Quebec, Alaska, Western Canada. ...

Whether it be proposals for sovereignty-association, entrenchment of provincial autonomy, regional economic development programs, or aboriginal self-government, Canadians have attempted over the years to develop new systems for dealing with our particular sociopolitical and geographical realities, which are unique to this planet. This unique aspect of the Canadian experience is proving to be a fertile source of inspiration for Canadian writers of speculative fiction like Gadallah.

SF AND FANTASY FOR THE YOUNG

Monica Hughes, who was born in England and has lived in Alberta for many years, has written close to twenty fine science fiction novels for young adult readers, making her the foremost writer of SF juveniles in Canada. She enjoys a large and enthusiastic fan following both here and in the British Isles. I highly recommend her work to readers of *any* age who enjoy a fast-paced, well-written science fiction story with thoroughly believable characters. I especially enjoy her resourceful and courageous young female heroines. But whether Hughes' stories feature a male or a female in the lead role, the young protagonist is always faced with challenges and situations which ultimately bring out the best in their character, although along the way he or she will frequently stumble and fail, and even break down crying, in an entirely human way. Hughes is best known for her Isis trilogy, beginning with *The Keeper of the Isis Light* (Bantam, 1981), in which space travelers from Earth who have set up a colony on the distant and beautiful planet Isis encounter its resident life forms and discover the differences and bonds between them.

Other fine examples of Hughes' work are *Devil on My Back* (Atheneum) and its sequel, *The Dream Catcher* (Macmillan, 1987), about a future Earth where people live in domed cities following the Age of Confusion, and the young protagonists must rebel against a rigid class system in order to break out of the restrictive dome society and reach are reconciliation with the people Outside. In *Sandwriter* (Methuen, 1986) and its sequel *The Promise* (Methuen, 1993), young women on a planet called Rokam, in the course of learning the arts of environmental control and resource management upon which the life of their planet depends, face the challenges of personal sacrifice and hard work needed to acquire the strength demanded of them. A world of climatic rigors and scarce resources that must be carefully husbanded, Rokam seems in many ways to echo the familiar concerns of Canadians. Similarly, *Ring-Rise, Ring-Set* (Methuen, 1983) tells of a future Earth in the midst of a new Ice Age. The young female protagonist leaves the comfort of her domed city to brave the harsh landscape of the Canadian North, and learns how to live among the people outside, who have preserved the Inuit way of life.

Suzanne Martel, of Québec, has written some fine juvenile SF which is available to English readers in translation from the original French. *Robot Alert* will appeal to very young readers with its cast of robots, aliens, and resourceful young humans. *The City Underground* (*Quatre Montréalais en l'an 3000*) (Douglas & McIntyre, 1982; originally published in French in 1964) is about the adventures of four boys living in an underground city called Surréal (from "Sous le Mont-Royal"), in a post-holocaust world where the surface is polluted by radiation and chemical poisons. A world of rigid, Big Brother-style social controls, the city of Surréal begins to crack under the weight of both geological and social forces, and the boys who are the story's heroes find themselves forced to venture outside to seek solutions for the crisis.

The fantasy novels of Ruth Nichols are remarkable for the magical beauty of their prose, and the mood of brooding mystery and wonder which the author manages to sustain throughout. Both *The Song of the Pearl* (Macmillan. 1976) and *The Marrow of the World* (Gage, 1972) should appeal to older teenagers (or adults) who appreciate a thoughtful, slower-paced story of great introspection and fine writing. Nichols has also written a blend of historical fiction and fantasy called *The Left-Handed Spirit* (Macmillan, 1978), about a young girl in ancient Rome who discovers that she has the paranormal talents of a seer and healer; her many adventures take her from Rome to China, where she eventually lives as an adult woman and discovers the blessings and the curses that her powers can bring, as well as learning to live amid the alien culture of her new people and her new family in a foreign land.

REALMS OF FANTASY

In 1985, Canadian readers voted Eileen Kernaghan, of Burnaby, British Columbia, the winner of a Canadian Science Fiction and Fantasy Achievement Award for her novel *Songs from the Drowned Lands* (Ace, 1983), which deals with the residents of a watery realm part fantasy and part SF. Her other works include *Journey to Aprilioth* (Ace, 1980); and a heroic fantasy novel with a female protagonist called *The Sarsen Witch* (Ace, 1989), which is set in the same universe as the one Kernaghan created for *Journey to Aprilioth*. Kernaghan is also the author of many short stories and poems published in such periodicals as *On Spec: The Canadian Magazine of Speculative Writing*.

Tanya Huff, of Toronto, made her entrance into the fantasy genre with a novel of Celtic sorcery called *Child of the Grove* (DAW, 1988). With a powerful sorceress as protagonist, the story covers all the traditional fantasy bases but manages to introduce refreshing new slants that are all Huff's own. For example, departing from the sword-and-sorcery tradition of glorifying the "arts of war," note the author's following remark at a point in the story where the army amassed by the forces of goodness goes forth to do battle with the army of Kraydak, the last evil Wizard: "No cheering crowd lined the road, for only fools and madmen cheer a war." *Child of the Grove* was so successful that Huff soon published a sequel, *The Last Wizard* (DAW, 1989), in which most of the action takes place in a wintry landscape of the kind with which most Canadians are chillingly familiar; snow and ice and mountain storms are the main forces against which the heroes must battle on their quest, in this tale. These books, along with her subsequent works, have established Huff's reputation for fantasy writing that is at once solid, imaginative, and playful.

It was with great delight, therefore, that I recall picking up Huff's next novel, *Gate of Darkness, Circle of Light* (DAW, 1989), and discovering that it makes the leap from the traditional ancient realms of fantasy writing to a modern-day setting — the streets of Toronto, to be exact (where I, too, happened to be living at the time). The wonderful cast of ordinary-extraordinary characters Huff assembles for the tale, and their interactions, are among its most memorable elements. She has followed up with a series of books about a vampire-detective team who battle supernatural enemies in the Toronto area. Beginning with *Blood Price* (DAW, 1991), this entertaining series follows the exploits of a young woman who is an ex-cop turned private detective, solving supernatural mysteries with the aid of a vampire who is actually the bastard son of Henry VIII.

CANADIANS IN A STRANGE LAND

L iving in Canada is more than just a matter of geography. Who we are and how we think is shaped as much by where we live (and by who else lives there) as by any other influences. Canadian speculative fiction reflects in many subtle ways the influences of the physical and cultural environment of this land upon the people who write it.

> "It's because nobody invited us," Noman said. "We're all foreigners here, we're all illegal immigrants. . . . I'm more foreign than you and I'm Kanadian. Maybe I'm the only real foreigner here."
> — Gwendolyn MacEwen, *Noman's Land*
> (Coach House Press, 1985)

If Canadian speculative fiction writers in general have proven to be particularly adept at exploring the theme of "alienation," of feeling like an "outsider," Canadian *women* writers of SF/F have really got it down to a fine art. Women of all races know what it feels like to grow up being treated like second-class citizens, with our concerns, our art, our very way of thinking and viewing the world too often treated by the dominant (male) culture as, at best, second-rate, or at worst, insignificant, irrelevant, and largely dismissible. Canadian women SF writers excel at stories told from the point of view of an alien life form — as, for instance, the cat-like telepathic beings in Phyllis Gotlieb's "Son of the Morning" (*Son of the Morning and Other Stories,* Ace, 1983). In Gotlieb's tale, as in Gadallah's *Cat's Pawn* and many other examples, the emphasis is on how beings who are alien to each other can learn to communicate (without benefit of *Star Trek's* magical "universal translator") and cooperate — themes which are certainly of immediate concern for all Canadians, in the here-and-now.

Another primary concern of Canadian women SF writers which surely springs largely from their Canadian consciousness is the degradation of the global environment and the depletion of natural resources — the fear of how far it might proceed and whether it might be irreversible, and the hope that somehow humanity might survive, in some form, in spite of it all:

> " . . . If the small, delicate organisms die, the large delicate organism that is the world will die . . . "
> — Candas Jane Dorsey, "Willows,"
> in *Tesseracts²*

> Successive *nuclear accidents, pollution,* small *wars* everywhere, and too many people. Barely enough to eat, and Earth itself becoming angry. Earthquakes, awakening *volcanoes,* changing *climates,* famines, epidemics, and finally the great *tides* that changed the *continents.*
> — Élisabeth Vonarburg, *The Silent City*

Time and again, we find Earthlings in the SF by Canadian women huddled together in underground cities or aboveground domes, at the mercy of technological constructs that control their lives, and then eventually breaking free of those artificial confinements to face the real environment outside directly — do or die.

When Canadian women SF writers decide instead to take humanity to the stars, we find them dealing with this popular science fiction theme in often rather unconventional ways that also seem to reflect definite aspects of the Canadian experience. Both *The Mind Gods* (Macmillan, 1976), by Marie Jakober, of Alberta, and *Dreams of an Unseen Planet* (Arbor House, 1986; Tesseract Books, 1994), by Teresa Plowright, of Vancouver, deal with the theme of space colonization in delightfully original ways. In both books, humanity finds itself forced to adapt in fundamental and unexpected ways in order to survive on new worlds. Jakober's book explores several different aspects of possible sociopolitical relations and conflicts amongst various separate colonies. In Plowright's story, the new planet is revealed to have a consciousness of its own, and ultimately speaks for itself, becoming a character in the book. Such aspects seem fundamentally related to the Canadian experience of trying to manage a country with a population relatively thinly spread out from sea to sea to sea — as difficult, perhaps, as managing any galactic federation might prove to be. As Eileen Kernaghan writes in her Author's Note at the end of *The Sarsen Witch*: "As I finish this book, archaeologists are moving toward a new prehistory, one in which the old notions of invasion and conquest give way to movement, influences and cultural process."

Ultimately, what seems to me most remarkable about the works of the women who write speculative fiction in Canada, looked at together, is their astounding diversity. Rather than tending to imitate the SF and fantasy writers of other nations, or even each other, each has produced work quite different from the others in style and thematic approach, each finding her own personal voice which shines through her work. Although there are common threads to be found, such as the typically Canadian thematic elements and sociopolitical preoccupations I have noted above, their work is ultimately as diverse as Canada itself. Writing such as this can only serve to enrich the field of speculative fiction as a whole, expanding its limits and opening up its dimensions of possibility in new directions.

Christine L. Kulyk's love affair with science fiction dates back to the 1960s, during her teenage years in her native Montreal. She became an active member of SF fandom upon moving to Edmonton, Alberta. Since moving back East to Ontario, she has made her living as a professional editor, writer, and researcher for books, magazines, technical manuals, and promotional materials.

WRITING WOMEN'S STORIES IN A MALE UNIVERSE
Reflections on Women and Science Fiction
by Francine Pelletier

⊁A MAN'S WORLD

The scenario is always the same: she is thirteen or fourteen years old, charming, reserved, possibly even shy. She walks towards me, alone or with a friend or two, and says, "You know, I don't like science fiction." After a moment's reflection, she adds, "But it's funny, I still liked your book."

No, this is not a recurring nightmare that haunts my nights as a SF writer. I experienced this very real situation over and over again during a five-year period — between 1989 and 1993 — years that I spent traveling around Québec (and part of Canada) when I did a series of "Meet the Author" sessions under various government programs. The "writers' tour" organized by the Québec Department of Education and managed by the Union des écrivains québécois, the Canada Council's program of meetings with Canadian authors, and the late lamented National Book Festival all provided me with opportunities to meet close to 11,000 students between the ages of eleven and seventeen over the five years, not to mention the informal meetings that took place at book exhibitions or writing workshops. I visited with these young people from all kinds of backgrounds in all manner of places, from the Magdalen Islands to Winnipeg, from Fort-Coulonge to Chibougamau.

As far as the boys are concerned, there is no problem. Although not many of them read novels, their limited numbers include some great lovers of science fiction. The most fanatical among them have read all of Sernine, all of Champetier, and they complain that Philippe Gauthier has not added a fourth volume to his trilogy. At age sixteen, even though girls of the same age find it "babyish," they devour the works in the Jeunesse-Pop series (the only series of works for young people in Québec that provides them with a regular diet of SF).

In the case of the girls, you can't miss it: "I don't like it," they say. And yet . . . Girls are good readers. By the age of ten they have read all of Lucy Maud Montgomery. By age eleven they have devoured *Les filles de Caleb* (both volumes, even though the first alone, the shorter one, has more than 500 pages!). At age twelve they read Harlequin romances or the latest Stephen King indiscriminately. So why not SF?

"In the movies SF films are always very violent," one of my hesitant readers told me. "I'm not interested in that," say most of them. "Too difficult," add others. "But," I reply, "have you actually *read* any?" "Well . . . no." So what's preventing you from trying? What invisible barrier is there between SF and its female readers?

Of course, the girls and boys I met on my tours offered me lots of advice to make my novels more attractive to them: more love, more horror, more kissing, and more hemoglobin . . . I should have listened to them, just to see what would happen!

Convinced that I could not get an answer from young people, I asked adult women readers who, like their younger sisters, admitted to a clear aversion to SF. "It's very hard to read," said one curious dabbler on the lookout for new authors. "We must create our own images, the stories do not relate to anything we have experienced." She is not exactly carried away. Do I dare suggest another title? "Not right away," she says cautiously. "You have to be ready for a book like that; you have to pay very close attention."

"Disconnected from reality" was the expression used by someone else. "Look," I said to this impassioned reader, "I thought you liked fantasy." Fantasy, yes, she admitted, but not *science* fiction. "The problem arises when the story is based on a gadget. When it's too technical, the whole story collapses if the hardware supporting it is outmoded." Stubbornly, I insist that she liked my novels, which contain their share of "hardware" after all. She likes Vonarburg, Le Guin . . . "Yes, but those are novels that tell a *story* above all else. The hardware is only secondary. Your novels don't age because they are first of all about characters. With a few wonderful exceptions, male authors write cold novels, which lack emotion."

There's no point in explaining that I do not share her opinion. I could quote a bunch of "wonderful exceptions" that are full of emotion by my male colleagues from Québec and abroad. At least I've identified, among the things that make SF off-putting to women, their desire to find in their reading *emotions* above all else.

To come back to the young female readers I described earlier, of course I often asked them *why*: why did they say they loved *my* novels if they disliked SF so much? "I don't know," was the inevitable reply. Whenever I try to find out more (always pressed for time, because, naturally, they come to see me at the end of the meeting), the response is in the negative. They liked them because "it's not violent like the movies," because they understood the technical aspects, because it wasn't too complicated. One day, I should like one of them to tell me that she liked one of my books because it was a masterpiece. Anyway, let's move on.

I then ask them whether, by chance, they might have liked my novel because the heroine was someone with whom they could identify. Their faces light up. "That's right. It's not a story about boys." Finally, the word is out: SF is a man's world.

But why on earth did you get involved in this business? If there is one question that keeps coming up at these meetings between author and readers, it is "Why do you write SF?" Teenagers cannot understand why a person would want to write, period. It is hard for them to imagine that a person can devote so much energy to an activity that pays so little. On top of this I have to explain why on earth anyone would write SF, a genre that attracts so few readers! Of course, I talk to them about *passion*; the need to tell the stories that dwell in me, to give life to the characters who haunt me . . . *Yes, but why do so through the medium of SF?* Most women who write imaginative literature in Québec stick to fantasy. Female SF writers, those who write mainly in this genre, are rare: the Vonarburgs and Rochons have few imitators. The name of Johanne Massé can be added to this short list as far as young readers are concerned. They are no more numerous in France, despite its greater population. In the United States, it is well known that a female author of fantasy is easier to find than one of SF.

If I were writing a scientific essay, I would ask my female colleagues what made them get involved in this field. However, that is not the case and my thoughts are personal. I shall limit myself to the one guinea pig I know most about. The reflections that follow are solely my responsibility and are not binding in any way on other female SF authors.

Why did I embark on this venture? I do not have any scientific training ("it shows," the wagging tongues will say). I was not a *Star Trek* fan as a youngster and didn't even read SF. In fact, I began to write science fiction before I had even read any. Of course, I used to watch some of the TV shows of that kind (*Voyage to the Bottom of the Sea, Lost in Space, Space 1999*), but it was not a passion of mine.

As a matter of fact, I wrote detective novels. One day, one of my stories took a turn that was pure science fiction. Without realizing it, I had been contaminated by my brother, who was a great reader and who told me so much about what he read that a seed was planted in my imagination. When he saw that I was writing SF (especially the piece of junk I had produced), he immediately suggested a few "classics" for me to read. Nothing doing! I wasn't interested. Since I was reading detective novels, in order to trap me, my brother surreptitiously slipped in Asimov's *Caves of Steel*. I was hooked.

All this leads me to suggest the following paradox: *women do not like science fiction because they do not read it*. To make it sound less contradictory: SF suffers from the prejudice that women have against it. Warning: reading one well-chosen book could lead to addiction . . .

Thus, after devouring all the Asimov my brother had, I dipped into the famous "classics" before forming my own tastes by reading Vonarburg, Le Guin, and other women authors. However, I never became the kind of unconditional and passionate reader that my friends are. When I took part in my first SF writing workshop in 1981 (moderated by Élisabeth Vonarburg), I thought I had a good knowledge of American SF writing. What a nerve! My male colleagues were incessant in their praise of this or that author of whom I had not read a single word. Even today, I am two decades behind literary developments abroad.

I must point out that, like the women readers referred to earlier, I find some male authors unreadable. "Sometimes I have the impression," I was told by one of these readers, "that the author has a clever scientific idea and says to himself: 'I'm going to make a novel out of this; now I have to find a story that will go with it.' *Women* authors, on the other hand, give an impression that *first* they create characters and emotions." This leads me to note the following obvious fact: *women readers prefer "soft" SF*, originating in the humanities, to "hard" SF, where technology sometimes has the lion's share.

However, all the considerations expressed so far will not solve the profound mystery underlying the situation of any SF author. Writing science fiction means locating the whole creative process in a specific mode of thought that involves formulating hypotheses, building worlds and thinking about the future each time there is a change in everyday life. Well, well! Are not the occupations traditionally regarded as being a "female" preserve those that involve *nurturing, taking care* of people, showing *concern* for people? Is the writing of SF based on the humanities not linked to a kind of atavism, a "maternal instinct" that leads the author to show concern for the future of humanity, just as a mother hen looks after her chicks? That would explain why Québec women authors, among others, place such importance on everyday life in the worlds they construct (it may also explain why I have absolutely no desire to have children . . . but that is another story).

Women are not of course the only ones who move the concerns of the here and now to another place and another time. The difference lies more in the *manner* in which this is done. It is said that women have their own way of doing things, pursuing a career, getting involved in politics. Why should there not be a feminine manner of *writing*? Hum. I am not sure that in a "blind test" it would be possible to distinguish between Pepsi and Coke, between a male and a female author. So I leave it to more audacious theoreticians than I am to open this particular Pandora's box. They should just be sure that they don't pinch their fingers under the lid! Be that as it may, where does this *manner* come from, if not from the models? It may be assumed that *if female models are held up for female readers, this should encourage the readers to continue their discovery of SF literature.* Having said this, I should point out that SF readers, whether male or female, will never be a majority of the population. Science fiction, at least in Québec, is not a genre that produces bestsellers.

And the lioness's share?

I read somewhere (no doubt in *Solaris*) that my female anglophone colleagues felt that they were barely tolerated by their male colleagues, that they were treated with condescension and later with animosity when they began to walk off with some of the most coveted literary prizes. In feminist circles I am greeted with scepticism when I say that Québec SF, in contrast, has always welcomed women authors. I have sometimes even had the impression that I get more attention because I am a woman who writes science fiction than because I am a woman writer, and that is rather annoying. Québec SF circles have always had, for example in their magazines, places of publication that provide considerable support for writers (support through their literary management, of course; I am not talking about financial support in the cultural field, where money is rather lacking). One thing is certain: a young woman writer of SF will receive support and encouragement from the whole community, which is possibly not true of other literary genres.

In this respect, being a woman in a male universe is not a burden. Let us just hope that such a new group of women writers will answer the call — and that a number of women readers can be persuaded to venture into the unknown, to take the *lovely risk* of opening a work of science fiction . . . whether or not it is written by a woman.

Francine Pelletier *has published some thirty short stories in reviews, anthologies, and collections, as well as a dozen novels for young adults, primarily in the pop-youth collection from Médiaspaul (formerly Éditions Paulines). In 1988, her collection* Le temps des migrations *won the Prix Solaris for best book and she won the short-story category of the* Grand prix de la science-fiction et du fantastique québécois *for "La petite fille du silence", a story from that collection. A member of the editorial board of the review* Solaris *from 1984 to 1990, Francine Pelletier has also worked on various periodicals, including* L'Année de la science-fiction et du fantastique québécois.

WOMEN AND SCIENCE FICTION
by Élisabeth Vonarburg

Author: The person who originates or gives existence to anything. The Creator. He who gives rise to or causes an action, event, circumstance, state or condition of things. He who authorizes or instigates. One who begets; a father, an ancestor. "The author of her being, her persecuted . . . murdered father."(Thackeray).
— *Oxford English Dictionary*

Do you think women and science fiction (henceforth SF) have little in common? If so, then you and the statistics for the non-English-speaking world agree. The statistics show that women read much less SF than men, are less interested in it, and write less of it. But the statistics are different for English-speaking cultures: according to surveys conducted by various English-language specialty mags, about equal numbers of women and men read SF, and while fewer women than men write SF, there are still many more women SF writers than in non-English-speaking cultures (about 25%, as opposed to 2% or 3%).

Nevertheless, in the collective imagination, SF is not really a field for women. The reasons are fairly obvious: SF, more than conventional literature, has recent origins in scientific and technological writing. The very definition of science fiction as "rational speculative literature" proposed by Pierre Versins, the pioneering encyclopedist of the genre, appears (given popular stereotypes) to dismiss women, the perennial champions of irrationality. Even today, in our so-called post-feminist Western societies, science and technology remain predominantly male fields, the province of hard Civilization and cold Logical Intellect, as opposed to soft Nature and the equally soft emotions, realms which are still essentially reserved, at the rear of the bus of progress, to the females of the species. In 1994 as in 1926 (the official birth of modern SF, the year in which the term "science fiction" was coined by Hugo Gernsback), women are apparently no more attracted to SF than to mathematics or rocket science, for so the stereotypes of patriarchal culture have decreed. But has not Zorro (in the form of triumphant capitalism, industrialization, and two world wars, thank you very much gentlemen) liberated them? Alongside the traditional three-headed image of "woman" (Our Lady of Nature, the Ice Virgin, and Mary the Whore) have not other heads sprouted? At the very least, the head of the citizen whose work and creativity equal that of men? If we are to believe SF texts, the answer is: not really or really not! The vast majority of SF still transmits the same age-old stereotypes as does conventional literature. The roles of women in SF narratives when women do appear in anything other than the traditional distant-backdrop roles of Warrior's Comforter or Keeper of the Hearth are, in descending order: (a) being kidnapped help! help! (the hero saves her); (b) screwing up help! help! (the hero rescues her); (c) trying to do the hero in (the hero triumphs).

As most SF *authors* are men, these conditioned reflexes are not so surprising; but as these men are writing SF, a genre whose essence consists of imagining how things could be otherwise, of challenging prejudices, or even, in the view of some critics, of promoting *change*, this does seem rather curious, a sign of deplorable laziness or alarming intellectual blindness in speculation, be it ever so rational!

We must, however, season this observation with a grain of diachronic salt. All things change, even SF. (It should be noted that the most popular SF writers on bookstore shelves are names from the 1940s and 1950s — Asimov, Clarke, Heinlein. Moreover cinema, now the leading vehicle for the dissemination of SF to the innocent public, is generally twenty to thirty years behind SF writing in terms of its subject matter and handling of themes.) The comments we have made hold entirely true for SF from the 1920s through the 1950s, but since the 1960s there have been major changes in the image of women in SF, essentially because, we would suggest, more women have started writing SF. Women writers burst onto the scene in the 1960s and their numbers increased exponentially between 1960 and 1980 (the rise has eased off since then). What they brought to the genre was, essentially, a new lucidity and new claims. The SF of the 1960s had Dad going to the office on Alpha Centauri in the year 3547 while Mom stayed home to run the vacuum robot and fix supper for their two-and-a-half kids after they ride their space-planes home from school. This, declared the new women writers, was an unacceptable violation of the very essence of SF, an unjustifiable blind spot in the imagination of the writers who dominated the field. If change was the driving principle of the SF imagination, if SF represented the revolutionary ferment of a metamorphosed future (we could add here a few other rather grandiose statements by certain SF writers of the day), then it was high time for SF to do some housecleaning, so to speak. And we can say without fear of exaggeration that the arrival of women on the American SF scene in the 1960s, combined of course with the social and political upheavals of that period, permanently changed the face of sf, if only by "sensitizing" some male authors. Inevitably, this gave rise to new, more politically correct stereotypes, but that does not detract in any way from the contribution of women to sf.

Not that women had not been "authoresses" before. Feminist research has turned up a number of female authors of utopias in the late nineteenth century and the first third of the twentieth century, at a time when male authors had practically abandoned the genre. And utopia is one of the immortal genetrixes of sf, with which it shares a vision of a different world. But the usual fate of the vast majority of works written by women before the advent of mass publishing and special collections befell these writings: they disappeared without a trace and did not serve to inform the collective consciousness of sf. They cannot be viewed as "seminal" (or ovular) works of modern sf. There were, however, several women writers of sf before the official birth of the genre. In the 1930s and 1940s, one woman was recognized as a "major sf author" — Catherine Moore. Her very first story, "Shambleau," was greeted as a masterpiece and published to critical acclaim. It was, however, published under the uncompromising initials "C.M. Moore." Similarly, "Leslie Stone," another woman sf writer of the period, and a little later "Andre Norton" had inoffensive names. Moore and Norton both came out of the closet fairly soon, without apparent damage to their careers. It should be noted here that a number of women authors of these "heroic" years say they never felt their sex was a handicap in sf circles, "on the contrary." A male comment on the period may help explain why: "there were so few of them!" (Things have changed since the 1960s. Not content simply to publish their work, women have started to win awards which previously went to men, and still more dangerously to occupy positions of power: literary editors, critics, and so forth. Comments from both sides have become less honeyed; as in any situation of cultural confrontation, when the Other nears twenty-five percent in numbers, we are approaching the limits of tolerance.)

So what did they actually write, this paltry handful of women who were so readily welcomed into the club (they did add some grace and beauty, after all)? Catherine Moore essentially told colorful space adventures featuring male heroes, similar to the stories of Leigh Brackett. Northwest Smith, the protagonist of "Shambleau" and a number of Moore's other short stories, had his hands full with female creatures who almost all belonged to the Mary the Whore category. (A Shambleau is a seductive extraterrestrial vampire who sucks the life force from her victims.) It is not surprising that these women writers were so readily accepted: they entirely bought into the dominant male stereotypes (pull a veil over my face).

But some qualifications are in order here. In a surreptitious fantasized revenge, these female figures subject the hero to grave physical and spiritual danger before they are finally defeated. And Moore's work quickly went beyond enthusiastic exploration of existing stereotypes, evolving towards more subtle themes up until the 1960s. In fact, her work seems to me to encapsulate almost all the phases of the progression of literary expression by women. First, there was the stage of *female self-denial*. Publishing under masculine pseudonyms or "neutral" initials, women wrote narratives with male heroes in which gender stereotypes were accepted, indeed sometimes celebrated. This was followed by the stage of *man-like revolt*: publishing under their own names, women authors wrote narratives in which the main protagonist is a heroine abundantly endowed with thinly-disguised male attributes. (Moore is fairly direct: one of her heroines is a warrior. As we know, in the beginning, muscle meant power.) I would call the third stage *female revolt:* narratives in which the heroine is clearly defined as a woman and asserts her femaleness. (Although, in the final analysis, it is often a stereotypical femininity of the Our-Lady-of-Nature/Savior-of-the-World type. Heroines with extra-sensory powers, especially telepathy, are a good example. See the short stories of Zenna Henderson.) "No Woman Born," a fine story by Moore, is another example of this tendency. A female singer (artists, even when they are male, often function as a positive symbol of femininity) who has been terribly burned in an accident, is given a new metallic body, thanks to the ingenuity of her (male) scientist friends. She has no face, only a smooth golden surface with amethyst crystal eyes. Her artificial body, obeying the commands of her undamaged brain, faithfully reproduces her attitudes, her voice, her "air." This body (today we would call the protagonist a "cyborg") opens up to the heroine the fantastic (and masculine) possibilities of strength and speed, gives her vocal power she did not previously have, and so forth, but also lends her an (emotional/"feminine") psychological power of empathy, which she uses to communicate her art to others. However, she must overcome the doubts of her scientist friends, who are afflicted with the Frankenstein complex and convinced they have created a monster, for she no longer fits their conception of who she is. (Indeed, one of them tries to kill her, so she must triumph over the scientists physically as well as morally.) The stage of female revolt may or may not be accompanied by a rejection of masculinity, which is a simplistic but inevitable reversal of the stereotypes: the man is presented as the Bad Guy (he is punished), the Incompetent (he is exposed), or as, in this case, the Weakling (he is rescued).

In a way, this story by Moore portends the last stage of our schematized typical development of women SF writers: ideal *gender integration*, which portrays "rounded" humans beyond stereotypes — beyond — sex? endowed with both intelligence and sensitivity, logic and emotion, etc., be they female or male. We must stress that this is an *ideal* stage of which we seldom find examples in reality. Similarly, the typical progression we have outlined comes from a mind's eye view; no writer has ever followed this course in exactly this way. These are, rather, possible fictional positions which each generation and each woman writer combines in its/her own way. They do, however, provide a useful schema for finding our way around in a text.

The question of *generations* of female authors is of some significance. The evolution of the utopian writing by women to which we referred above followed the peaks and valleys of the feminist movement of the late nineteenth century and early twentieth century. The same applies to SF written by women, and perhaps still more characteristically so, for this field is perceived as masculine on two counts: as *literature* and as literature dealing with *science and technology*. We might well assume that this two-fold challenge would attract specific types of women, and we should not be surprised to find that these women subjected the aporias of masculinity/femininity models to searching scrutiny in the 1940s and

1950s (see, for example, the short stories of Judith Merril, Anne McCaffrey, Katherine McLean), while in the 1960s and 1970s they became "flaming feminists" (Joanna Russ, *The Female Man*; Suzy McKee Charnas, *Motherlines*), "thoughtful feminists" (Ursula Le Guin, *The Left Hand of Darkness*; Joan Slonczewski, *A Door into Ocean*), or "ambivalent feminists" (Marion Zimmer Bradley, the *Darkover* series), and then in the 1980s more-or-less "post-feminist" (the novels of the American writers Sheri Tepper and Pat Cadigan, and of the British writer Gwyneth Jones). Influenced by the spirit of the times, each generation modulated and appropriated the themes and motifs of SF in its own way, but the patterns have been sufficiently consistent through the generations that we may speak (cautiously) of "Women's SF."

We should point out here that the same themes and motifs do appear in the work of male authors as well. Any attempt to draw a distinction between "women's SF" and "male SF" must focus on the relative *frequency* of themes and the *way they are handled*, more than on the subject matter as such. A study of that nature could be expected to reveal differences in tone, modulation, connotation, and *proportion* between texts written by women and by men, which unfortunately are beyond the reach of the simple listing of themes which I shall present here.

Bearing this cautionary note in mind, we do find, first of all, that themes related to *physicality* are prominent in SF written by women (not surprisingly). "Cyborgized" women, whose bodies (and hence minds no dualism here!) have been mutilated by invasive technology, are a frequent motif from the 1950s through the 1970s: we encounter working women whose eyes have been removed and replaced by implants which see only in black and white ("Spectra" by Vonda McIntyre), women bereft in more ways than one who are caught between social stereotypes of beauty and the technology which enables them to conform to those stereotypes or not ("The Girl Who Was Plugged In" by James Tiptree Jr.). (It should be noted here that this female author, "James Teptree Jr.," a staunch feminist, published with great success under a male pseudonym for about ten years for a variety of reasons, and indeed pretended to be a man. She fooled all of U.S. sci-fi-dom until she finally revealed her female identity:

Alice Sheldon. James Tiptree Jr., winner of numerous prestigious awards, one of the best authors of American SF of the day, triumphantly brandished by male writers in response to feminists as a symbol of the liberated man, was a woman! The news sent strong and lasting shock waves rippling through the American SF scene and through the consciousness of women everywhere who are interested in SF.)

We also find, again in connection with physicality, themes related to *sexuality* and *reproduction*. Here too, women often appear as victims. In Kate Wilhelm's "Baby, You Were Great," new technologies permit increased exploitation: a female artist of a new type carries a transmitter to allow one and all to share her experiences, which unbeknownst to her are arranged to be exciting, titillating, or emotionally painful. In other cases, women are victims of doctors and medical technology, of a society which would control their reproduction (often through the use of eugenics), or simply of the physically unlivable world left by the excesses of military-industrial society, as in Judith Merril's simple but incisive 1948 story, "That Only a Mother": the protagonist, the wife of a nuclear technician, gives birth to a girl with marvelous intellectual and musical gifts but no arms or legs. Apparently oblivious, the mother writes glowing reports to her husband. It is the father (and with him the reader) who realizes upon his return that the girl is deformed.

Another motif related to physicality which has been immensely popular with both male and female authors over the past ten years is genetic engineering — cloning, sex changes, improving the human body. Women writers generally have a more ambivalent attitude towards this subject than men. For example, when dealing with cloning, many male writers seem fascinated by the narcissistic thrill of the *duplication of self*, while women are more interested in the problem of the clone's individuation, its attainment of independence (Ursula Le Guin, "Nine Lives"; Pamela Sargent, *Cloned Lives*). On the possibility of changing sex at will, men seem to be interested primarily in the broadening of experience and the elimination of all questions of sexual identity, since "the mind has no sex," whereas the problem of identity does concern women, who are more cautious about ranking the importance of mind and body.

Women writers are also ready to tackle broad-ranging studies of entire societies (witness the writing of utopias by nineteenth- and twentieth-century feminists, discussed above). One of the trailblazing works of this type is undoubtedly Ursula Le Guin's *The Dispossessed*, which gave the utopian genre new life in an SF guise. It bore the revealing subtitle "An Ambiguous Utopia"; unlike the classic utopias, which were atemporal and static, this utopia was subject to *change in time*, closing the gap between utopia and SF.

There has also been a kind of forced convergence between women's concerns and the utopian genre as practiced today within the framework of SF — and I would go so far as to say between women and SF as such. On the one hand, women are in a sense compelled to take a detour by way of the future to represent their concerns and proposals in more concrete form than theorizing and manifestos, for the past and present are burdened by social and psychological deadweights too heavy to cast off. In conventional literature, the only paths open to women authors are protest, condemnation, and revolt; to undertake *creation*, to ask new questions, or to ask old questions in a different, constructive way, they must enter a new time and space. And they have taken full advantage of the opportunity to do so in SF, with results which are sometimes disturbing for male readers but always thought-provoking (unlike escapist literature). We find societies where women outnumber men or where men have entirely disappeared (mutations, viruses), "separatist" societies in which men and women live in distinct worlds, most often with hostility on one or both sides, which must be resolved in one manner or another. This last theme highlights generational changes among women writers. In the 1960s and 1970s, they demanded separation with some measure of ferocity (Joanna Russ, "When It Changed"). In the 1980s, they sought complementarity (Pamela Sargent, *The Shore of Women*). In the 1990s, they contemplate separation impassively, confident they will be able to survive. Thus, in her recent novel *Ammonite*, the young writer Nicola Griffith asks the same question as did her sisters of previous generations: what remains when all members of one sex (in this case men) are removed from society? But she replies with a certain serenity (based on a speculative variant of parthenogenesis made possible by current progress in genetics): there remains a full and whole society which works just fine.

At the same time, if as I have suggested there is a convergence between women and SF as such (and not only its utopian current), this is so because in contemporary society, woman remains the Other of man. We need only think of the anguished (or exasperated) question "What do women want?" or Master Freud's ruminations on the "dark continent." And SF is precisely that: the literature of the Other, of difference, of otherness, other places, other times. Considered from this point of view, it is not surprising that one theme which appears prominently and idiosyncratically in the work of women writers is the theme of the Other in all its guises: extraterrestrial, mutant, robot, android, cyborg. Whereas in SF written by men, the Other is often automatically the protagonist's enemy in a territorial conflict (extraterrestrial), a menacing inferior who poses a threat to identity (robot, android), or a being who raises overly sensitive questions about what it means to be human (mutant, cyborg, or again extraterrestrial), the protagonists in SF by women take a rather less antagonistic stance, more readily accepting the Other as a person whose identity humanity is unjustly denied. "The Women Men Don't See," a fine story by "James Tiptree Jr." all etched in shades of gray, illustrates this convergence: an unmarried woman and her daughter (both ordinary, neither beauties nor ugly ducklings), lost in the jungle with the narrator, the pilot of a small plane (he too is ordinary, neither exceptionally handsome nor particularly macho) are offered a chance to leave the Earth in an extraterrestrial vessel and they accept, to the stupefaction of the narrator, who cannot understand that they should prefer life among non-humans to life with men who do not see (that is, who "love" or marginalize or despise) women.

Once again, all these texts are more indicative of the individual development of their authors than of female SF as a whole (not "feminist SF," as if women writers always had political agendas!). And it should not be thought that women writers explore only "soft" themes drawn from the social sciences (sociology, psychology), which surged into SF as a whole during the revolution of the 1960s and were dubbed the "New Wave." It is just that when they deal with the sciences, and especially the traditionally "hard" technologies, they do so from a more critical and ambivalent point of view than their male colleagues. The greatest revolution of the twentieth century, or at least the deepest and most lasting, has been wrought by the invention of the pill, and thanks to electronics, biceps are no longer a prerequisite for operating a steam shovel. Women know that they stand to benefit from the progress of science and technology, and not just because household appliances will make housework easier! (This may be why more women read and write SF in the United States, a country which traditionally has been fascinated by technology and still considers itself to be at the cutting edge of technological progress.) On the other hand, women also know that, despite significant progress, they are not the ones who decide new directions for scientific research or define new technological choices, as things stand now. This ambivalence naturally finds expression in SF, and indeed women are not alone in expressing it. If there is a conclusion which may be drawn from a survey of contemporary SF in the mid-1990s, it is that the common ground between male and female authors, in terms of their concerns and their ways of fictionalizing them, is broader than it was twenty years ago. Things do not change as quickly as SF imagines or hopes, but all things do change at least, that is a conviction we hope men and women can share!

*Élisabeth Vonarburg is the author of three collections of short stories in French; a dozen stories have been published in English in Canada and the U.S.A. as well as three novels (*The Silent City, The Maërlande Chronicles/In the Mother's Land, *and* The Reluctant Voyagers). *In 1990 her story "Cogito" won a Canadian Casper Award (now Aurora Award) for Best Short Film in French. She is working on several other projects and still lives in Chicoutimi, Québec.*

THE FEMALE UTOPIA IN CANADA
by Guy Bouchard

It is too easy to associate the concept of utopia with the fool's paradise, or the prison camp, and those who do so are too comfortable in their disdain.[1] Utopia is the daughter of dream, but the dream is also part of reality: as distortion or escape, but sometimes too as innovative ferment. To treat the concept of utopia as a dream of a better life may therefore be a function of metaphoric approximation, but an approximation pregnant with meaning, and one not to be dismissed simply because associations between dream and fool's paradise, or prison camp, are likewise too easy to establish.[2]

And then there is society. It is the task of realistic political thought to describe it as it is, in theoretical terms. But there is another "politics", a *heteropolitics* one might say, which is no longer concerned with society as it is, but as it might be: whether in theory, as in *Le nouveau monde amoureux* (Fourier), whereupon we speak of a *para-utopia*, or in fiction, in the form of a story with invented characters, as in *Voyage en Icarie* (Cabet), whereupon we speak of a *utopia* in the strict sense of the term. A utopia is therefore a fiction which presents, on a basis of implicit or explicit criticism of actual society, a society that is idealized or demonized compared with the existing one. If idealized, it is embodied in a *eutopia*, as in the aforementioned novel by Cabet; if demonized, it takes the form of a *dystopia*, as in Orwell's *1984*. Historically, the utopia has undergone a double mutation: originally to a very great extent eutopian and masculine, in the first half of the twentieth century and some years thereafter it became resolutely dystopian, although certain feminist novelists resurrected the eutopia between 1960 and 1990, metamorphosed by new values incompatible with the patriarchal society. It is in light of this evolution of the genre that it may be interesting to briefly examine a few Canadian utopias written by women, whose merit has been recognized by various literary prizes, one official-language translation, and even a film adaptation: *L'Euguélionne* by Louky Bersianik, *Le silence de la cité* and *Chroniques du Pays des Mères* by Élisabeth Vonarburg, *The Handmaid's Tale* by Margaret Atwood, and *L'espace du diamant* by Esther Rochon.

1. *L'EUGUÉLIONNE* (1976)
BY LOUKY BERSIANIK

In principle (because she symbolically represents the situation of women on Earth), the heroine of Bersianik's novel is an Extraterrestrial. Having set out in search of a life-affirming planet and a male of her species, it is not long before she realizes that Earth can offer neither. She learns that in the beginning, the men forcefully seized power and lobotomized the women. Hence they now control the economy, the family, and public affairs. Hence they have converted the human race into capital by usurping its name and establishing themselves as the owners of women's bodies. Hence too they have converted knowledge into capital, thereby producing the sexist language and misogyny of the male culture. Euguélionne discovers all this, not only by observing people's behavior, but also by systematically investigating every sphere of our civilization. Earth women, she concludes, are no better off than the females of her own planet: they live in a condition of slavery. But the realization of oppression is the prerequisite for liberation. Consequently, Euguélionne preaches revolt against the patriarchal yoke. Upon being publicly assassinated, she is reborn and rises to heaven in a parody of the crucifixion, resurrection, and ascension of Jesus of Nazareth. Galvanized by her message, the women and a few positive men rebel and shatter the tables of the phallic law, thus opening the possibility of a new way of life based on equality of the sexes, freedom, respect of oneself and others, and justice. Euguélionne thus fulfils the mission assigned to her by a prophecy before she was even born: announce the good news of the end of a certain kind of slavery on Earth.

It is this novel's accomplishment to bring us to understand that, in terms of sexual politics, that is, the balance of power between the sexes, for women the world as it was in the early 1970s and, at least in part, as it still is, is a dystopia. The political regimes in place may profess themselves to be liberal democratic or socialist, but they are all simply variants of male power, of androcracy. The revolt preached by Euguélionne thus initiates a passage from an androcratic dystopia to an inchoate androgynous eutopia, that is, one founded on equality of the sexes, as symbolically represented in the novel by a small community of men and women who learn to live together according to new values.

2. *LE SILENCE DE LA CITÉ* (1981) BY ÉLISABETH VONARBURG

Nuclear accidents, pollution, minor wars, overpopulation, famine, volcanic eruptions and tsunami have brutally transformed the face of the Earth. A number of the privileged have taken refuge in subterranean cities. On the surface, the survivors, some of whom have undergone mutations, live as tribes. Since far more women than men are now born, they are eliminated at birth or reduced to slavery. As in *L'Euguélionne*, the basic situation in terms of sexual politics is therefore that of a dystopian androcracy.

Also as in that novel, the situation has not been finalized. The novel presents two possible outcomes. The first lies in simple inversion: replace the androcracy with a gynocracy. Judith has fled her tribe and founded Libéra, the city of free women. On behalf of all women, she demands power proportional to their numbers, and to get it she is prepared to unleash a war of the sexes.

Yet this is not the outcome that the novel advocates. Through genetic experiments, one of the last survivors of the underground cities has created a woman capable of self-regeneration and metamorphosis. After eliminating her "father" who has become a dangerous lunatic, Elisa generates children endowed with the same power as she has. After testing what it means to be a woman, those of her children who will join the surface tribes as men will not only transmit their genes to their descendants, but contribute to the advent of a new society, which in the end may come to resemble the democratic and egalitarian commune where they have lived with Elisa. Once again, then, the expected result is an androgynous society.

3. *THE HANDMAID'S TALE* (1986) BY MARGARET ATWOOD

While Vonarburg's story takes place several centuries after ours, Atwood's is set in the near future, in a time when the extreme right in the United States has taken power and established a totalitarian monotheocracy. The most remarkable feature of this society, given a declining population caused by increasingly widespread sterility and deformed births, is its exacerbated sexism. Overnight, thanks in large part to the replacement of cash with computer cards, women found themselves stripped of economic power, a law having transferred all their property to their closest male relative, and without access to paid employment. In the Republic of Gilead, a woman's place is now the home, and her destiny is tied to her biology — directly if she is fertile, and indirectly if she is not. In concrete terms, this means that women are divided into different castes, according to their reproductive ability and social rank.

Offred is a handmaid. The task of such a handmaid is to copulate once a month, ceremoniously and without pleasure, with a Commander whose wife is sterile. But Offred has had experience of the age prior to the Republic of Gilead, when despite the threat of rape and the hunt for a husband, women used to enjoy a degree of freedom and relative independence. The difference between the two societies enables Offred to realize her oppression and to foster a rebellious spirit, which she expresses by keeping a clandestine private diary, indulging in illicit activities with the Commander who lodges her, trying to establish contact with a resistance network, and having a liaison with the Commander's driver. Finally, by staging a false arrest, the Commander allows her to escape and record her memoirs for posterity.

The end of the novel, which is moved forward several decades into the future, has sometimes been misunderstood. In 2195, the Republic of Gilead no longer exists. Through a conference held on the specific subject of Offred's memoirs, we realize that the sociopolitical situation and the condition of women have changed, and that this age strangely resembles our own. Some critics have seen this as an apology for the *status quo*, but if one notices the highly satirical nature of this denouement, and the ineptitude of the learned speaker who has been unable to discover the narrator's real given name, this return to a peri-utopian society, that is, one which is neither idealized nor demonized, can be interpreted as a new chance that is given to us: the dystopia has shown us the features in our society which resulted in Gilead, and it is for us to eliminate these characteristics to the benefit of the positive aspects of our society, so as to make possible an androgynous eutopia.

4. *L'ESPACE DU DIAMANT* (1990) BY ESTHER ROCHON

Destitute and scantly populated, the archipelago of Vrénalik has for many centuries suffered under a curse prohibiting its inhabitants from leaving, until Taïm Sutherland finds the statue of Hatzlén and puts an end to it. Strénid, the chief, is the first to go to the South, where he lives for one year. During that time, he enters Catadial, a country whose inhabitants are linked to the Asvens people by the ancient voyage of Queen Suzanne, by a linguistic heritage, and by a treasure held in trust. Strénid negotiates an agreement with Emperor Othoum: the Asvens who so wish will be able to come and settle in Catadial, in a city to be built for them, on condition that Taïm Sutherland serves the emperor for twelve years. Taïm accepts, fulfils his contract, and the Asvens come and settle in the Red City.

In addition to Vrénalik and Catadial, the planet has other countries, including Ister-Inga, formerly founded by Asvens emigrants. In view of its "ordinary, mediocre position, which is that of most places on the planet," Ister-Inga may symbolize those places. This would make Vrénalik a peri-utopia at the crossroads. Once the curse is lifted, the archipelago becomes easy prey for the unscrupulous industrialized countries interested in its forests and other natural resources: its inhabitants are threatened with a dystopian invasion if they refuse to change. In this case, change means leaving for Catadial and joining a eutopian society whose social system is such that it allows people to grow and develop, and profit from each other's talents. This integration is not unilateral, since Catadial must serve as an example to the other countries and so open itself to them, and both Taïm Sutherland, who has already "opened" Vrénalik, and the Asvens themselves, by their presence and their travels, contribute to this openness.

In terms of sexual politics, Catadial is an androgynous society where almost all functions are in principle accessible to both women and women, even though it appears that in practice the queen governs only in replacement of the emperor or his eldest son, and the army is reserved for men only. There is no indication of any subordination of one sex to the other, and such institutions as legal vagrancy for those under fifty years of age and the raising of children by parental groups suggest very great autonomy for women, who even when married seem to have full rights over their own bodies.

5. *CHRONIQUES DU PAYS DES MÈRES* (1992) BY ÉLISABETH VONARBURG

We are now somewhere in the early fourth millennium, in the same sort of future as *Le silence de la cité*, and almost the same post-catastrophic setting. Lisbeï tells her story, from the age of five until her death. Her autobiography, together with her letters and those of other characters and a document written by the secret master of her destiny, introduces us to four different ages and four different models of society.

First, the age of the Harems: after the catastrophe, the men, although fewer in number, hold the power, and the women are reduced to slavery. Next, the age of the Hives: the women rebel, seize power by force, and it is the men's turn to be at their mercy. Third comes the dominant age of the story, that of the Motherland [*Pays des Mères*]: the women still hold power and remain in charge of all important activities; and although the men are initially defined in terms of their reproductive abilities, this domination is made less oppressive by the dissemination of a pacifist religion and philosophy. Finally, thanks in large part to Lisbeï and above all Kélys-Cheïré, the metamorph who has used her, and other individuals produced by him without their knowledge to influence the fate of the Motherland, a fourth age begins, that of a community in which power is increasingly shared between the sexes, which consider each other as equals.

If we agree to call a repressive domination a *black dystopia* and a domination that is as benevolent as possible a *pink dystopia*, these ages may be characterized as follows. The androcracy of the Harems, a black dystopia for the women, is replaced, in the mode of inversion, by the gynocracy of the Hives, equally dystopian and equally black, but this time for the men. This is followed by the gynocracy of the Motherland: it is still dystopian for men, but a pink dystopia, which has begun to transform into a eutopian androgynous society.

BY WAY OF CONCLUSION . . .

A utopia may be stable or unstable, depending on whether the social model it embodies is changed or not. If we overlook this distinction and the sometimes inchoate nature of the new emerging society, and if we focus solely on the dominant model in a given story, we may have the impression that four of the five novels we have just analyzed feature dystopias, and therefore contradict the evolutionary scheme outlined in the introduction. On the other hand, if we take into account the potential instability of the models, two groups are clearly distinguished: on one side, the book by Esther Rochon, where we move from a peri-utopia to an effective androgynous eutopia; and on the other, the other four novels, where the initial androcratic dystopia gives way, directly or after certain mediations based on the inversion of the domination, to an androgynous inchoate eutopia. If we note that the patriarchal power is immediately disqualified in *L'espace du diamant*, we can conclude that the female Canadian utopias, whether their authors claim to be inspired by feminism or not, are structured on the same values: refusal of masculine domination, refusal of a simple inversion of the domination as a final solution, and apology for the androgynous society. In this sense, they are a magnificent illustration of the feminist renaissance of the eutopia.

NOTES

1 This text is based in part on research done for a project (1989-92) funded by the SSHRC on the *Philosophie hétéropolitique du féminisme*. The concept of the utopia outlined here has been developed and justified in the following texts: G. Bouchard, L. Giroux, G. Leclerc, *L'utopie aujourd'hui* (Montreal: Presses de l'Université de Montréal, 1985); G. Bouchard, "L'art de la définition: l'utopie", *Recherches sémiotiques*, 7, 3 (1987): 329-366; and *Les 42,210 univers de la science-fiction* (Quebec City: Le Passeur, 1993). On feminist utopias: G. Bouchard, "Les utopies féministes et la science-fiction", *imagine . . .*, 44 (1988): 63-87, and "Charlotte Perkins Gilman et la métamorphose du concept d'utopie", *Protée*, 17, 2 (1989): 89-96. These references are provided to compensate for the brief portrayal of the theoretical framework.

2 See Ernst Bloch, *Le principe espérance*, Vol. 1 (Paris: Gallimard, 1977): 19.

Guy Bouchard, *a professor in the Faculty of Philosophy at Laval University, has published two novels,* Vénus via Atlantide *(1961) and* Les Gélules utopiques *(1989 Prix Boréal), and a number of short stories, including* "Andropolis" *(Prix Septième Continent) and* "Si la vie vous intéresse" *(1993 Prix Septième Continent). His theoretical works include* Le Procès de la métaphore, L'Utopie aujourd'hui *(co-author),* George Orwell et "1984": trois approches *(co-author),* Femmes et pouvoir dans la "cité philosophique", Relire "L'Utopie" de Thomas More *and* Les 42,210 univers de la science-fiction *(Prix Aurora and Prix Boréal).*

THE ALIEN AT THE FEAST
The Publishers of and the Audience for Fantastic Literature in Canada
by Phyllis Gotlieb

At first thought I was going to title this piece: Alien Finds Utopia in Canada! to express my belief that our country, which is blessed with so much to praise and enjoy, is a place where an alien, say, Xtkubt, a stone-carver from the planet Pthak, could land in her space flivver and become part of our community the way so many immigrants have done. Except for aboriginals all of us here are immigrants or descended from them, and I tend to think of the science fiction community — producers, readers, fans — as such a descendant because it started out with foreign ideas and worked on them until they became distinctively Canadian. As a group we are still very young, but happily, we have grown greatly since the arid years over three decades back when I made up the very uneasy majority of one active native-born science fiction writer in Canada, and we are gathered here in this Volume to celebrate our numbers: writers, as well as graphics artists and film-makers.

Many of our science fiction ideas originated in the United States and Britain, as those of our francophones developed from French themes. We cannot avoid having been influenced by the English themes of Mary Shelley, H.G. Wells, and Rudyard Kipling and from America those of Hugo Gernsback, Robert Heinlein, and Isaac Asimov. It is mainly the American Engine of Progress that has dragged us alongside it the way it drags our businesses and stock markets. In spite of these overbearing influences we've managed to develop what I believe is a distinctive voice, a voice — like that of all Canada — wider-ranging than the English one because of our vastnesses east, west, and north; more civil and more free-minded than the American one, and certainly less blood-hungry. This clear and transparent voice echoes in all our arts, in the vastness of our paintings and the civility of our writings, and the writers we have attracted from the U.S. and U.K. have been of like minds.

Listen to the mild hum of our detective fiction and you find good stolid Canadian cops who enjoy a nice summer barbecue — no wild crawdad expeditions here — and our Private Eye, Benny Cooperman, walks no mean streets — you could believe we had no triads or Mafiosi here in sweet Canada — he's a nice Jewish boy who ingests nothing more dangerous than egg-salad sandwiches, and you could bring him home to your mother. Even our vampires are sober citizens who'd hardly make a ripple on a Toronto street. But it is significant that no matter how or whether our identity troubles us, our civil works are enjoyed in other countries and in many foreign translations.

So to look at us, we are not British, we are not American, and yes, we and many other countries appreciate our differences in the ways we live and behave.

But I am writing here not only to celebrate how far we have come but to remind us of the long, long way we have to go. Our bookstore and library shelves may have comfortably absorbed science fiction, but to my mind there are still distinct — and distant — aliens in Canada who are called not Xtkubt and her hatchlings, not detective story or mainstream or essay writers, but Science Fiction Writers. They are Us, more grammatically, We who have written these essays. We may be appreciated and enjoyed in Canada but we are hardly ever published here.

In Canadian publishing, science fiction is the alien that couldn't. Exceptions are the brave souls out west at Tesseract Books, out east at Pottersfield Press, and around the middle, at the magazine *On Spec* (with perhaps at most another fledgling or two) who have dared to bring us SF as Canadian as Molson's Blue. And small presses cannot provide the advertising and other promotional activities that will spread our news.

The few science fiction books that manage to achieve hardcover publication with the larger publishers here are handled with tongs and quickly dropped. Even the SF hardcovers published in the U.S. and imported for distribution by Canadian publishers are not only left to wither but bought in batches at cheap bulk prices that leave writers with at least twenty-five percent lower royalties than their contracts are supposed to guarantee. They might as well have been published in Canada. This spiritual separation began as early as the late nineteenth century, when mainstream writers in Canada as well as Britain, France, and the U.S. were increasingly producing a body of futuristic fiction prophesying the War that actually was to come. Our first Canadian classic, James De Mille's *A Strange Manuscript Found in a Copper Cylinder* (1888), was published in New York, and the work of his compatriot, Grant Allen, appeared in New York and London.

A hundred years later we are forced to depend on American paperback publishers so that Canadians will read us. And they do read us. The Canadian sales of my own American-published books have regularly added up to one fifth of their total in North America, not one tenth as the population figures might indicate, and I dare guess that other writers would find similar numbers. But these sales don't bring us much profit when as a foreign market we get only half of the royalties on American sales, even less than we get on hardback copies. Our stores and even library shelves are crammed with mass market paperbacks bought by millions of people, but except for Harlequins and Bantam Seal reprints almost none of them originate here, and until they do Canadian writers of all literary forms will continue to be cheated.

Another of our difficulties is that science fiction in Canada is plagued with the usual perceptions of the medium as disreputable, to be stowed away on some shelf next to the porn. Even Margaret Atwood's now famous dystopian novel *The Handmaid's Tale* was considered a great risk for her when it was first published in Canada.

Of course we're not alone. This situation has afflicted American writers up to the last thirty years or so — it originated there, with Hugo Gernsback, who in 1926 with his *Modern Electrics* and *Amazing Stories* magazines innocently did more harm to fantastic literature than ten thousand snobs could do, by trammeling it into the rigidity of dependence on science and mechanical gadgetry to the detriment of everything else: plot, character, and the thoughtful development of its ideas.

From the 1920s through the 1940s American writers were trapped in the ghetto of a great cluster of pulps with no hardcover relief until the early 1950s. I was born in the same year as *Amazing Stories*, and I made my first sale there, so I am not going to look down at it, but by 1959 its editor was publishing Gene Wolfe and Ursula Le Guin; more literate magazines like *Galaxy* and *Fantasy & Science Fiction* had appeared along with the hardcover publisher Gnome Press. Soon SF writers were liberated by rapidly expanding paperback production, followed by a great rise in successful hardcover publishing.

This universe has shown no sign of shrinking. But not in Canada. Here there has been no universe to expand. I know it's little use moping and complaining when solutions are so difficult to find for three very difficult problems.

1. There has always been a shortage of money for publishing, especially in a recession, and publishers depend on government grant programs. Almost every Canadian publication that has contained a piece of my work, poetry or prose, has been subsidized. And I am grateful for that too!

2. Our communities are scattered along the edge of the American giant like beads on a string. Even Québec — a self-enclosed community with a population the size of New York City and a vibrantly flourishing European-style culture that gives a hearty welcome to science fiction — is but one more bead where there are no more funds available than in TROC and dependence on French and U.S. markets (in translation) is heavy.

3. Canadian attitudes to genre fiction are cautious. The detective genre has tiptoed into publishing by being neat but not gaudy. In mainstream fiction there is only one wild man — no wild women — and that is Mordechai Richler. *Solomon Gursky Was Here*, with its fantastic overtones, is every bit as *outré* as the best science fiction, and we need to be a little wilder, not fearful and frozen by the vastness of our winter country.

When I was in London recently I was walking along Charing Cross Road to look in all the bookstores. In one big window I saw autographed copies of Iain Banks's new SF novel *Feersum Endjinn* among the mainstream books. Banks writes mainstream novels that are on the edge of science fiction, and science fiction that is over the edge. Yet his and Brian Aldiss's and Michael Moorcock's books have not been pushed into a corner and labeled. As a poet who has often been looked at sideways for writing science fiction, I looked at Banks's book, and though I felt no need to press my nose against the windowpane, I did think it must be bliss to be treated like that.

I know there are science fiction writers who earn their livings producing novels in long series or in pre-owned universes, and who need to be labeled, for their particular readers, but I want a wider span of readers for all of us. Fantastic literature is not only a genre. It has been and always will be the Engine of the Imagination. Sir Philip Sidney said it three hundred and fifty years ago when he defended "Poesie" against the-obligation to produce merely sober descriptions of life:

> Only the poet, disdaining to be tied to any such subjection, lifted up with the vigor of his own invention, doth grow, in effect, into another nature, in making things either better than nature bringeth forth, or, quite anew, forms such as never were in nature, as the heroes, demi-gods, cyclops, chimeras, furies, and such like; so as he goeth hand in hand with nature, not enclosed within the narrow warrant of her gifts, but freely ranging within the zodiac of his own wit.

Though I have no power to solve our problems, I can look for hope:

1. What science fiction writers need most in Canada is mass-market paperback publishing that produces originals and then sells them to publishing houses in the U.S. and abroad. How can we achieve that when publishers must depend on grants? Why can't our publishers use some of their grant money to put out popular literature that might really sell. Who knows? If they tried they might make real money. And become truly Canadian publishers instead of branch plants.

2. Yes, we are lined up on a thin string along the back of the elephant to the south, but with today's communications choices that needn't keep us beads apart forever if we really want our community to prevail. We have hundreds of thousands of readers out there along that string.

3. No, we cannot change peoples' attitudes to science fiction by wishing, but fantastic and visionary literature has always found its due place in the world and there is no reason to give up hope on its place in Canada.

In the end I would say that my attitude towards writing SF in Canada for forty years is one of devotion — in its sense of faithfulness and hope, not Joan Crawford in some movie weepie. There is some hope here, in the increasing number of writers, the growing membership in our SF Canada association, even in the ever lengthening list of Canadians who belong to Science Fiction Writers of America, and especially in this anthology where we can speak our minds. Where I began as one there are now many.

But we must be a publishing community of fantastic literature laying out our feast in our own house. Then we can celebrate more joyfully than ever. For if no one in Canada will publish our work, how can we truly find our places in, how can we really enrich this Canadian Library?

Phyllis Gotlieb, co-editor of Tesseracts[2], *has been writing SF and poetry for over twenty-five years. She is one of the major figures of Canadian science fiction, with books such as* Sunburst *(1964) and* O Master Caliban! *(1976) translated into six languages. Her latest writing is* Heart of Red Iron.

WRITING AND PUBLISHING IN THE MARGINS
Canadian Science Fiction from the Eastern Perimeter
by Lesley Choyce

Somewhere in the 1960s I decided that I was no longer all that interested in the so-called "mainstream." Anything that was too popular was not to be trusted. This went for clothing, music, books, and politics. I was much more interested in what was happening in the wings; I was attracted to all the excitement, freedom, chaos, and energy that existed on the fringe. And it was clear to me that once something or someone became too popular, too commercially successful, there was a dilution process, a watering down and ultimately a demise.

So, as a writer, and ultimately as a publisher, I sure as hell wanted to insure that I stayed hunkered down on the perimeters of mass culture. I could feed off it but I didn't want to fall into the trap of producing something purely for the sake of commercial success.

I had been writing bad SF stories ever since I was twelve years old and first encountered Jules Verne's *Journey to the Centre of the Earth*. I'd seen the movie (with Pat Boone who I thought was pretty cool back then) and then I read the book, dense as it was, and became a real Jules Verne freak. After that came Andre Norton, Harlan Ellison, Asimov, Heinlein, Bradbury, Van Vogt, and the rest. But as I got older I stopped reading those writers — who of course I cynically saw as being "established" and therefore not to be trusted. Instead, I started reading the fringes: Beat poets, strung out novelists, avant garde this and that. My own writing was a mixed bag of SF, fantasy, surrealism, Kerouac rambling prose, and poetry. I successfully avoided commercial success by cleverly not fitting into any single genre and therefore was published rarely and wandered so far around in the headspace of my own fringe that I had almost no audience at all.

Living too close to one of the major centers of all things popular (New York), I realized one day that if I was going to prevail happily on the fringe, then I better relocate. So in 1978 I moved to Nova Scotia. I kept writing weird stories, poems, and novels, but I also thought it was time that I paid my dues as other literary types had by starting my own small press. I called it Pottersfield. A potter's field in medieval times was where all the poor people got buried — thieves, pickpockets, prostitutes, and a lot of artists and writers. The potter's field was invariably a field of clay; eventually someone would dig up the clay which had high calcium content from the dead writers' bones and make something useful out of it.

I would not publish my own stuff because it was important to continue to suffer and scoff at the mainstream publishers who rejected my work. But I could at least come to the aid of other writers: Nova Scotians in particular, Canadians in general — because I had now become one of them, a citizen of the far north fringe, a refugee from the fevered vortex of mass-market American pop culture.

Soon I discovered just how far out on the margin of the page this province of Nova Scotia was. Canada had discovered Can Lit but there was very little room for recognition of Atlantic Canadian Literature (AtCanLit). Pottersfield Press attempted to round up Atlantic writers and publish them regularly, for it was important to me that we showed the world (the one which preferred to stay tuned to American sitcoms) that we were a bunch of wildly creative Yahoos who would not be easily labeled. No more lobster trap stories, no more tales by old geezers sitting on fishing wharves.

In 1980, the offbeat introduction to volume two of *The Pottersfield Portfolio* began, "The year is 2081. A young man from Inverness, Cape Breton sits nervously in the departure terminal. Canada's space colonization program is in full swing. The trip itself won't be so bad but the waiting around can be hell." That year, I think I had "discovered" Cape Breton and Newfoundland and realized what intense and marginalized islands they were. Great writing and large living were byproducts of being marginalized. I knew for sure that literature (and someday space travel, too) was going to be whole lot more interesting once we got more Cape Bretoners and Newfoundlanders involved.

Like Pat Boone, crawling down into the supposed bowels of the earth, I wanted to go further down and explore more of the living and dead literature of this region. I was beginning to discover that, to a great extent, "literary" writing meant boring writing — stuff you would read because it was supposed to be good for you. If possible, I would avoid becoming a press that published boring literary writers and try to concentrate on writing that was challenging, weird, expressive, anarchic, active, and adventurous. The *Portfolio* published a number of science fiction short stories by non-legendary contemporary writers like Jon Welland and Gary Eikenberry and Wade Kenny. Like me, they were operating in their own peripheral vacuums; we were all still scribbling madly on the fringes of the Canadian page.

I would seek out whomever was out there and encourage them, usher them into print. My nose had me pointed exclusively to the present and the future until I stumbled one day across a guy named John Bell, holed up in the Archives of the Killam Library at Dalhousie University. He wrote SF, he was publishing a 'zine called *Borealis,* and, in the world of subcult SF, he was light years ahead of me in knowledge. I was impressed and maybe a little in awe until he asked me if I knew anything about the *tradition* of science fiction and fantasy writing in Atlantic Canada?

I wanted to explain that I wasn't *into* tradition. I was a nontraditionalist, ya know. I wanted to know where we were going, not where we've been. But why not put them both together? he suggested, blow everybody's mind by proving that Atlantic Canada has been a maniacal hotbed of outrageous SF and F writing for over a hundred years!

In the end we started working on a project. John and I both saw our region as being "marginalized." I had personally always felt marginalized, so my identity expanded to embrace this place. We lived in a part of the world, a part of the country, pretty well ignored and taken for granted by the rest. And we were on the edge of the continent. There would be this anthology (the second or third Canadian SF anthology ever to be published) called *Visions from the Edge.* In the introduction, John writes with a big honest chip on his shoulder, "if Canada as a whole suffers from a marked colonial mentality which depreciates our national culture, the Atlantic region is in an even more disadvantaged position. At this juncture the nation at least has only one inferiority complex to contend with, namely that involving the United States. In the region, however, we have to maintain our identity in the face of two homogenizing, dominating centers: the United States and Upper Canada." Boy, we sure didn't want to be dominated or homogenized back then. The book appeared in 1981 and John probably deserves the credit for including writers I was only vaguely familiar with.

Now I was already friendly with some of my newfound compatriot marginalized writers in the region who were alive and writing science fiction. Spider Robinson, for example, was another immigrant from New York. If I understand it correctly, one day Spider gave up his security job guarding a big hole somewhere near the city, started writing science fiction under the influence of marijuana and coffee, and soon moved to the Annapolis Valley of Nova Scotia. H.R. Percy, a respected novelist living in Granville Ferry, had produced a dynamite alternate history about a Francophone North America, and William Kotzwinkle (later of *E.T.* novel notoriety) was living in the woods in New Brunswick. Elizabeth Mann Borgese (daughter of Thomas Mann) was a famous oceanographer near Halifax who was teaching dogs to play classical music on the piano and had been publishing SF stories since the 1950s.

But for me, the real eye openers where the old dead dudes — the Atlantic writers who had come before us, writing from the margins for (oh no!) American pop culture. In fact, many of them had made very successful careers writing for the U.S. pulp magazines. Lucy Maud Montgomery had written pop stories about contact with the spirit world because she allegedly needed the money. Francis Flagg of Halifax contributed to *Amazing Stories, Weird Tales,* and *Astounding* back in the 1920s and 1930s. We included in *Visions* a harrowing tale of encounter with an alien crystaline entity that would put *Star Trek* writers to shame. It seemed that a whole pile of Atlantic Canadian writers had an end-of-the-world story with a different twist. A lot of these stories involved submerging New York or evaporating Los Angeles, which I found personally uplifting.

Alexander Graham Bell's lawyer, a chap named H. Percy Blanchard, lived in Ellershouse, Nova Scotia, and he had produced a strange, obscure novella called *After the Cataclysm,* wherein the polarity of the earth changes and the planet tilts sideways so that the area around the Great Lakes ends up with a Mediterranean climate. A man from the past awakens in this post-holocaust future to discover an androgynous society full of beautiful women who aren't the slightest bit interested in sex. We decided to include the whole thing in the anthology.

Simon Newcomb, one of the world's preeminent astronomers, was from Wallace, Nova Scotia. In 1903, he too had fictionalized where we were going in his aptly titled story, "The End of the World," wherein he documents how a comet coming our way does in the planet, despite the fact that we're warned ahead of time by kindly beings on Mars who are sending Morse code messages to earth with giant lights, telling us, "Hey, look out. There's this big thing headed straight towards you." In this particular future, the earth had become a dull place, lacking the spunk to meet the challenge. For, as Newcomb wrote of it, "almost every scientific discovery had been made thousands of years before, and inventions for their application had been so perfected that it seemed as if no real improvement could be made in them."

Sometimes, however, Atlantic Canadian writers envisioned a future humanity that was up to the challenge of total annihilation. My personal favorite comes from one Laurence Manning of St. John, New Brunswick and a founding member of the American Rocket Society who, in 1934, published a story called "The Living Galaxy" in Hugo Gernsback's *Wonder Stories* for mass American consumption. I think it must have been a heyday of SF enthusiasm when each writer tried to outdo the next with larger insect mutations, more bizarre alien encounters or scientific convolutions. Manning had read stories set fifty years in the future, or a hundred years in the future, or even a thousand years in the future. He then decided he would outdo them all. He would make the leap, a leap of faith beyond all the other pulp SF writers who peered ahead. As he states in the introduction to his tale, "the date is very far into the future — more than 500,000,000 years and the sun, Earth, Mars, Venus and other things have long since died." (He doesn't say how they died; they just died.) The story is a real lesson about envisioning the future from the 1930s. People live to be a hundred million years old — "You expect to live forever, except for risk of accidents." Strangely enough, in this opening scene, Manning notes that they are still using *books* in the classrooms of the far future.

But it's Manning's leap that is so exciting, and the scope of this Maritimer's vision is stupendous. The problem in the story is this: there's a galaxy (and he doesn't just mean an old Ford) about to collide with our galaxy and it will mess things up for good. So a heroic scientist named Bzonn has to build really big space ships made from scooped out planets (it takes 2100 years) and they shoot off at "100,000 miles a second" on a trip that takes a mere four million years. ("It is regrettable that the colonization idea was not considered until a million years had elapsed.") In the end, this noble crusade is a success and the living galaxy does not gobble up home our galaxy. It's safe to say that Manning is a little heavy handed with the ending, but then he was writing for the American mass market and blasting things was a popular way of solving problems back then.

Visions from the Edge marked my coming of age in the world of Canadian SF. I went on to write a book of SF stories, *The Dream Auditor* (Ragweed Press) and edit an anthology of Canadian fiction set in the future, *Ark of Ice* (Pottersfield). But I gained a healthy respect for all those writers, alive or dead, who had created their works from the margins, for I was now one of them. I tried to figure what aspect of Manning's wonderful and outrageous story was peculiarly Maritime. Maybe it was the resourcefulness of Bzonn, the sense of self-reliance. Those are qualities that still persist here in my Canadian Far East.

Perhaps in the future, writers like me, trying to get off the beaten track, will set up shop on the dark side of the moon or on a cosy asteroid hollowed out for human habitation. But for the twentieth century, the farther shores, places like Lawrencetown Beach in Nova Scotia or Tofino or even Iqaluit up north, might be the perfect vantage points from which to challenge mainstream North American culture. I like to think that the best of the really inventive science fiction will find its way into print from the small presses and by writers who themselves are not living the life at the center of the madness of contemporary urban life. And I'm hoping that all those visions from the various edges of our civilization, geographically or otherwise, will find voice and ultimately engender an audience, that forever-audience of seekers for whom the so-called "best" of popular fiction is never quite satisfying enough.

Lesley Choyce was born in New Jersey in 1951 but moved to Canada and became a citizen when he was a young man. He teaches part-time at Dalhousie University, runs Pottersfield Press, and has forty books in print. He lives in a two-hundred-year-old farm house at Lawrencetown Beach overlooking the ocean. He also hosts a TV show in Halifax called Choyce Words.

SOLARIS
Twenty Years of Québec Science Fiction
by Joël Champetier

The birth of Québec science fiction, as an organized cultural community, is generally recognized as having occurred in September 1974 with the founding of a fanzine called *Requiem*, created by some college students under the direction of Norbert Spehner, a French teacher at the Cégep Édouard-Montpetit in Longueuil.[1] *Requiem* would later become *Solaris*.

We must first of all acknowledge that Canadian and Québec science fiction written in French certainly existed prior to the founding of *Requiem*. We need not exhume such works of folklore as *Mon voyage à la lune* by Napoléon Aubin (1839) or the popular serials of the mid-twentieth century, for it is easy to find a number of SFQ books in the 1960s and 1970s, apparently written by authors who were conscious of writing SF. One might cite *La Cité dans l'oeuf* by Michel Tremblay (1969), *Si la Bombe m'était contée* by Yves Thériault, or the trilogy *Compagnons du soleil* by Monique Corriveau (1976). Furthermore, many authors who are still active today did not wait for *Requiem/Solaris* to publish, or published without necessarily expressing a desire to be part of the magazine or a community. This was certainly the case with Esther Rochon when she published *En hommage aux araignées* (1974); Jean-François Somain (or Somcynsky), the author of a diverse body of work; Jacques Brossard, the author of *Le Métamorphaux* (1974); and Alain Bergeron, the author of *Un été de Jessica* (1978), a novel which was also serialized in *Le Soleil*, Québec City's daily newspaper.

But all of these were isolated, almost sporadic events. *Requiem/Solaris* was to be the first structural nucleus for an attempt at a genuine literary community freely modeled on the anglophone example, with its magazines and fanzines, its anthologies and collections, its annual conventions and literary prizes.

The first issue of *Requiem* took the form of a typewritten fanzine of amateur construction, with a rather naive cover illustration. However, it had two characteristics which already distinguished it from most of the anglophone fanzines flooding the United States. First, the print quality was excellent, indicating the care that had gone into its production. Second, it already contained fiction. We know that, on the English-speaking side, the fanzine is mainly a forum for discussion of the genre and the community. Very little fiction is published, doubtless because fiction is properly served by a large and diversified publishing industry. As the situation in Québec was definitely not so favorable, the young team immediately realized that it was practically its duty to provide a vehicle where writers interested in the genre could publish. The articles, criticism, and fiction that went into the new magazine at the time thus represented an initial establishment of effective contact with a potential readership.

Naturally, the first steps of a newborn are always somewhat wobbly. Those old issues now prompt a smile of condescension. The humor is at times heavy-handed, and the fiction at a very amateur level. But that was to be expected: Norbert Spehner and the rest of the team started from scratch; they had to invent from the ground up. However, improvement in terms of both layout and content was constant and rapid. Between 1974 and 1978, *Requiem* featured the first published work of those who were to become the major authors of SFQ: Jean-Pierre April, René Beaulieu, Michel Bélil, Jean Dion, Esther Rochon, Daniel Sernine, Élisabeth Vonarburg. And for most of them, that initial appearance took the form of reportage, articles, and letters — a reminder that SFQ writers are often analysts and critics. Furthermore, almost all of these authors are still very active today, particularly April, Rochon, Sernine, and Vonarburg.

Requiem became *Solaris* in the summer of 1979, with issue number 28. The magazine was already receiving grants from the Canada Council and was continuing to evolve toward semi-professional status. One sign of this maturity was that it ceased to be the almost exclusive creation of just one person. Norbert Spehner retained his position and continued to do an enormous amount of work, but he was now seconded by Élisabeth Vonarburg as literary editor, and shortly thereafter by Luc Pomerleau as head of the comic strip section. Humor and familiarity did not disappear, but found a more appropriate register, becoming discreet when called for by the content.

One cannot underestimate the importance of the groundbreaking work done by Élisabeth Vonarburg during her eleven years as literary editor of *Solaris*. She was responsible for publication of the work of a second generation of SFQ writers: Jean Barbe,

Annick Perrot-Bishop, Camille Bouchard, Joël Champetier, Michel Lamontagne, Marie-Claire Lemaire, Stanley Péan, Francine Pelletier, Claude-Michel Prévost, Marc Provencher, and later Harold Côté, Stéphane Langlois, Yves Meynard, and Jean-Louis Trudel. This forum for creativity and training was nourished and encouraged by an annual literary award open to young authors. Initially called the Prix Dagon, it became the Prix Solaris in 1981, and for some years was extended to all Francophone authors, both Canadian and European.

All of these changes to *Solaris* were the reflection of a ferment passing through the entire sFQ community. The year 1979 saw the first sFQ convention, Boréal, organized in Chicoutimi under the direction of Élisabeth Vonarburg, as well as the birth of two important magazines: *Pour ta belle gueule d'ahuri*, established by a group of students from Sainte-Foy college in Québec City, and *imagine . . .* , founded by former contributors and authors of *Requiem/Solaris*, Jean-Marc Gouanvic, Esther Rochon, Claudomir Sauvé, Jean-Pierre April, and Michel Bélil. Although short-lived, *Pour ta belle gueule d'ahuri* remains one of the four major sFQ magazines, because of the graphics quality of its six issues and primarily because it brought together a nucleus in Québec City which has since remained active, with certain members now on the *Solaris* team. As for *imagine . . .* , not only does it still exist, but like *Solaris* it has established itself in its field as one of the central magazines of La Francophonie. *L'Année de la science-fiction et du fantastique québécois* (Le Passeur/Logiques) is also an excellent periodical which has been inventorying and analyzing all sFQ production since 1984.

In this connection, if *Solaris* had ceased to evolve after issue 28, it would still be considered one of the finest magazines of La Francophonie. There was in fact no major change for a number of years, apart from a refinement of the project. Spurred on by competition, the magazine gradually became more embellished, comic strips took on more importance, and the editorial content became increasingly solid. The pool of contributors formed or prompted by its existence provided the magazine with dynamic, varied content, giving shape to an objective clearly stated in issue 45: "to give as faithful an account as possible of developments in the field of SF in Québec." And not only in Québec, one might add, since *Solaris* continued to report on what was happening in Europe and the English-speaking world. For example, over its twenty years, *Solaris* has published almost seventy-five interviews with an international array of French- and English-language authors, artists, comic strip writers, and publishers, from Brian Aldiss and Jean-Pierre April to Gene Wolfe and Berni Wrightson. This period reached its peak in 1982 with the publication of a fiftieth issue, a fiction special featuring the authors discovered by the magazine.

But this issue was also an occasion for taking stock and for reflection. After all his years of volunteer service at the helm, Norbert Spehner took his well-earned rest after issue 52. Co-ordinated by Élisabeth Vonarburg, a team comprised of the core contributors took over the reins: Joël Champetier, Claude Janelle, Charles Montpetit, Germain Plante, Luc Pomerleau, Daniel Sernine, and Élisabeth Vonarburg. Over time, Mario Giguère, Francine Pelletier, Marc Pageau, Gabriel Rochette, Raymond Côté, Fabien Ménard, Julie Martel, Simon Dupuis, and Yves Meynard were added, or filled vacancies. These contributors were sometimes transient, sometimes permanent. There was no dramatic break in the magazine's direction, but this rather abrupt editorial change resulted in a certain indecision, with the immediate consequence of a delay in publication and notable variations in the layout (such as four modifications to the cover-page dummy from issue 53 to issue 61). This proved no obstacle to the celebration of the magazine's tenth anniversary in issue 58, demonstrating that the new team had managed to get up to cruising speed all the same.

But they were cruising on a rather turbulent sea. The equipment side of things suffered a blow in issue 60 with the move to dot printer typography after the breakdown of the typesetter that had previously been used. Faithful readers had to wait for two years, until issue 73, before the magazine adopted laser composition. Luc Pomerleau also replaced Élisabeth Vonarburg as co-ordinator and Claude Janelle left the magazine. Despite a few jolts to the layout, the magazine underwent no major transformations, apart from appearing to consolidate its editorial consistency. In its critical discourse, *Solaris* was increasingly less concerned with full coverage of sf in all of its manifestations — something which had become impossible — in favor of a more thorough exploration of the subjects it treated.

Solaris came of age around 1989, with Luc Pomerleau as co-ordinator and Élisabeth Vonarburg as literary editor. This was evident with the publication of issue 87, a fifteenth anniversary special which, in addition to a large fiction section and a new logo (the one still used today), offered a number of testimonials and self-assessments on Solaris and sfq in general. A great deal of progress had been made since Élisabeth Vonarburg's lament twelve years earlier (in Requiem No. 15) at the scarcity of sf in Québec and her puzzlement at the apparent aversion of Québec authors to adopting speculative fiction as a literary genre. Since the mid-1970s, the trajectory of sfq has more or less followed that of Solaris. This is not to say that Solaris has done it all, but simply that it seems to have been a relatively accurate reflection of the phenomenon it has observed and promoted.[2] Many of the community's vital components took shape over the years, allowing sfq to spread through other channels: numerous fanzines sprang up and died, and collections specifically devoted to sf were born, one of them being Chroniques du Future, at Préambule, edited by Norbert Spehner, who published the Aurores boréales anthologies, most of which consisted of texts that had appeared in Solaris. Another formative activity was the annual presentation of the Grand Prix de la science-fiction et du fantastique québécois, accompanied by a large monetary award: this helped to make sfq slightly better known to the literary establishment, despite the latter's relative indifference.

Another, doubtless even more important sign of maturity is that Solaris has made its way to a one hundredth issue, then to its twentieth anniversary, and is still continuing, having absorbed the constant reduction in grants, two new taxes, two changes to the literary editorship (Joël Champetier replaced Élisabeth Vonarburg and has in turn just been replaced by Yves Meynard), a change in publication frequency (the magazine is now a quarterly), and the departure of Luc Pomerleau, who has been replaced at the crucial co-ordinator's position by Joël Champetier. Solaris' pool of contributors is extensive enough and its infrastructure solid enough for it not to be overly affected by personnel changes. Apart from all aesthetic, editorial, or financial considerations, this is one of the most significant distinctions between the fanzine, often the ephemeral creation of a single individual, and the so-called professional magazine, where, without denying the individual contribution of each collaborator, it is the overall result that matters — what the reader is given to read.

In a way, even though the magazine is now in its twenty-first year of publication, there has been no fundamental change in its editorial mission since the first *Requiem. Solaris* exists for and through SFQ. It has been said that if English-speaking SF were to disappear, its 'fandom' would continue to function as if nothing had happened. If — God help us — SFQ were to disappear, *Solaris* would lose all reason for existence. On the other hand, if *Solaris* had never existed, clearly the present situation of SFQ would be very different. In what way? Let's just say that the sad state of most European fandoms, where the local SF has not been given stable support, gives one reason to reflect . . . And so, long live *Solaris*!

NOTES

1   Strictly speaking, it would be more accurate to speak of *French-Canadian* science fiction, since the Francophone science fiction community in Canada includes certain Francophones outside Québec. Furthermore, in order not to burden this article with complex (and sometimes controversial) terminology, readers are asked to accept the acronym SFQ as covering such various manifestations of imaginative literature as SF, fantasy, horror, and weird tales.

2   The author of this history has drawn liberally from two articles originally published in *Solaris*: "Historique de la SFQ" by Daniel Sernine (*Solaris* No. 79) and "Splendeurs et misères d'une revue de SF" by Mike Archaw (*Solaris* No. 87), both of which are highly recommended to readers who wish to further investigate the history of *Solaris* and of SFQ in general.

Joël Champetier has published some twenty short stories, as well as nine novels for adults and young adults in the fields of science fiction, fantasy, and horror fantasy. He has been a member of Solaris since 1983 and the co-ordinator since 1992.

A SHORT HISTORY OF THE SCIENCE FICTION MAGAZINE *imagine...*

by Marc Lemaire

FOREWORD

No literary or paraliterary genre more tellingly bears witness to the passage into modernity (or post-modernity) which Québec intellectuals have wrought in their cultural journals than science fiction. And no magazine better illustrates the process than *imagine* . . . As Andrée Fortin questions, then answers in *Passage de la modernité:*

> Cultural renewal? What appears at first glance as a drift in genres and concerns converges, here again, into a fragmented, pluralistic subject, immersed in daily experience, which is at most a witness to events (I am tempted to say a fellow traveler), an actor, but on the stage of daily life. The sense that one's actions are pathetic, or simply the suspicion that one's words and deeds are ineffectual, yields humor or fantasy.
>
> New genres dominate: literary journals shift from literature to paraliterature and the boundaries between literature and the visual arts become blurred.
>
> In the seventies, therefore, the writers of SF, fantasy and comic strips shared with their feminist contemporaries a sense of humor and a collective existence with its daily highs and lows, which they felt pressed to explain. This did not prevent them from aiming high and seeking to expand their group as much as possible across Québec and even the continent. [1]

At the same time, the cultural ferment surrounding *imagine* . . . has been a reflection of the politically and socially fragmented post-modern era.

THAT'S ALL SCIENCE FICTION!

From its first issue in 1979, *imagine* . . . billed itself as a magazine of Québec science fiction, without ever defining SF (we shall return later to the significance of the qualifier "Québec"). As Jean-Marc Gouanvic wrote in the first issue of the magazine:

Thus, a third science fiction magazine, *imagine* . . . (the title is intended as an invitation) is born . . . .The imagination needs space to expand; we mean to provide this space. The magazine will be open to all the currents which make up the genre of "science fiction," from hard science to more speculative or avant-garde quests. No tendency is barred. *imagine* . . . will also be open to science fiction from around the world.

Clearly, the Québec and francophone readership of 1979 was sufficiently well versed to accept the "science fiction" label without explanation. The content of the first issue did not further enlighten novice readers as to any definition of the science fiction the magazine intended to publish: it included a New Thing piece, in which the text's unusual shape reflects the theme, a speculative fiction, and the first instalment of the novel *L'Epuisement du soleil* by award-winning Québec SF writer Esther Rochon, strongly marked by the social and political climate of the Bourassa era. (Rochon began working on this novel around 1963, completed it in early 1980, and published it during the post-referendum period. Each period is reflected to some degree in the novel.)

What was clearer was the magazine's focus on fiction, in terms of both quality and quantity (and French-language fiction at that). Aside from a short article on the first Québec SF convention, the only non-fiction piece dealt with the invasion of Europe by American SF in the 1950s! *imagine* . . . had set out to prove that Québec and French-language SF was as good as the U.S. product. Québec's third SF magazine thus delimited its field before defining it. The time was the period leading up to the first referendum on independence.

The second issue, dated December 1979, maintained the same philosophy, welcoming all varieties of science fiction. This issue contained the first of many stories by Jean-Pierre April which would appear in the magazine, as well as an article by April tackling, at this early date, the "prospects for Québec SF," in which he condemned the pernicious influence of the American writers whose work dominated all markets. April marked out three directions for the development of Québec science fiction: semi-fantastic literature with roots in the oral tradition; science fiction stemming from the Quiet Revolution of the 1960s and Québec's opening up to the world; and a syncretic science fiction produced by a combination of genres and styles, which April would discuss at length and write, but which hardly anyone would practice.

Benoit Breton's first text, "L'3trang3 m3caniqu3 d3 monsi3ur mort3l," appeared in the same issue. Written by a narrator whose hands had been amputated and whose typewriter replaced all e's with 3's, it subverted typographical conventions and refused to stay within any margin. *imagine* . . . was (re)inventing science fiction, reshaping the form to reflect the idea, championing revolt against tradition. The period was the end of the punk rock era in music but a decade before cyberpunk.

The magazine never did define science fiction. That did not prevent it and every other SF magazine, not to mention every SF author, from attempting at some point to lay claim to having been the first to publish or to write SF in Québec, no doubt in a bid for legitimacy.[2] However, in science fiction, what counts is the future, not the past.

In its next few issues, *imagine* . . . broadened its scope to embrace cinema and illustration. In 1981, the magazine announced that it would henceforth be subsidized by the Canada Council and Québec's department of cultural affairs. *imagine* . . . had entered the circle of recognized cultural magazines.

THEORETICAL DEBATES

Against this background, *imagine* . . . decided to publish an annual issue every September devoted to theoretical work on science fiction, under the title *Regards sur la science-fiction et les littératures de l'imaginaire* (Perspectives on Science Fiction and Imaginary Worlds). It was not surprising that a magazine put out by scholars from various disciplines should end up on more theoretical ground, although its vocation remained to promote a literature of greater vigor and greater confidence in its own potential. In the editorial to No. 17, editor Jean-Marc Gouanvic declared:

> If there is a magazine which offers its readers fictional texts of quality and quantity, it is *imagine* . . . But that is not

enough: a magazine must promote discussion in its particular field, publish critical studies. This is imperative if we are to establish and win recognition for science fiction in Québec and the French-speaking world.

The editorial board was seeking to legitimize what was considered a minor literary genre, viewed always through the prism of cinematographic images (*Star Wars* and *Star Trek* were never far from mind) and preconceived ideas (science fiction was still found in the supernatural section on bookstore shelves). *imagine* . . . therefore devoted entire issues to the acts of various SF congresses held in Québec (No. 25 and 28), to studies funded by the Social Sciences and Humanities Research Council of Canada, and to excerpts from M.A. and Ph.D. theses (No. 53).

TRAVELING THROUGH TIME

There was Québec literature based on imaginary worlds long before *imagine* . . . appeared on the scene. For example, Jules-Paul Tardivel's *Pour la Patrie*, a utopia set in Québec in the year 1945, was published in 1895, and Ulric Barthes' *Simila Similibus* was published in 1916. Science fiction serials appeared in the 1960s. It would therefore be simplistic to date the birth of Québec SF from 1974 or 1979.

To prove the point, Michel Bélil contributed a series of articles on the history of science fiction in Québec to the magazine. The first, dealing with fantastic literature in Québec in the nineteenth century, appeared in *imagine* . . . No. 6, accompanied by Wenceslas-Eugène Dick's classic story, "Une Histoire de loup-garou." Jean-Marc Gouanvic suggested the following parallel in this same issue:

As we read the article by Michel Bélil, we are struck by the distance between that era and our own (and the story by W.E. Dick is significant in this connection), between fantastic literature, a popular genre rooted in a rural society deeply influenced by religious belief, and science fiction, which has accompanied urbanization in Québec and replaced faith in the beyond with non-metaphysical beliefs. Bélil calls for a "new fantastic literature." It is our view that science fiction, in the broadest sense, can be that literature.

Bélil's first article was followed in subsequent years by others containing increasingly detailed analyses, as he proceeded to compile past examples of the genre (No. 22, 31, 49).

The magazine printed other examples of French Canadian SF from the nineteenth century: "Mon voyage à la Lune" by Napoléon Aubin (1839) in No. 8-9 and in No. 19 "La Tête de Saint-Jean Baptiste, ou Légende pour nos arrières-petits-neveux, en 1980," written by Wenceslas-Eugène Dick in 1880. "Lettre écrite de la Lune" by Louis-Joseph Doucet (1911) was published in *imagine . . .* No. 16 and "Les Hommes sphériques," from Louis Champagne's serialized novel *Les Aventures futuristes de deux savants canadiens-français* (1949), appeared in No. 26.

NATIONALISM IN SEARCH OF QUÉBEC IDENTITY IN *imagine . . .*

The author Jean-Pierre April exerted the greatest influence on the magazine's literary identity. His classic short story, "Le Vol de la Ville" (The Theft of the City), published in *imagine . . .* No. 3, dealt with what would become one of his favorite themes: Canadian and Québécois specificity as expressed in science fiction. The city of the story's title is Montréal. April also contributed a major satirical text to No. 7, "Le fantôme du forum" (The Phantom of the Forum), which lampooned Québecers' favorite pastimes: hockey and beer.

No. 7 introduced what would become a common theme among contributors to *imagine . . .*, Québec nationalism. In his article "Vive le Québec libre! Le séparatisme québécois dans la science-fiction de langue anglaise" (Vive le Québec libre! Québec Separatism in English-language Science Fiction), Dalhousie University archivist John Bell observes that English Canada has always been concerned about U.S. domination and the national unity issue. He suggests that four events in Québec politics have left an impression on English Canadian literature: De Gaulle's "Vive le Québec libre" speech of 1967, the October crisis of 1970, the PQ victory of 1976, and the 1980 referendum (which had just been lost). Perhaps to even things out, in No. 19 (1983) Bell contributed an annotated bibliography of science fiction and fantastic literature written by English-speaking writers born or living in Québec. Donald Kingsbury, author of *Courtship Rite*, is undoubtedly the best known.

In No. 40 (June 1987) *imagine* . . . published "Un pas de plus" (One More Step) by Geoffrey Edwards, a story about an independent Québec which has become a major player in the space race and in which men and women are equal.

A regular feature entitled *Planète Québec, lectures de la* SFQ (Planet Québec: Readings in Québec SF) began running in *imagine* . . . No. 18. As the name indicates, it was devoted to criticism of Québec science fiction. Written by Jean Barbe and Marc Provencher, the column was distinguished by its literary quality. The two authors cast their literary criticism in the form of narrative: they would tell a story while criticizing the stories of other writers.

In opposition to the hegemonic U.S. model, *imagine* . . . opted (perhaps involuntarily) for distinctly Québec or francophone SF (with rare exceptions), reflecting the upheavals on the national unity front over the years, during a period when barriers were shifting or breaking down. In calling itself a "Québec science fiction magazine," *imagine* . . . indicated both the origin and goal of the literature it sought to promote.

THE NORTH: THE FIRST GREAT CANADIAN MYTH?

"The North," editor Jean-Marc Gouanvic wrote in *imagine* . . . No. 4, "may be the 'new frontier' of our America: James Bay, technological prowess, the quest for the top of the world (as in Jules Verne), individual and collective adventure, an unknown land (imagine what may be concealed intact under the thickness of the ice), the ancestral land of the Inuit, and much more. In short, there is no need to venture fictionally to stars as yet inaccessible when we have the North close at hand." *imagine* . . . No. 10 was devoted to the North, the unknown land of ice, at once real and imaginary, which all Canadians imagine and fear, the land which has inspired so many fantastic tales. Did not the first great Québec hero in *Maria Chapdelaine* die of cold in the terrible North?

In "KébéKéleKtrik," Jean-Pierre April compellingly intertwines the conquest of the North with the unstated theme of Québec's technological success. This technological conquest embraces an aspiration of the Québec people but also its fear of failure, of defeat at the hands of Nature or inertia. April's short story, built on the first great Québec myth, expresses the full force of his Québec brand of science fiction.

ONE PICTURE IS WORTH A THOUSAND WORDS

Science fiction admits fanciful images of the unknown spawned by the author's fantasies. *imagine* . . . soon realized the power of the image in the realm of the imagination and opened its pages to creative visual artists. Illustration really entered the magazine in *imagine* . . . No. 6, which included three portfolios presenting the work of Pierre D. Lacroix, Mario Giguère, and Richard Coulombe. In No. 21, prompted perhaps by the fact that artist Catherine Saouter-Caya had become Editor-in-Chief, the magazine's editorial board launched the "Imagitextes" series, in which authors wrote texts based on an artist's drawing. This idea gave birth to a tradition which was carried on in No. 33/34, an oversize issue containing illustrated stories (Histoires en emages), and in an oversize special issue for which authors were asked to write the beginning and end of a novel based on three illustrations published in May 1994 under the title *Décollages* and the subtitle *récits imcomplets*. Literary experimentation was thus wedded to illustration. In No. 56, the magazine also began publishing SF photography.

FOREIGN SHORES

Although *imagine* . . . declared itself open to science fiction from around the world in its first issue, it more realistically confined itself to French-language SF, of which it quickly became one of the leading vehicles. In the 1990s French, Belgian, Swiss, and other writers, lacking attractive vehicles in their own countries in which to publish their work, have often appeared in the pages of *imagine* . . .

Numbers 13 (devoted to science fiction from France), 30 (the French-speaking world), 54 (Belgium), and 63 (Switzerland) are anthologies of the best science fiction writing from those countries. The magazine subsequently established a tradition of publishing at least one French-language science fiction text from outside Québec in each issue. Local writers benefited from the opportunity to compare their imagination and craft to that of foreign authors.

In No. 16, *imagine* . . . launched the *Échos de sFonie* feature, devoted to international science fiction writing, focusing on French-speaking countries.

ALTERNATE WORLDS AND UTOPIAS

Jean-Pierre April's marvelous story "Canadian Dream" in No. 14 is an example of an alternate world, based on an alteration to an historical event: what if Jacques Cartier had discovered Canada in Cameroon? In another example of the genre, Pierre Corbeil's "La Concession" (No. 55-58) asks, what if France had conquered North America?

Utopian literature is undoubtedly one of the oldest forms of writing based on imaginary worlds; it has tantalized humankind since the Epic of Gilgamesh (3000 BC). Closer to our own age, *imagine* . . . has devoted many pages to more recent utopias, publishing a number of utopian short stories and critical texts.

Women have fascinated and perplexed some contributors to the magazine. *imagine* . . . has published both studies and short stories on the theme of women and feminism, from Guy Bouchard's feminist utopias to a study of power relations in fiction by women writers of sf. *imagine* . . . has also published pastiches, sf radio plays and sf short stories for children. It has put out issues devoted to eroticism, technology, childlike fantasies, the Middle Ages, and the bonsai (as theme and form). The best writers were invited to contribute texts to these issues based on a single theme, which served as both inspiration and guide. *imagine* . . . also attempted an issue on the typical Québécois hero Roger Tremblay. That attempt failed, perhaps because nobody was sure what a Québécois really is.

THE SEVENTH CONTINENT

To stimulate literary creativity, *imagine* . . . created its own literary award, the "Septième continent" (Seventh Continent), which is awarded each year to the best manuscript submitted to the jury. The winner receives a stipend and the winning text is published in a European magazine. The sextant was chosen to symbolize the award, both as a navigational aid towards the future and in tribute to the explorers who used the instrument to discover the New World. The first winner was Jean-Pierre April's "La Survie en rose." In the ten years of its existence, the award has gone to important writers from Québec, French Canada, France, and Belgium.

EPILOGUE: TOWARDS POST-MODERNISM

A massive influx of new authors — that is how the magazine's literary editor, Jean-Marc Gouanvic, described the scene in 1986 (No. 37). Over the previous year, he had seen many new Québec SF writers appear in the pages of the magazine. In order to thrive, a literary genre such as SF needs original ideas, the injection of new blood, the emergence of writers who can tell the same stories differently. The cyberpunk movement did just that: in harnessing the potential of computers to create its own universe, it continued the exploration of the virtual realities which the hippie generation before it had explored with drugs and the post-industrial generation with time machines and vessels traveling faster than the speed of light.

imagine . . . therefore had a duty to support the development of new Canadian and Québec talent and to welcome young writers to its pages. No. 37 marked a turning point in this respect, but the process had begun earlier and would continue with the work of Agnès Guitard, Jean-Louis Trudel (a Franco-Ontarian), Bertrand Bergeron, Pierre Corbeil, Victor Corbeil, Victor Frigério (of Toronto), Jean Pettigrew, Annick Perrot-Bishop (of Newfoundland), Claude-Michel Prévost (of British Columbia), Pierre Sormany, and others. During its fifteen years of existence, *imagine* . . . has often sought its contributors outside the confines of science fiction:

Jean Marcel, Paul Zumthor, André Berthiaume, Evelyne Bernard, Claude D'Astous, Pierre Bec, Marie-José Thériault, Roger Des Roches, and Jeanne Terracini are all non-science fiction writers who agreed to try their hand at the genre.

Modern science fiction is a monster, said Jean-Pierre April (No. 61). A monster which, over the past 20 years, has devoured everything in its path, feeding on influences of all kinds, modern and ancient, without regard to predefined generic limits. From its first issue, *imagine* . . . advocated breaking down the barriers between science fiction sub-genres. Later, it challenged the barriers between all types of literature based on imaginary worlds; hence its current subtitle, "science fiction et littératures de l'imaginaire." Now, like science fiction itself, the magazine is progressing towards post-modern fragmentation. *imagine* . . .'s era has been a time of anarchy and uncertainty, play and irony, doing rather then being. In this respect, *imagine* . . . is a creature of its time.

 NOTES

1 Andrée Fortin, *Passage de la modernité. Les intellectuels québécois et leurs revues* (Montréal Presses de l'université Laval, 1993): 336, 343.

2 On this interesting subject, see Guy Bouchard, "L'Image de la SF au Québec: 1960-1984," *imagine* . . . 65. Bouchard discusses the dispute among Québec SF magazines as to which was the first on the scene and slips in a claim for himself as the first (or almost the first) writer of science fiction in Québec.

3 Guy Bouchard, "Disruptions," *imagine* . . . 45 (October 1988) and "Andropolis" (winner of the Prix Septième continent, 1989), *imagine* . . . 48 (June 1989); André Trognée, "Flash 17," *imagine* . . . 52 (June 1990). *imagine* . . . 31 was devoted in large part to utopias and dystopias, including an article entitled "L'Utopie en domaine français au Canada: aperçu historique." See also Guy Bouchard, "Les Utopies féministes et la science-fiction," *imagine* . . . 44. *imagine* . . . 55 (September 1990) was partly devoted to feminist utopias, including Margaret Atwood's *The Handmaid's Tale*.

4 See Guy Bouchard, "Les Déesses elles-mêmes," *imagine* . . . 49 (September 1989), and "Sexisme et utopie," *imagine* . . . 61 (September 1992). See also *imagine* . . . 53 (September 1990).

Marc Lemaire is an insurance and copyright lawyer by day, editor-in-chief of imagine . . . by night. He was also literary editor of Carfax and editor-in-chief of L'Aristide. Some days, he has been known to mix up literature and law in the same text, and he now spends more time on his computer than in reality.

FILLING THE EMPTY AIR WITH DREAMS
By William Lane

Dew. (sb)
The moisture deposited in minute drops upon any cool surface by the condensation of the vapor in the atmosphere . . .
Formerly supposed to fall or descend softly from the heav-
ens, whence numerous current phrases, figures and modes
of speech . . . "
                              — *Oxford English Dictionary*

Growing up in Canada in the 1950s, our sense of the form
and shape of our country was ineffably defined by the leg-
endary "DEW Line" which spanned the Arctic from sea to
sea. DEW, of course, stands for Distant Early Warning. And in reality, this "line" was nothing more than a system of twenty-one
radar tracking stations pointed uselessly towards Siberia. A later
generation would be wise enough to relegate the DEW Line to the
same trash heap of rusting weaponry along with Star Wars and
particle beam weapons. But growing up in the 1950s and 1960s, it
was something much more mysterious . . . a line in the air that no
one could see, defining the northern boundary of our nation in a
way which was almost impossible to imagine, with a technology
which seemed to transmute thin air into a fine web of deadly
frost. The DEW line was an outward and visible sign of an inward
and spiritual terror always lurking just beneath the surface of
postwar Canadian life. For many, it was the closest they would
ever get to "thinking of the unthinkable." That terror was as close
as the frozen ether.

A later generation would forget the DEW Line, and instead be
forced to dream over and over again of dew point. Dew point was
the outward and visible sign of our battle with the environment.
Its role was to guarantee the exact temperature at which moisture
would condense on highways and windshields — often just short
of freezing point. This new measure of our barometric confidence
was actually conceived in England, back in the 1830s, but it
achieved popular currency in Canada very late in the twentieth
century, primarily on the Weather Channel, where it began to
appear alongside the temperature during winter broadcasts. An
imaginary concept, it battled with an invisible enemy . . . the
dreaded *black ice*, frozen patches of glare ice that would form
without warning on the highway. And like the DEW Line, its

genius was pure mystification. That is, no one could understand exactly *what* it was. At winter gatherings all over Canada, people would ask each other . . . what *is* dew point, anyway? The principle of control and certainty had reconstituted itself in the form of a mystery.

DEW Line, Dew Point . . . many strange and perilous phantasms can be conjured out of the dew, it seems . . . out of the empty air. Especially in Canada, there are powerful forces lurking just beneath the surface of perceptual experience.

Arcular. (adj)
1. Of the form of an arc.
        — *O.E.D.*

Mr. Arcularis finally leaves his hospital bed after barely surviving a serious operation, and sets off on a magical sea cruise to Europe. It's the journey he has always dreamed of taking. But as he moves steadily east, it becomes more and more obvious that something is wrong. For one thing, it's much too cold for July. And for another, Mr. Arcularis is repeatedly paralyzed by a "feeling of vagueness and dizziness." Sometimes he is overcome by a powerful swooning melancholy, like the strains of the *Cavalleria Rusticana*. As the days go by, it gets colder and colder. His teeth chatter, and his hands begin to turn blue. Outside, "a cold fog surrounded the ship," and the ship itself seems "anchored among walls of ice and rime."

In truth, of course, Mr. Arcularis has never left the operating room. As he gradually begins to understand, he is dying on the operating table, while dreaming of a hopeless journey through an arctic wasteland.

Mr. Arcularis is a very simple but oddly powerful short story by Conrad Aiken. Written in 1931, the story was introduced to many Canadian teenagers through a leading high school anthology published in 1961 and reprinted every year throughout the 1960s. And it was also the subject of a famous CBC radio adaptation by Gerald Noxon in 1948, which was repeated in 1949 and again in 1953, and less than a decade later, there was another adaptation by Robert Herridge, heard on both *Startime* and *Encore* in 1960. All in all, a very popular story.

Conrad Aiken was born in Savannah, Georgia, and educated at Harvard — a long way from the snow fields of the Canadian North. He was much more interested in "depth psychology" and the concept of the "divine pilgrim." But Mr. Arcularis somehow managed to articulate our Canadian preoccupation with this landscape of frozen death. In this landscape, the ether becomes a fourth dimension, a zone where every thought, desire and fantasy can become utterly real. Mr. Arcularis may not have been a Canadian citizen, but he nevertheless became the patron saint of several generations of Canadian radio artists, who peopled this frozen landscape with phantasms of their own, hanging in the empty air like ghostly premonitions.

Canada . . . as in many countries, the secret fantasy is a cruel inversion of the public face. On the surface, a new country full of potential, and just under the surface, the fantasy is a death wish fulfillment, the landscape of gentle annihilation.

Mr. Arcularis was long gone by the time I came to work at CBC Radio in 1982. But Bill Howell was still producing *Nightfall,* and one of his personal favorites was the one where the central character ripped his own heart out of his chest, a fine example of the kind of imagery that would be nothing more than grotesque and ridiculous on film, but which achieves an almost poetic intensity and grace on the radio. And the first production I observed during my week of technical orientation was a production by Fred Diehl about a patriotic soldier who comes back from the dead, to drink to the Allied victory in the Second World War. Canadian gothic, in other words, was still very much alive in the ether.

Ether (also aether)
1. The clear sky, the upper regions of space beyond the clouds . . . the element breathed by the gods.
4. . . . . as a general name for extremely subtle fluids, the existence of which was imagined or inferred.
— *O.E.D.*

Radio, it has often been noted, is the perfect medium for fantasy and the imagination. It moves as quickly as air and as lightly as thought. It enjoys a special and trusted relationship with the listener, just on the edge of the subconscious. One survey after another has shown that people still turn to radio in times of crisis, and they tend to believe what they hear. What's more, radio is still very cheap and quick to create, compared to other forms of dramatic production, so it's possible to take wild and crazy chances on the imagination of writers who can't be trusted not to tell amazing and fascinating lies.

In our land, too, radio has long enjoyed the reputation of national authority. It has been the secret network connecting Canadians across the country, our national theater before we had much theater to speak of, our secret identity even before we began to investigate properly our reasons for lacking an identity.

When I conceived the idea for *Vanishing Point* in 1985, inviting our listeners to "expect the unexpected," I felt our work was inspired as much by its Canadian ancestors as it was by Rod Serling and the *Twilight Zone*. At the same time, Serling's philosophy for *The Twilight Zone* suggested some powerful analogies to the Canadian situation. He draws our attention to the idea of speculative drama as a forum for the discussion of unpalatable truths. It's a way of thinking which may have some relevance in a country which often seems to prefer to air its disagreements in private.

For Serling, fantasy was a vital antidote to the "kind of prolonged, unbelievable double-talk" that already filled the airwaves even in 1957. It was a arena where he could explore subject matter too serious for television, in a form that made it accessible to the widest possible audience. It was storytelling on a knife edge between the greatest seriousness and the most free-spirited imagination. It's a particularly sophisticated way of hedging your bets, creatively speaking. A similar impulse, perhaps, to the one that informs what some critics have dubbed the "Canadian ironic" style.

In truth, of course, there are almost as many Canadian styles of "fantasy" radio as there are Canadian dramatists of talent and imagination. Some of our best writers dream of the dead landscape or Mr. Arcularis, while others choose to people that landscape with visions that are absolutely positive and life-affirming. Some write of characters who are irrevocably lost in a universe of simple truths, while others write of new and undiscovered ways to find oneself at peace in the midst of whirling chaos. The diversity of vision is itself a sign of life. In radio art, as in every other branch of human culture, the freedom to dream is the freedom to be truly alive.

William Lane *is a theater director, writer, critic and radio producer. He was the first director to win the Pauline McGibbon Award. His work as a playwright includes* The Brides of Dracula *(1978). Since 1982, he has been an Executive Producer at CBC Radio, where he conceived the very popular* Vanishing Point *series of half-hour dramas, which ran from 1985 to 1992. He is currently Executive Producer of Studio '95.*

PEEKING UP THE SKIRTS OF THE END:
Speculative Content in Canadian Pop Music
by Michael Skeet

The world has been waiting for the definitive survey on the subject of science fictional and fantastic elements in Canadian popular music. It is still waiting. What follows is a purely subjective look at one writer's experience through nearly three decades, first as listener, then as radio producer, and finally as pop music journalist.

That science fiction is often described as "a literature of ideas" would seem to make it a very unlikely subject for adaptation to the pop music form, popular music in the second half of the twentieth century being devoted as it is to sensation and hormonal flux rather than any form of contemplation or intellectual exercise. In large part, that has indeed been the case. Indeed, science fiction and fantasy did not really enter into pop music's glossary, in Canada at least, until after the explosive growth of science fiction in the visual media sparked by *Star Trek* and *2001: A Space Odyssey*. Like *Star Trek* and its many imitators and followers, the pop music which emerged from the explosion of visual-media SF concentrated on the surface appeal of SF rather than any in-depth discussion of ideas. Even as pop music became more sophisticated through the 1970s and into the 1980s, the lyrical content of many songs with SF themes offered little more than surface references to SF subjects and themes. SF readers looking for music that somehow related to the emotional attachment they felt to the genre as often as not had to listen to music with no obvious lyrical connection to visual or literary SF. (Motion-picture soundtracks and such tone-poems as Holst's "The Planets" often filled the void.) Nevertheless, some pop songwriters have successfully melded SF ideas and images to the structure of popular music. Canada has produced a disproportionate number of these lyricists, writing for pop music groups which are among the foremost in the world in terms of utilizing SF images and/or themes in their music.

The earliest SF-related pop music was of a more or less pure novelty nature; one thinks of the Byrds' "Mr. Spaceman," for example. In the 1960s, the 45rpm single was the dominant form of pop music, and this was a form that did not easily lend itself to SF subjects. It's perhaps significant that John Stewart's 1969 moon-landing single, "A Man Named Armstrong," did not chart particularly well.

The first Canadian pop music single with an identifiably SF theme is probably The Five Man Electrical Band's "I'm a Stranger Here" (1973), a trite but nevertheless effective protest song utilizing a visiting space alien as a viewpoint character. "Effective" is not really a word that could be used to describe Prism's "Spaceship Superstar" (1974). This song is almost legendarily peurile; in the writer's opinion, only Zagar & Evans's "In the Year 2525" (1969) is harder to listen to.

As a rule, SF and fantasy are not the bricks of which hit singles are made. The Five Man Electrical Band's 1974 followup to "I'm a Stranger Here," "Werewolf," and Prism's cheesily apocalyptic "Armageddon" (1979) stand as rare exceptions. But this is of little matter, since by 1974 the long-play record had superseded the single as the predominant pop music format, and the stage had been set for a series of Canadian groups which would successfully utilize SF themes and imagery in the longer song-forms made possible by the LP album.

It is this writer's contention that the growth in the use of SF imagery in pop music in the mid-1970s was neither accidental nor coincidental. The children who had watched *Star Trek* during its initial run on NBC, and who spent their early adolescence reading the fantasy novels that emerged from the mid-sixties popularity of Tolkein, brought a love for, and familiarity with, science fiction and fantasy tropes to the pop music scene. One can almost see a gestation at work: following David Hartwell's assertion that "the golden age of science fiction is twelve," the twelve-year-olds watching *Star Trek* in 1966 were, by the early to mid-1970s, in their late teens and early adulthood. Some of them were forming pop and rock bands. It is no surprise that it was the early 1970s that saw the founding of such groups as Prism, FM, Saga, and the most successful of the Canadian producers of SF-related music, Rush.

Rush, when it began recording in 1973, was just another power trio at a time when Canada had something of a reputation for hard-edged rock groups. But when drummer Neil Peart joined the band in 1974, he brought with him a love of SF and fantasy that very quickly found voice in the lyrics he provided for bassist/lead singer Geddy Lee's music. Very quickly, Rush was recording interlinked sequences of songs that were (relatively) complex musically and, if not so complex lyrically, at least based in more than a superficial way on SF themes and images.

In the mid to late 1970s, Rush evolved from a power trio to an art-rock band, in a fashion similar to the many imitators of the English bands Genesis and Pink Floyd. Led by Peart's SF-inspired musings, Rush recorded in this period three albums dense with SF imagery: *2112; A Farewell to Kings;* and *Hemispheres.* The albums were thematically linked, through the device of a sentient space ship, Cygnus X-1. *2112* in particular is something of a landmark, featuring as it does a song-cycle which is unabashedly science fictional in content: in a grim future, a Randian hero (the cycle was ostensibly inspired by Peart's enthusiasm for *The Fountainhead*) provokes a revolution through his music.

Having said all this, though, it must be added that these albums are not particularly inspiring as SF. The lyrics are over-earnest and clichéd, and the music is as pompous and bombastic as any of the worst of the art-rock movement's excesses. In 1980, anxious to leave behind what Lee described as the "fog" of art-rock, Rush re-made itself again and, with the album *Permanent Waves*, abandoned the SF concept album as a vehicle. Had the three above-mentioned records been the extent of Rush's contribution to the genre, the band might have been worthy of little more than a footnote in a catalogue such as this.

In fact, however, Neal Peart has continued to evolve as a lyricist as Rush has evolved musically. The images and language of SF continue to appear in two or three songs on each Rush album, but the way in which they are used is much more sophisticated than the more earnest but simplistic lyrics of the 1970s. The lyrics of such songs as "Dreamland" (from the 1991 album *Roll the Bones*) are more ambiguous, impressionistic. More importantly, they give equal place with ideas to the human beings who create, and suffer the consequences of, those ideas. At his best, in his lyrics to "Animate" and "Alien Shore" (both from the 1993 album *Counterparts*), Peart achieves what the best of literary SF does: he uses SF images to pull the listener into songs that are in fact resolutely rooted in the here and now.

While Rush stands as the pre-eminent Canadian practitioner

of pop-music SF, a number of other groups must also be cited. FM was formed in Toronto in 1976. The band's recording debut, *Black Noise* (originally recorded for the CBC) featured such titles as "Phasors on Stun," "Slaughter in Robot City" and "Aldeberan." FM's music was originally a wildly eclectic melange, led by the eccentric multi-instrumentalist Nash the Slash (born as Jeff Plewman). Over the years, the band's music moved steadily away from SF influences and into the musical mainstream. Slash has continued to combine SF and music, though, as a solo artist. His post-FM career has been notable for his composing and performing music scores for SF films. He has even appeared at SF conventions (where his stage presence, head completely wrapped in bandages, does not look all that unusual by comparison), performing the scores he has composed for such classic silent films as *Metropolis* and *The Cabinet of Dr. Caligari.*

The Vancouver group Strange Advance set out from its inception to write SF-flavored songs. Like both Rush and FM, Strange Advance began as a trio, though after its first album the group continued with just two members, Darryl Kromm and Drew Arnott. In a 1982 conversation with the author, Kromm and Arnott were quite outspoken about the influence of literary SF on their writing. That first album, *Worlds Away* (1982), can be interpreted as a song-cycle set in a giant arcology. The album is subtle, though, being open to a number of interpretations. Even the SF content of such songs as "Worlds Away" and "One Chance in a Million" is understated rather than overt.

In 1985, Strange Advance achieved a success of some note when their single "We Run" (from the album *2WO*) became a hit both on radio and in dance clubs, the first Canadian hit single with SF content in over half a decade. As with the songs on *Worlds Away*, "We Run" is primarily a song about people. The SF nature of the lovers' dilemma behind the song is only apparent from a careful perusal of the lyrics. Other songs on this album ("Nor Crystal Tears," "Running Away") are more obvious in their SF content, but are still effective. More obvious but somehow less effective are the SF-influenced songs on *The Distance Between* (1988), to date the last original album from Strange Advance.

Klaatu was yet another trio. (What is it with pop trios in

Canada?) This group, active from the mid-1970s to the early 1980s (the band re-formed for a single performance in Germany in 1988) is most notable for the controversy surrounding its purported origins and for a cover version of one of its SF songs by American MOR stalwarts The Carpenters. The controversy concerned rumors that the group (named for the alien in the classic SF film *The Day the Earth Stood Still*) was actually the Beatles, re-united and recording under a pseudonym. Klaatu, composed of Toronto-area musicians, denied the rumors as loudly as possible. Since the band followed each denial with a refusal to discuss the actual identity of the group's members, and since Klaatu had in fact deliberately set out to sound Beatle-esque on several tunes from their first album, the denials only served to amplify the rumors further. *Rolling Stone* magazine named Klaatu "Hype of the Year" in 1977. A year later, The Carpenters had a top ten hit with their version of "Calling Occupants," originally recorded by Klaatu on their 1976 album *3:47 E.S.T.* Lyrically, the song is banal, though it's pleasant enough to listen to. Sales of the band's first album were buoyed by hype, and each subsequent album sold fewer copies than its predecessor until, sometime after 1981, Klaatu just faded away.

One of the Canadian bands most consistently identified with fantastic imagery is also one of the relatively few Canadian bands less successful at home than outside the country. (It's also one of the few groups in this survey that has never been a trio, though there are three core members — Ian and Jim Crichton and Michael Sadler — who have been with the band in all of its various incarnations.) Saga was originally known as Pockets when founded in Toronto in the mid-1970s. By the time the band recorded its first album in 1978, though, the name had been changed. Almost immediately, Saga's epic live performances and its synthesizer dominated art-rock became popular in Europe, where Saga continued to be a top draw into the 1990s. In Canada, the band is less well known (though a number of its albums have sold well by Canadian standards).

There are, in addition to the groups and songs mentioned above, innumerable Canadian pop musicians who have at one time or another recorded music with some sort of hook to SF. John

Mills-Cockell's synthesizer band Syrinx, for example, recorded the theme to the (then) forward-looking TV series *Here Come the Seventies*, and followed this with a number of albums (*Tillicum* comes most notably to mind) of SF-related instrumental music. Even the vocal group Moxy Früvous can be included in this collective, by virtue of their post-apocalyptic "The Drinking Song" (the live version contained on their independent cassette is superior to the studio version included on their 1993 debut album, *Bargainville*), which makes for interesting comparison with Prism's "Armageddon." The latter is all about institutions and bombast; "The Drinking Song" puts a human face on its SF — if, indeed, SF is what it is. For this writer, at least, the best SF pop music is that which makes the least overt connections to the genre.

Michael Skeet is a writer and broadcaster living in Toronto. He has written several hundred articles on music and film and has a syndicated film criticism spot on CBC Radio. He began writing science fiction in 1986, and in 1992 his short story "Breaking Ball" won an Aurora Award. The following year, Skeet shared another Aurora with Lorna Toolis (his wife), for their work editing the anthology Tesseracts[4]. *He is a founding member of SF Canada (the Canadian science fiction writer's association) and for two years served as the organization's vice president.*

PRISONERS OF GRAVITY
Gregg Thurlbeck

I suspect that, like many other Canadian readers of speculative fiction, I was first drawn to the genre by writers from other countries. I first started to read SF seriously in the early 1980s and, in my case, the authors in question were Ray Bradbury, Ursula K. Le Guin, John Varley, and Roger Zelazny.

I was a terrible reader throughout my school years, my mind wandered constantly and I would often reach the end of a page only to discover that I had no idea what I'd supposedly just read. It really didn't matter whether the book was a math text or a novel assigned for English class, I just couldn't keep myself interested in all those words. And so, after completing my university degree in Communication Studies, I simply stopped reading entirely.

Luckily, less than a year after my graduation, I became good friends with one of my co-workers at the community television station in Winnipeg where I was getting my first professional experience in television production. MTV had just gone on the air in the U.S., and she would notice me spending hours glued to the satellite signal. I was enthralled. Watching rock and roll heroes getting into strange situations and negotiating the surreal visual landscapes dreamt up by the creators of this new medium. Bowie's *Ashes to Ashes*, *Fade to Gray* by Visage, Ultravox in *The Thin Wall*. This was exciting, inspiring stuff. My friend, seeing that I was unaware how many of these "new" images and ideas weren't really so new, suggested that reading too could be an enjoyable way to fill my leisure time. I rather reluctantly agreed to try to read a couple of collections of science fiction short stories which she thought would somehow manage to hold my interest. Ray Bradbury's *The Illustrated Man*, Roger Zelazny's *The Doors of His Face, The Lamps of His Mouth*, and John Varley's *The Persistence of Vision* all sat untouched beside my bed for several weeks before I finally decided to get on with the task of doing battle with all those words.

And suddenly I could read. The stories were full of surreal landscapes and heroic people in strange situations. I would reach the bottom of a page without having drifted off somewhere in the midst of the second paragraph. I didn't have to reread everything two and three times before it would stick. I was actually enjoying myself. And a hundred thousand new worlds were formed in the night sky.

Part of the reason short speculative fiction succeeded for me where other forms of literature had failed was the primacy of plot. Exciting things happened in these stories. But there was a second important feature that set these tales apart — relevance. Often the heroes of these stories found themselves in situations that twisted the dilemmas that we were dealing with in this world. My favorite authors might set their stories elsewhere or elsewhen but they never lost site of twentieth century Earth. I remember that I was particularly impressed by how John Varley's story "Options" managed this. The story takes place on the moon and centers on a woman who decides to undergo a sex change operation much to the dismay of her husband. I read "Options" at the very time that I was being politicized regarding gay issues through my work on a television series called *Coming Out*.

Speculative fiction seemed to me to be taking risks. It was challenging in the same sort of way that the music I liked best — Elvis Costello, The Clash, The Specials — was challenging. And so I stuck with it, always holding a particular fondness for short stories. Each year I would pick up both Terry Carr's and Donald Wollheim's Best SF of the Year collections. When I ran across an author whose work I particularly enjoyed, I'd search out one of their novels and give that a try. As well, I worked my way through the list of Hugo and Nebula Award winning novels. I was still a very slow reader, but for the first time in my life I was, in fact, a reader.

It was a decade later, in Toronto, that I was given the opportunity to merge my career with my love of speculative fiction. Another co-worker, my former boss on thetelevision series *The NewMusic*, was looking for someone to help salvage a project called *Prisoners of Gravity. PoG,* as it was rather less than affectionately known among the staff at TVOntario, had been created one year earlier by a group of people who felt that speculative fiction and comic books were important forms of literature which deserved much more respect than they tended to receive in the mainstream media. They also understood that the growing audience for genre fiction would appreciate a show that didn't take itself too seriously, so long as the work itself was treated with due respect. The only problem was that the team did not include anyone who had both the time and the experience to produce and direct the series. An outside producer was brought in to fill this void but he, unfortunately, did not share the team's vision for the show. The result could be termed chaos were it not for the fact that chaos has turned out to produce some very interesting, thought provoking visuals. Luckily, the powers that be at TVOntario realized that the reason the show wasn't working had nothing to do with the concept of the series and everything to do with a failure to realize that concept. At the conclusion of the first season, I happened to be looking for work, the *PoG* team were looking for a worker, and from that starting point we set about turning *Prisoners of Gravity* into a series of which we could all be proud.

Over the course of the next four years we produced 111 half hours of television which managed to celebrate SF while not being afraid to criticize the genre for its shortcomings. We explored themes rather than profiling people because we felt that ideas were what SF was all about. The *PoG* team (Commander Rick Green, Mark Askwith, Shirley Brady and myself) interviewed hundreds of speculative fiction authors from Douglas Adams to George Zebrowski. In the process we traveled to science fiction and comic book conventions in London, New York, Orlando, San Francisco, San Diego, Seattle, Niagara Falls, and Calgary.

Canadian writers were an important and frequent part of the mix on Prisoners of Gravity, not only because they were often easily accessible to us, but also because their work was exciting and adventurous. When Tanya Huff, Sean Stewart, or Charles de Lint appeared in an episode along side their more famous American or British counterparts, it was because they and their fiction deserved to be there. Canadians have become an important part of the world of speculative fiction.

But it is a *world* of speculative fiction. And while it's wonderful to see that it is now possible for a Canadian SF writer to set their tale in Ottawa, Vancouver, or even rural Nova Scotia without editors fretting over whether readers will be capable of identifying with a Canadian protagonist, I prefer to think that this, if any, form of literature can and should be larger than national boundaries. After all, the alien arriving from space cannot see those lines on the globe and the inhabitants of the land of Faerie seldom carry passports.

And just what constitutes a Canadian speculative fiction

author anyway? Among the ranks you'll find people such as A. E. Van Vogt, S. M. Stirling and Judith & Garfield Reeves-Stevens who were all born here but now make their homes in the United States. As well, we lay claim to Judith Merril, William Gibson, Michael Coney, and Spider Robinson, all of whom were born elsewhere but now reside in Canada. Does this make these authors less Canadian than Robert J. Sawyer, Élisabeth Vonarburg, and Barbara Delaplace? Canada, unlike the United States, does not adhere to the melting pot philosophy and so Canadian speculative fiction is as varied as the smorgasbord of Canadian people who create it.

While there are certainly texts that could be cited as representing a distinctly Canadian speculative perspective, I for one have not run across the Canadian SF equivalent of Pierre Berton. Nor do I feel particularly drawn to the notion of seeking such a person out. For me, speculative fiction succeeds best when such nationalist boundaries are dismantled. And I have found that my favorite SF authors of the past few decades have been tearing down these walls. Kim Stanley Robinson's Mars (Red Mars, Green Mars, Blue Mars) is not the reflection of American suburbia that Ray Bradbury pictured for that planet in the 1950s. In fact, Robinson's Mars feels considerably less American than the Mars that Michael Skeet envisioned in "Breaking Ball," a story that won the Aurora Award for best English language Canadian SF short story. Robinson's Mars is home to Arabs and Russians; the Japanese, Swiss and French are likewise represented. It is a vision of the future that reflects the ways in which speculative fiction itself has changed.

At the time that Ray Bradbury wrote *The Martian Chronicles*, SF tended to be written by Americans for Americans. Speculative fiction authors who lived anywhere else still tended to write like Americans because they too were writing for the American market. But eventually the readership grew, spreading beyond the borders of the U.S., and many of these foreign authors began to move away from the "can do" American style of speculative fiction writing. The British "new wave" writers of the 1960s expanded SF geographically as well as stylistically.

So, in the 1970s did Canadians ask themselves; if an SF story set in London, England can be successful in the States why not a story set in London, Ontario? The question may seem straight forward enough but we Canadians have always seemed to lack the confidence to define ourselves as being truly distinct from our powerful neighbors to the south. And this certainly colors (or should that be colours) the way they see us. During a recent Olympics an American friend of mine was shocked to discover that, since there wasn't a Canadian athlete in the finals for a particular race, I wasn't automatically cheering for the American. After all we're on the same side. I assured him that for most of the people I knew beating the Americans at the Olympics was far more important than beating the Russians, or anyone else for that matter. Even when we're not American, we're more not-American than we are Canadian.

So when Canadian SF authors don't set their books in London, Ontario, I don't despair. The time when speculative fiction needed that kind of move is three decades past and the Brits took care of it for us. Now is a time when SF needs to think in more global terms. And maybe we Canadians with our lack of any consistent identity are ideally suited to the task. The future is ours for the taking, all we have to do is imagine it.

Gregg Thurlbeck began working in television in 1979, and he moved to Toronto in 1982 to work on CITY TV's series The NewMusic. *He was hired to produce and direct the second season of* Prisoners of Gravity *in 1990, which was twice nominated for the Gemini Award, won a Silver Medal at the New York Festivals of Television (for the "Zero Population Growth" episode), and received the International Reading Association's Broadcast Media Award for the Ray Bradbury Profile episode. He is currently developing a new series called* E-Space Velocity *which "explores the intersection between technology and the arts." A pilot episode has been produced for the Canadian Discovery Channel.*

. . . THEY PROMISED ME A FUTURE . . .

Michael Cherkas and Larry Hancock

-3-

THE END

Michael Cherkas *was born in Oshawa, Ontario. He now lives in Toronto with his wife and two children, where he works as a free-lance designer and illustrator. His comic book work includes* The Silent Invasion, Suburban Nightmares, *and* The New Frontier.

David Lawrence (Larry) Hancock *resides in Toronto, where he is employed by day as a chartered accountant. In his after-hours, he is the writer of the science fiction comic book series* The Silent Invasion *and* Suburban Nightmares. *He is past-chairman of The Friends of The Merril Collection of Science Fiction, Speculation and Fantasy. He met he wife Jody on a science fiction fan tour of Australia prior to the 1985 WorldCon in Melbourne.*

Heather Spears *provided the sketches of the authors for this book. Her books* How to Read Faces *(1986) and* The Word for Sand *(1988) both won the Pat Lowther Award.* The Word for Sand *also won the Governor General's Award for poetry; and poems collected in* Human Acts *(1991) won the CBC Literary Prize. She was educated at the University of British Columbia and the Vancouver School of Art, and now studies at the University of Copenhagen. In 1989 she began to write science fiction, both short stories and novels, including the Twinworld series:* Moonfall *(1992),* The Children of Atwar *(1993), and* The Taming *(1995).*

ACKNOWLEDGMENTS

The idea of *Out of This World*, the National Library of Canada's science fiction and fantasy exhibition, was conceived in 1992 — almost by accident as the result of a casual conversation between National Library and Toronto Public Library's Merril Collection personnel. It unleashed a torrent of creative ideas. This anthology developed when the exhibition curatorial team were exchanging "what ifs" after a long discussion of the exhibition content and storylines.

I was charged with approaching authors to ask whether they would be interested in contributing to an anthology of science fiction and fantasy essays reflecting the themes of the exhibition. The enthusiastically positive response delighted us. My sincere thanks to all the authors for their unique input and invaluable support. It goes without saying that we couldn't have done it without you.

Thanks, too, to the curatorial team of Hugh Spencer, Allan Weiss, and Lorna Toolis, and to all members of staff of the Toronto Public Library's Merril Collection and the National Library involved. There were many. A special thanks to the project miracle worker, Margo Wiper, the Library's Director of Marketing and Publishing, and her team. And thanks to Bob Hilderley at Quarry Press for sharing in our excitement about this anthology. This project had a way of growing.

Andrea Paradis

BIBLIOGRAPHY

Books Displayed at the National Library of Canada Out of This World *Exhibition*

The Identity Variations

Individual Identities

Hémon, Louis. *Maria Chapdelaine*. Boucherville, Québec.: Éditions de Mortagne, 1983.

Herbert, Frank. *Dune*. Philadelphia: Chilton Book Company, 1965.

Hughes, Monica. *The Keeper of the Isis Light*. [London?]: Collins Educational, 1980.

Kingsbury, Donald. *Courtship Rite*. New York: Timescape Books, 1982.

Laurence, Margaret. *The Stone Angel*. Chicago: The University of Chicago Press, 1993.

Roberts, Charles G.D. *The Heart of the Ancient World*. Toronto: McClelland and Stewart, 1974.

Stewart, Sean. *Passion Play*. Victoria, B.C.: Beach Holme Publishers, 1992.

Wilson, Charles Robert. *The Divide*. New York: Doubleday, 1990.

Cyberindentities

Gibson, William. *Count Zero*. New York: Arbor House, 1986.

Gibson, William. *Neuromancer*. New York: Ace Science Fiction Books, 1984.

Ryan, Thomas J. *The Adolescence of P-1*. New York: Ace Books, 1979.

Weiner, Andrew. *Distant Signals and Other Stories*. Victoria, B.C.: Porcepic Books, 1989.

Wilson, Robert Charles. *Memory Wire*. New York: Bantam Books, 1987.

Machines and Robot Identities

Asimov, Isaac. *I, Robot*. New York: Gnome Press, 1950.

Capek, Karel. *R.U.R. (Rossum's Universal Robots): A Fantastic Melodrama*. Translated by Paul Selver. Garden City: Doubleday, Page & Company, 1923.

Dorsey, Candas Jane. *Machine Sex . . . and Other Stories*. Victoria, B.C.: Porcepic Books, 1988.

Gotlieb, Phyllis. *O Master Caliban*. New York: Hagerstown, 1976.

Martel, Suzanne. *Nos amis robots*. Montréal: Héritage, 1981.

Sernine, Daniel. *Chronoreg*. Montréal: Éditions Québec/Amérique, 1992.

Shelley, Mary Wollstonecraft. *Frankenstein, or, The Modern Prometheus*. New York: Dodd, Mead and Company, 1983.

Willer, Jim. *Paramind*. Toronto: McClelland and Stewart, 1973.

Alien Identities

Barcelo, François. *Agénor, Agénor, Agénor et Agénor*. Montréal: Quinze, 1980.

Coney, Michael. *Brontomek!* London: Victor Gollancz, 1976.

Mantley, John. *The Twenty-Seventh Day*. London: Michael Joseph, 1956.

Robinson, Spider and Jeanne. *Stardance*. New York: Dell Publishing Company, 1980.

Rochon, Esther. *Coquillage*. Montréal: La Pleine Lune, 1985.

Vogt, A.E. van. *Slan*. Sauk City, Wisconsin: Arkham House, 1946.

Wilson, Robert Charles. *The Harvest*. New York: Bantam Books, 1993.

Family and Ethnicity in Canadian Fantastic Fiction

The Family

Bouchard, Guy. *Les Gélules utopiques*. Montréal: Éditions Logiques, 1988.

Green, Terence M. *The Woman Who Is the Midnight Wind*. Porters Lake, N.S.: Pottersfield Press, 1987.

Herbert, Frank. *Dune*. Philadelphia: Chilton Book Company, 1965.

Vogt, A.E. van. *Slan*. Sauk City, Wisconsin: Arkham House, 1946.

Ethnicity

Dann, Jack. *More Wandering Stars: An Anthology of Jewish Fantasy and Science Fiction*. New York: Doubleday & Company, 1981.

Saunders, Charles R. *Imaro*. New York: Daw Books, 1981.

Women and Canadian Science Fiction and Fantasy

Gotlieb, Phyllis. *Sunburst*. Dee Why West, N.S.W.: Eclipse Paperbacks, [197?].

Hughes, Monica. *The Keeper of the Isis Light*. [London?]: Collins Educational, 1980.

Kernaghan, Eileen. *Journey to Aprilioth*. New York: Ace Books, 1980.

MacDonald, Flora. *Mary Melville the Psychic*. Toronto: Austin Publishing Company, 1900.

Martel, Suzanne. *Quatre Montréalais en l'an 3000*. Montréal: Les Éditions du Jour, 1961.

Merril, Judith. *Daughters of Earth: Three Novels*. Garden City, N.Y.: Doubleday & Company, 1969.

Merril, Judith, editor. *Tesseracts*. Victoria: Press Porcépic, 1985.

Pelletier, Francine. *Le Crime de l'enchanteresse*. Montréal: Éditions Paulines, 1989.

Pelletier, Francine. *Le Temps des migrations*. Longueuil, Québec.: Éditions du Préambule, 1987.

Perrot-Bishop, Annick. *Les Maisons de cristal*. Montréal: Les Éditions Logiques, 1990.

Speculative Feminist Fiction

Atwood, Margaret. *The Handmaid's Tale*. Toronto: McClelland & Stewart, 1985.

Dorsey, Candas Jane. *Machine Sex ... and Other Stories*. Victoria: Porcepic Books, 1988.

Vonarburg, Élisabeth. *Le Silence de la cité*. Paris: Éditions Denoël, 1981.

Political Identities

Ballem, John. *The Dirty Scenario*. Don Mills, Ont.: PaperJacks, 1974.

Centennius, Ralph. *The Dominion in 1983*. Peterborough, Ont.: Toker & Company, 1983.

Grove, Frederick Phillip. *Consider Her Ways*. Toronto: MacMillan, 1947.

Lawrence, W.H.C. *The Storm of '92*. Toronto: Sheppard Publishing Company, 1889.

MacLennan, Hugh. *Voices in Time*. Markham, Ont: Penguin Books, 1981.

Moore, P.S. *Williwaw*. St. John's, Nfld.: Breakwater Books, 1978.

Powe, Bruce. *Killing Ground: The Canadian Civil War*. Toronto: Peter Martin Associates, 1968.

Tardivel, Jules-Paul. *Pour la patrie*. Montréal: Hurtubise HMH, 1975.

Fantastic Voyages . . . and Incredible Journeys

Berger, Michel and Luc Plamondon. *Starmania*. Scarborough, Ont.: WEA, 1978.

Bryant, Edward and Harlan Ellison. *Phoenix without Ashes*. Greenwich, Conn.: Fawcett Publications, 1975.

De Mille, James. *A Strange Manuscript Found in a Copper Cylinder*. London: Chatto & Windus, 1888.

Edwards, David. *Next Stop — Mars!: A Novel of the First Space-Ship Voyage to the Red Planet*. New York: Greenwich Book Publishers, 1959.

Hill, Douglas. *Deathwing Over Veynaa*. London: Victor Gollancz, 1980.

Sawyer, Robert J. *Golden Fleece*. New York: Warner Books, 1990.

Trudel, Jean-Louis. *Un Trésor sur Serendib*. Montréal: Médiaspaul, 1994.

Time Travel

Green, Terence M. *Children of the Rainbow*. Toronto: McCelland & Stewart, 1992.

Manning, Laurence. *The Man Who Awoke*. Toronto: Ballantine Books, 1975.

Trudel, Jean-Louis. *Le Ressuscité de l'Atlantide*. [S.L.]: Éditions Fleuve Noir, 1994.

Wells, H.G. *The Time Machine: An Invention*. New York: Random House, 1931.

New Environments

Abbey, Lloyd. *The Last Whales*. Toronto: Random House, 1989.

Heine, William C. *The Last Canadian*. Markham, Ont.: Simon & Shuster, 1974.

Kilian, Crawford. *Icequake*. Vancouver: Douglas & McIntyre, 1979.

New Technologies, New Challenges

Card, Orson Scott. *Ender's Game*. Toronto: TOR, 1985.

Service, Robert W. *The Master of the Microbe: A Fantastic Romance*. New York: Barse & Hopkins, 1926.

Wilson, Robert Charles. *The Divide*. New York: Doubleday, 1990.

New Perceptions

Gotlieb, Phyllis. *The Kingdom of the Cats*. New York: Ace Science Fiction Books, 1985.

MacDonald, Flora. *Mary Melville the Psychic*. Toronto: Austin Publishing Company, 1900.

Robinson, Spider. *Telempath*. New York: G.P. Putnam's Sons, 1976.

Vogt, A.E. van. *Slan*. Sauk City, Wisconsin: Arkham House, 1946.

Strange Worlds and Strange Peoples

Utopias and Dystopias

Atwood, Margaret. *The Handmaid's Tale*. Toronto: McClelland & Stewart, 1985.

Bradbury, Ray. *Fahrenheit 451*. New York: Ballantine Books, 1953.

Cohen, Matt. *The Colours of War*. New York: Methuen, 1977.

Holden, Hélène. *After the Fact*. Ottawa: Oberon Press, 1986.

Huxley, Aldous. *Brave New World*. Harmondsworth, Middlesex: Penguin Books, 1955.

Leacock, Stephen. *Afternoons in Utopia: Tales of the New Time*. New York: Dodd, Mead & Company, 1932.

MacLennan, Hugh. *Voices in Time*. Markham, Ont.: Penguin Books, 1981.

More, Thomas. *Utopia: Containing an Impartial History*. London: D.I. Eaton, 1795.

Pedley, Hugh. *Looking Forward: The Strange Experience of the Rev. Fergus McCheyne*. Toronto: William Briggs, 1913.

Plato. *The Republic*. London: J.M. Dent, 1976.

Stewart, Sean. *Passion Play*. Victoria, B.C.: Beach Holme Publishers, 1992.

After the Apocalypse

Cohen, Matt. *The Colours of War*. New York: Methuen, 1977.

Drew, Wayland. *The Gaian Expedient*. Toronto: Random House of Canada, 1985.

Gotlieb, Phyllis. *Sunburst*. Dee Why West, N.S.W.: Eclipse Paperbacks, [197?].

Holden, Hélène. *After the Fact*. Ottawa: Oberon Press, 1986.

Hughes, Monica. *Invitation to the Game*. Toronto: HarperCollins, 1992.

Martel, Suzanne. *Quatre Montréalais en l'an 3000*. Montréal: Les Éditions du Jour, 1961.

Spears, Heather. *Moonfall*. Victoria, B.C.: Beach Holme Publishers, 1991.

Parallel Worlds

Lint, Charles de. *Moonheart*. London: Pan Books, 1990.

Stirling, S.M. *Marching Through Georgia*. New York: Baen Publishing, 1988.

Weiner, Andrew. *Station Gehenna*. New York: Congdon & Weed, 1987.

Wilson, Robert Charles. *Gypsies*. New York: Doubleday, 1989.

Prehistoric and Posthistoric Worlds

Bessette, Gérard. *Les Anthropoïdes*. Montréal: Les Éditions La Presse, 1977.

Manning, Laurence. *The Man Who Awoke*. Toronto: Ballantine Books, 1975.

Roberts, Charles G.D. *In the Morning of Time*. London; Toronto: J.M. Dent, 1923.

Wells, H.G. *The Time Machine: An Invention*. New York: Random House, 1931.

Alternate Histories

Hood, Hugh. *Around the Mountain: Scenes from Montreal Life*. Toronto: Peter Martin Associates, 1967.

Gibson, William and Bruce Sterling. *The Difference Engine*. New York: Bantam Books, 1992.

Stirling, S.M. *Marching Through Georgia*. New York: Baen Publishing, 1988.

Québec Fantasy and Science Fiction

Le Fantastique

Bednarski, Betty, translator. *Selected Tales of Jacques Ferron*. Toronto: Anansi, 1984.

Benoit, Jacques. *Les Princes*. Montréal: Stanké, 1981.

Leclerc, Félix. *Carcajou*. Montréal: Éditions du Jour, 1973.

Major, Henriette. *La Ville fabuleuse*. Saint-Lambert, Québec: Les Éditions Héritage, 1982.

Turgeon, Pierre. *Un, deux, trois*. Montréal: Les Quinze, 1980.

Vonarburg, Élisabeth. *Chroniques du pays des mères*. Montréal: Éditions Québec/Amérique, 1992.

Yance, Claude-Emmanuelle. *Mourir comme un chat*. Québec: L'Instant même, 1987.

Québec Science Fiction for the Young

Chabot, Denys. *L'Eldorado dans les glaces*. Montréal: Bibliothèque québécoise, 1989.

Champetier, Joël. *La Mer au fond du monde*. Montréal: Éditions Paulines, 1990.

Rochon, Esther. *L'Épuisement du soleil*. Longueuil, Québec: Éditions du Préambule, 1985.

Rochon, Esther. *L'Étranger sous la ville*. Montréal: Les Éditions Paulines, 1986.

Sernine, Daniel. *À la recherche de Monsieur Goodtheim: novellas de science-fiction.* Montréal: Les Publications Ianus, 1991.

Sernine, Daniel. *Les Contes de l'ombre.* Montréal: Presses Sélect, 1978.

Sernine, Daniel. *Quand vient la nuit.* Longueuil, Québec: Éditions Le Préambule, 1983.

Trudel, Jean-Louis. *Aller simple pour Saguenal.* Montréal: Éditions Paulines, 1994.

The Genre Variations

High Fantasy

De Lint, Charles. *Moonheart.* London: Pan Books, 1990.

Duncan, Dave. *The Coming of Wisdom.* New York: Ballantine Books, 1988.

Gedge, Pauline. *Stargate.* New York: The Dial Press, 1982.

Kay, Guy Gavriel. *A Song for Arbonne.* Markham, Ont.: Penguin Books, 1993.

Kay, Guy Gavriel. *The Wandering Fire.* Toronto: Collins, 1989.

Kay, Guy Gavriel. *Tigana.* New York; Markham, Ont.: Penguin Books, 1991.

Kernaghan, Eileen. *Journey to Aprilioth.* New York: Ace Books, 1980.

Kilian, Crawford. *Eyas.* Toronto: McClelland & Stewart - Bantam, 1982.

Tolkien, J.R.R. *The Fellowship of the Ring: Being the First Part of The Lord of the Rings.* Toronto: Methuen, 1971.

Dark Fantasy

Blais, Marie-Claire. *La Belle Bête.* Montréal: Cercle du livre de France, 1968.

Colombo, John Robert and Michael Richardson, compilers. *Not to be Taken at Night: Thirteen Classic Canadian Tales of Mystery and the Supernatural.* Toronto: Lester & Orpen Dennys, 1981.

Davies, Robertson. *High Spirits*; Markham, Ont.: Penguin Books, 1982.

Hébert, Anne. *Les Enfants du sabbat.* Paris: Éditions du Seuil, 1975.

Huff, Tanya. *Blood Price.* New York: DAW Books, 1991.

Huff, Tanya. *Gate of Darkness, Circle of Light.* New York: DAW Books, 1989.

Hutchison, Don, ed. *Northern Frights.* Oakville, Ont.: Mosaic Press, 1992.

McCormack, Eric. *Inspecting the Vaults.* Markham, Ont.: Penguin Books, 1987.

Reeves-Stevens, Garfield. *Blood Shift.* New York: Warner Books, 1981.

Ruddy, Jon. *The Running Man.* Don Mills, Ont.: General Publishing, 1976.

Magic Realism

April, Jean-Pierre. *Berlin-Bangkok.* Montréal: Éditions Logiques, 1989.

Findley, Timothy. *Not Wanted on the Voyage.* Toronto: Viking, 1984.

Hancock, Geoff, ed. *Magic Realism.* Toronto: Aya Press, 1980.

Kinsella, W.P. *Shoeless Joe.* New York: Ballantine Books, 1983, 1982.

Moore, Brian. *The Great Victorian Collection.* New York Farrar, Straus and Giroux, 1975.

Roberts, Charles G.D. *The Heart of the Ancient World.* Toronto: McClelland & Stewart, 1974.

Watson, Sheila. *The Double Hook.* Toronto: McClelland & Stewart, 1989.

The Borderlands

Jolicoeur, Louis. *L'Araignée du silence et autres nouvelles.* Québec: L'Instant même, 1987.

Yates, J. Michael. *Man in the Glass Octopus.* Vancouver: Sono Nis Press, 1968.

Fantastic Fiction for Children and Young Adults

Buffie, Margaret. *Who is Frances Rain?* Toronto: Kids Can Press, 1987.

Clark, Catherine Anthony. *The Golden Pine Cone.* Illustrated by Claire Bice. Toronto: MacMillan Company of Canada, 1950.

Fernandes, Kim. *Zebo and the Dirty Planet.* Toronto: Annick Press, 1991.

Green, John F. *There's a Dragon in My Closet.* Illustrated by Linda Hendry. Richmond Hill, Ont.: Scholastic-TAB Publications, 1987.

Layton, Aviva. *The Magic Stones.* [Toronto]: Magook Publishers, 1977.

SMCL

3 5151 00128 7069